KU-300-268

# Ways of Exchange

An important *tee* network consisting of Kaketao (Sauli clan, with pig) Kama (Mamagakini), Kuliana (Yauwani), Lapai (Poreyalani), and Wereya (Malipani). The pig is of European breed and came from Wapenamanda along a well-established "*tee*-road" of men.

# Ways of Exchange

## The Enga *Tee* of
## Papua New Guinea

D.K. FEIL

University of Queensland Press

First published 1984 by University of Queensland Press
Box 42, St Lucia, Queensland, Australia

© D.K. Feil 1984

Typeset by University of Queensland Press
Printed in Hong Kong by Silex Enterprise & Printing Co.

Distributed in the UK, Europe, the Middle East, Africa, and the
Caribbean by Prentice Hall International, International Book
Distributors Ltd, 66 Wood Lane End, Hemel Hempstead, Herts.,
England

Distributed in the USA and Canada by Technical Impex
Corporation, 5 South Union Street, Lawrence, Mass. 01843 USA


**Cataloguing in Publication Data**

*National Library of Australia*

Feil, D.K. (Daryl Keith), 1948–
    Ways of Exchange

    Bibliography.
    Includes index.

    1. Enga (New Guinea people) – Rites and ceremonies.
    2. Barter – Papua New Guinea. I. Title.

390'.0899912


*Library of Congress*

Feil, D.K. (Daryl Keith), 1948–
    Ways of Exchange

    Bibliography: p.
    Includes index.
    1. Enga (New Guinea people) – Commerce. 2. Enga (New
Guinea people) – Rites and ceremonies. 3. Ceremonial
exchange – Papua New Guinea. I. Title.
DU740.42.F42      1984      306'.0899912      83-23414

ISBN 0-7022-1994-0

My parents have given constant support from afar. My wife, Rose, deserves much more than mere dedication.

# Contents

## x   *Contents*

# Photographs

# Illustrations

## TABLES

# FIGURES

# MAPS

# Acknowledgments

Much of the research upon which this book is based was under-taken while I was a Research Scholar in the Department of Anthropology, Research School of Pacific Studies, Australian National University. From 1979 onwards, the Department of Anthropology and Sociology, University of Queensland has sup-ported my research in Papua New Guinea. I owe both of these institutions a considerable debt of gratitude for their financial support.

I wish to thank the Papua New Guinea government and officials of the Enga Province for permission to do research there. I was also shown many kindnesses by the Australian and European members of the Kompiama community during my early stays: Frank and Glenn den Oudsten, Russell Mumme, Mike Itlsceff, and Bert and Alice Weizer.

My earliest teachers in New Guinea anthropology were Paula Brown and John Barnes, and I wish to remember their contribu-tion however belatedly. While I wrote my doctoral thesis, and subsequently, Andrew and Marilyn Strathern, Anthony Forge, Roger Keesing, Derek Freeman, and Annette Weiner con-tributed much inspiration and necessary criticism. Michael Young supervised my thesis with care, and Marie Reay and Paul Alexander have read parts of this book in other, much earlier form. They are all, of course, immune from the defects which remain.

The Mamagakini people welcomed me with friendliness and tolerance and my debt to them can never be adequately reciprocated. They taught me much more than *tee* things, and I can only hope that this account of their lives proves of some small value to them, and conveys the respect and affection I hold for them. I mention my closest friends and patient assistants: Maku, Kale, Kama, Ango, Pimbiki, Kepa and Komba. The women, Pyakeyame, Kupame, and Wapuyame instructed a male in women's ways with patience and good humour.

# Introduction

## Themes

Ceremonial exchange institutions are one of the most striking features of Papua New Guinea societies. Since Malinowski's description of the *kula* in *Argonauts of the Western Pacific* (1922), they have been widely reported throughout the area and Melanesia generally, and in the Highlands especially, most ethnographers have noted the significance of exchange and reciprocity in the economic, political, and ritual life of the communities they studied. (See for example, Luzbetak 1954; Bulmer 1960a, b; Ryan 1961; Salisbury 1962; Criper 1967; Rappaport 1967; A.J. Strathern 1971; Meggitt 1974). In this book I analyze an outstanding example of a ceremonial exchange system: the *tee* among the Tombema-Enga of the Western New Guinea Highlands. Of all systems of exchange so far described, the *tee* is perhaps the most elaborate and highly developed in terms of number of distinct communities involved and their interlocking dependence, in its geographical extent, and its organizational rules and requirements. With the adjoining Melpa *moka* (A.J. Strathern 1971) and Mendi *mok ink* (Ryan 1961) which interdigitate with the *tee*, more than 200,000 people are linked into a system of similarly structured exchange activities.[1]

Descriptive accounts of the *tee* date from 1951 (Bus 1951). Elkin (1953) described the *tee* he witnessed at Wabaga (see map 4) after only a short visit, and his account remains a valuable source. Kleinig (1955) and Meggitt (1974) have also studied aspects of the *tee*. In part, my aim here is to contribute to the ethnography of the *tee* and related institutions, to analyze its complex workings, and to demonstrate its significance for wider Enga culture.[2]

While drawing on these earlier works, a more important aim of the present study is to attempt to put the *tee* into an historical and comparative perspective. Most earlier analyses of ceremonial exchange have focussed almost solely on the functional value of transactions for maintaining or expressing social relations; the transactions themselves have been seen as secondary. The monographs of A.J. Strathern (1971), Young (1971), and more recently Sillitoe (1978), have shown ceremonial exchange to be a "social contract" between groups and individuals, promoting social control and, on balance, being a positive integrating force in societies lacking formal judicial procedures. This approach, consistent with a synchronic structural-functional analysis has shown convincingly what exchange "does" in New Guinea societies. Equally, as a dominant organizational principle, exchange has also provided a measure of comparability to an otherwise bewildering range of variation in Melanesian societies. The analysis of exchange activities has shed bright light on political and economic institutions and behaviour. In short, exchange, like descent in African studies, has become a theoretical concept of prime importance for anthropologists working in Papua New Guinea.

Without denying the functional value of exchange, a major theme of this book considers the material side of transactions. Sahlins has noted that "a material transaction is usually a momentary episode in a continuous social relation" (1972:185). In this dominant view, social relations are primary, the exchange transactions themselves are secondary. With such priority therefore, it matters little what is exchanged, and the relations between persons producing the things exchanged are left further in the background. Social relations are defined by exchange; the social concomitants of exchange rather than production are generally the point of departure, a view recently criticized by some economic anthropologists (Frankenberg 1967; Meillassoux 1972, 1978; Clammer ed. 1978). In this analysis of the *tee*, its structural and functional character is placed in historical context and is seen as the outcome of both material and sociopolitical forces. The present configuration of the *tee* then cannot be studied aside from its historical roots, nor apart from the material importance of its transactions. I argue, in part, that only by considering what are the exchange items of value, how they are produced, and what are the resulting relations between people who produce them, can one understand and explain major differences between exchange institutions, and related social, political, and economic phenomena. Significant contrasts in this book will be drawn with other New Guinea Highlands exchange systems to highlight the place of the *tee* in a wider comparative framework.

The historical and material dimensions of the exchange system provide the context for a second major theme: a detailed analysis of the social relations of exchange within the workings of the *tee* institution. Here the present study adopts a different analytical approach when compared to earlier work on the *tee*, especially to that of the influential writings of M.J. Meggitt (1972, 1974). In his investigation of the *tee*, as in his accounts of Mae-Enga social structure (1965a), religious order (1965b), leadership (1967, 1971) and, more recently, warfare (1977), the basic unit of analysis is the corporate descent group. In none of these studies is there a place for individuals: a person's behaviour and allegiance is assumed to be determined by his group membership and epiphenomenal of it. His choices are seen as constrained and conditioned by that structure, while individual variation is downplayed or ignored altogether. In Meggitt's view, an individual's participation and decision-making in the *tee* is likewise an outcome of his membership of a descent group. This assumption that descent groups are the predominant units involved in ceremonial exchange, remains the prevailing view among anthropologists who have worked in the Highlands and elsewhere in New Guinea (but compare Sillitoe 1978).

But is the *tee* institution amenable to this kind of highly structured analysis? I argue here that a behavioural, individual-centred approach to *tee* phenomena provides a better framework for understanding ceremonial exchange generally, and produces insights which structural analyses mask.[3] The very essence of the *tee* is its broadening, non-parochial outlook: the important ties affirmed by the reciprocal exchange of valuables reach well beyond the narrow confines of a person's own group. These ties are created by individuals alone and are in no sense "held" collectively. All members of a particular group may present valuables on the same occasion, but exchange relationships in Tombema–Enga society are highly personal, private affairs and, I argue, group motives and concerns have little relevance to the strategies of individual *tee* partnerships. Thus, while I do not deny that descent group membership influences individuals' behaviour in certain activities in Tombema society, it plays a decidedly secondary role in the social practices which are the concern of this book. For the individual, ties of exchange provide a parallel, but not "supplementary" (Boissevain 1968:544) set of relationships to those of descent. As Keesing has noted (1976:482), "all societies are organized in both more formal and enduring groups and *ad hoc* coalitions; it is their relative importance and spheres of relevance that vary". *Tee* partnerships and ties of exchange are not "*ad hoc* coalitions"; rather they parallel clanship as a second, separate but equal, structure of relationships in Tombema society. The significance of these relationships in exchange dealings is a major theme of this work.

Providing a label for these ties of exchange which conveys some understanding of the basis on which they are formed presents immediate difficulties. I frequently call them friendships. In contrast to conventional views in which exchange ties in the Highlands are portrayed as the simple outcome of cognatic kinship and affinity, I argue that the social significance of kinship and affinity are determined primarily by performance and conduct in the *tee* system. A person is regarded as a relative only if he is also an exchange ally.[4]

The emerging literature on friendship (see for example, Eisenstadt 1956; Burridge 1957; Cohen 1961; Wolf 1966; Holzberg 1973; Leyton 1974; Paine 1974; Schwimmer 1974; Brain 1977; and Marshall 1977)[5] distinguishes two aspects of friendship which are relevant to this study: the "affective/moral" component and the "instrumental/utilitarian" component. *Tee* partners are friends, their partnerships emphatically have a moral component and I continually emphasize that partnerships "do" things that other relationships cannot (compare Evans-Pritchard 1933; Firth 1936). Tombema distinguish *tee* partners as a separate category of persons. The content and structure of *tee* relationships also conform to frequently cited criteria of friendship (as opposed to kinship relationships): they are voluntary, dyadic, and intimate (for example Marshall 1977:646). Friendships are also often characterized as temporary and mutable. Paradoxically, however, the very nature of the ties binding *tee* partners in Tombema society makes them less mutable, more enduring, than other relationships. The sentiment of amity which exists between *tee* partners is undeniable, if difficult to substantiate. The established structural analyses of the *tee* and similar institutions obscure or deny the affective and instrumental aspects of partnerships validated by exchange.

An analysis of *tee* partnerships leads us back to the problem of social control and integration. Young (1971) studied how, on Goodenough Island, offended parties shame rivals and wrongdoers by giving them massive gifts of food. Such gifts, it was argued, redress the social balance and deter persons from committing such offences in the future.[6] In Melpa society (A.J. Strathern 1971), the exchange of valuables preserves tenuous political alliances between groups; without it, warfare and aggression are likely and alliance impossible. In Meggitt's account of the *tee* (1974), a clan's *tee* performance demonstrates its strength to other clans and, if the display is good enough, suggests to neighbouring and therefore, threatening clans, that they should look elsewhere for land to expropriate. In all of these studies, ceremonial exchange and warfare/aggression are treated as similar activities, almost as functional equivalents. It is often argued that after the ban on warfare in New Guinea by the colonial administration, ceremonial exchange activities expanded and flourished because they took over the role of warfare (Salisbury 1962). Thus, social control and the integration of groups is achieved by aggressive giving: exchange relations between givers and receivers are not based on trust, but on latent competition and rivalry which might surface at any time.

My analysis here also argues that ceremonial exchange contributes to integration and social control. But, I argue, social control does not arise from precarious alliances and tenuous relations of competition between givers and receivers, nor from the shame incurred from being forced to accept a large gift; rather, individual *tee* partnerships are alliances of friendship which cut across clan boundaries and ultimately reduce the efficacy of clans as war-making units. In Tombema-Enga society, warfare and exchange are opposing principles: the *tee* has never been an instrument of hostility and aggression between groups, because exchanges are not the concern of corporate groups. Ceremonial exchange has few implications for intergroup relations. Only friends can exchange, exchange is a symbol of their friendship, and, as I will show, *tee* partners are not competitors but allies. In the *tee*, competition for prestige is channelled inward, a man's surest support comes from outside his immediate descent group. The arena of greatest competition is among close agnatic clansmen. Clan solidarity is thereby undermined by exchange (see Uberoi 1962:159; Hallpike 1977:97) but, at the same time, exchange alliances between individuals from warring groups are strengthened. Taken together, these processes tend to reduce tension between rival groups. Structural analyses have concentrated on the significance of ceremonial exchange for groups and therefore have failed to explore adequately what happens within groups. Interclan warfare is a feature of most New Guinea societies and it is not surprising that competition between clans in ceremonial exchange has been emphasized. I approach the problem by investigating individual alliances of exchange which promote stable, secure partnerships between men of different, opposing groups.

Thus, while I argue that the *tee*, like other exchange systems is functionally important for social control, I locate its source in interpersonal transactions rather than in intergroup prestations. Furthermore, the importance of individual transactions and the overall functional character of exchange systems like the *tee* are a direct reflection of the production process and the material nature of the transactions themselves. A comparison of the *tee* with some other exchange systems will make this proposition apparent.

A third major theme of this book is the embeddedness of *tee*-related activities and interests in nearly every Enga social practice. The *tee* is an archetypal "total prestation" (Mauss 1954), expressing and encapsulating the range of Enga social and cultural values. All Enga transactions are related to the *tee*, and it to them; the boundaries between *tee* and other prestations are arbitrary and heuristic only, for they form a single continuum in Enga way of thinking. This book will demonstrate the systematic interconnection of *tee* and related transactions which in turn provides the political and economic framework of Tombema–Enga society.

The Enga have elaborated ceremonial exchange and concomitant pig production beyond that of other New Guinea Highlands societies (Feil 1984). This elaboration includes both the interlocking of many communities, widely spread geographically, and also the interconnection of all contexts of exchange, including for example, bridewealth (Feil 1980, 1981). This book then, attempts to show how the *tee* permeates Tombema-Enga society, how exchange relationships are the key economic and political relationships, and how all production and exchange decisions have the *tee* as backdrop.

After a brief description in chapter one of the Tombema-Enga people, their ecology and social structure, chapter two delineates the important parameters of the *tee* institution. The phases of *tee*-making, the type of valuables exchanged, the relationship of the *tee* institution to other contexts of giving and some macro aspects of the *tee* are described, as a prelude for the analysis of *tee* partnerships. Chapter three examines the production of pigs for the *tee*, and compares this process with that of the neighbouring Melpa *moka*. In the latter system, pearlshells rather than pigs are the most valuable exchange items. Chapter four carries forward the comparison by examining the place of women in the *tee*, both as producers of the most important wealth items − pigs − and their role in the distribution of them. The implications of a basic distinction between "house-raised pigs" and pigs from "exchange roads" is explored.

Chapters five and six analyze *tee* partnerships in depth. In the first of these chapters, the patterns of Tombema exchange relationships are examined: what *tee* partners do, who they are, and the kinds of ties that bind them together. The concepts of symmetrical and complementary relationships, following Bateson (1936 [1958]), are used to illustrate patterns of interaction between *tee* partners and those who do not exchange. Chapter six describes the contexts of competition in the *tee* and the competitive units involved in *tee*-making. An individual *tee* is analyzed and a brief account of recent *tee* history in the Kompiama area is provided. Chapter seven briefly analyzes the reasons for the dissolution of *tee* partnerships. While they are essentially stable and secure relationships, disputes do occur which dissolve partnerships. The death or divorce of a woman who links men as *tee* partners may also lead to the collapse of an exchange relationship. The conclusion offers an answer to the question of the meaning of the *tee*, and the significance of it and *tee* partnerships for Tombema society.


**Fieldwork Conditions and Methodological Note**

I arrived in Kompiama early in February 1974 and set out almost immediately with a government patrol which was investigating public works and hearing disputes in the surrounding area. I quickly learned that the Sau River forms a rough cultural-linguistic boundary between Mai-Enga and Tombema-Enga speakers. Some very minor differences in dialect and custom distinguish the two peoples and are mentioned briefly in chapter one. The first weeks were spent with Mai speakers and when we crossed the Sau River, northeast of the patrol post, and entered Tombema country for the first time, I decided, without undue deliberation, to settle immediately. One minor consideration influenced my choice: I preferred to settle in a Tombema speaking area rather than in a Mai one. Mai-Enga were already well-known in the literature and I wanted to discover any differences that might exist between the two groups. I found few.

The Tombema people whom I first encountered, members of the Mamagakini clan, were friendly and offered me a place to build a house. There was a road linking the area to Kompiama twenty miles away, and more importantly, I noticed recently planted *tee* sticks at a *tee* ground. I lived twenty-nine months with Mamagakini, from February 1974 to April 1975; from July 1975 to August 1976, and for the month of July 1977. I returned in 1980 for a further two months' study.

I began fieldwork almost immediately; taking a census of the clan's 535 permanent members, eliciting bits of information like kinship terminology along the way and beginning to learn the language. Melanesian pidgin was used in the early months. Language learning was a neverending task, and although I became reasonably proficient in Enga by the second stage of fieldwork, I was never fluent. I could understand most conversations and respond, if haltingly. During the census-taking my attention was constantly diverted to *tee* activities. Everyone talked about it incessantly, publicly and privately. Rumours were rife that the *tee* was about to arrive, and so on. Men were constantly away to "talk *tee*". It became obvious to me that the *tee* was the central concern of their lives at that time, and information about it was easily obtained. The *tee* had received far too little attention in Enga studies and I decided early to concentrate my research in that direction.

With the census completed, I selected a sample of men from Mamagakini whose *tee* activities I would explore and monitor closely and from whom detailed information both past and present would be sought. In the end, the sample included 45 men, about one-third of Mamagakini resident adult men. They were not chosen randomly. I assumed that bigmen would be the most active participants in the *tee* and so I sought to include all recognized bigmen from Mamagakini in my sample. Sixteen out of eighteen assented. All subclans are represented. Details of the same kind were also collected from five bigmen in other clans who have kinship or affinal ties with Mamagakini. I also decided that details of an entire subclan's members were needed for a subclan makes the *tee* at the same time and place. I was living with the Mapete subclan (21 adult male members) and each member became an important informant. Later still, I decided to collect details on all father-son pairs who were making *tee*, to measure continuity in *tee* partnerships. The tables used throughout this book are based on this sample of men.

Information on a wide range of *tee* activities was collected from this sample of men. I came to know each man well and after cross-checking most of their responses in the beginning and finding them very accurate, I accepted later answers at face value. Data on *tee* payments, both past and present, are precisely remembered, and some individuals could recount with amazing accuracy minor details of *tee* transactions which occurred fifty years earlier. Complete details of *tee* partnerships, past, present, and dissolved were also collected from these men.

A complete pig census was also conducted for all Mamagakini households (see Appendix 1). It was based on both observation and interviews. I travelled to the Wapi, the Wale-Tarua, Wapenamanda, Wabaga and the Tsaka valley to record details of *tee* exchanges and to trace *tee* routes. I witnessed *tees* throughout the Enga area, not just in Kompiama, and I believe that it operates similarly in all the areas I visited. The chain-like structure of the *tee* and *tee* partnerships made it necessary to collect information on individuals linked only remotely to men in my Mamagakini sample. The *tee* community is a commonwealth, and collecting information from a sample of men in one clan only was just the beginning.

## A Note on Orthography

Wherever possible, I have followed the orthography for Enga words given by Lang (1973) based on the Enga orthography conferences of 1965 and 1970. To simplify presentation, I have omitted tonal markers.

This orthographic use, unfortunately, necessitates some changes in the spelling of Enga words which have become popularized in the literature: for example *te* is now written *tee*; *Mae* is now written *Mai* (except where I refer explicitly to Meggitt's work); and *Laiapu/Raiapu* is now rendered *Laiapo*.

## Notes

1.   The *tee* is sometimes referred to as *maku pingi. Tee* talk (*maku pii*) is "to boast loudly" (*maku lenge*). The words *maku, moka,* and *mok ink* are clearly cognates or loan words and suggest a common origin of the ceremonial exchange institutions of Enga, Melpa and Mendi.
2.   Meggitt and Elkin worked among the Mai-Enga at Wabaga, Bus among Laiapo-Enga near Wapenamanda, and Kleinig on the Laiapo/Mai border near Biripi. With Kompiama these three areas form a triangle in which most *tee* activity takes place.
3.   In this book, I have drawn implicitly on the vast literature of network analysis (for example Mayer 1966, Boissevain 1968) and transactional analysis (for example Barth 1966, Bailey 1969, and Kapferer 1976). Individual- centred alliances are the most important units involved in *tee*-making. These alliances do not exist only in the "chinks in the social structure" (Boissevain 1968:544) nor are they "subinstitutional" (Kapferer 1976:19). And, while *tee* networks are composed of ego-centred, maximizing, manipulating individuals, *tee* relationships also have a highly constraining, moral component.
4.   Both A.J. Strathern (1971) and Meggitt (1974) show that some exchange partners are unrelated. These are, however, mostly partners of bigmen who go beyond the immediate community to establish alliances. For Meggitt

(1974:188) these alliances between unrelated bigmen are formed because they "may be of political and military utility to their own clans".

5.  Paine (1974) argues that friendship is found only in technologically advanced, complex societies. Others (for example, Schwimmer 1974) suggest that friendships are important in all kinds of societies, for example in "particularistic" ones (Parsons and Shils 1951), characterized by lineages, clans, age-sets, and castes.

6.  This short summary does not do justice to Young's (1971) intricate analysis. Those of A.J. Strathern (1971) and Meggitt (1974) are treated more fully in later chapters.

# ONE

# The Setting: The Kompiama Area and the Tombema–Enga People

## The Kompiama Area

Until the Kompiama patrol post was established in October 1953, the location was known as *yukutesa*, after a cordyline plant abundant near the site. The name was changed to Kompiama, perhaps the European approximation of the Tombema word *kopona*, meaning "warm place" or "low-lying region". The patrol post itself is located at a lower altitude (1,371 metres above sea level) than surrounding mountains which rise to 2,610 metres or more. From the central Enga areas of Wapenamanda and Wabaga, the Kompiama area is relatively "low-lying": habitation occurs more frequently at lower altitudes, and crops characteristic of warmer climates are plentiful. *Kopona* contrasts with the central Enga areas, known as "cold places" (*mandaka*), without many food varieties.

Four separate census divisions are administered from Kompiama[1] (see map 2): the Wale-Tarua, northwest of the patrol post; the Wapi, to the north; the Lower Sau, on the west and north sides of the Sau River; and the Upper Sau, on the east and south sides of the river. It will be pointed out that the Sau River, flowing eastward from sources midway to Wabaga, forms a rough cultural-linguistic boundary between the Upper and Lower Sau residents, the former speaking the Tombema dialect (see Elkin 1953:162), the latter the Mai dialect. These are just two of up to twelve or more dialect divisions among Enga speakers. Thus Tombema refers more specifically to those people living in the Upper Sau census division. The name

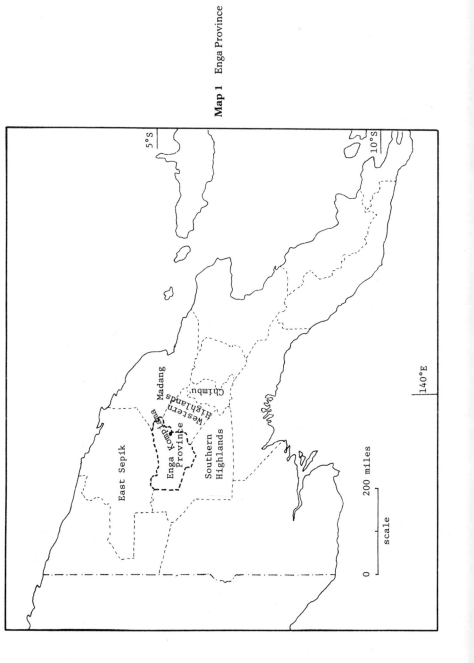

**Map 1**  Enga Province

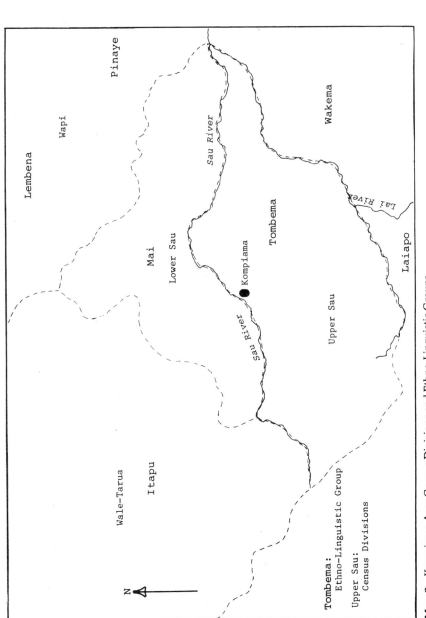

**Map 2** Kompiama Area Census Divisions and Ethno-Linguistic Groups

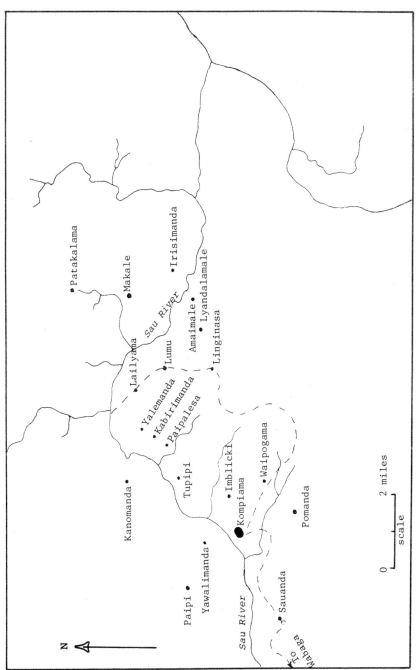

**Map 3** The Kompiama Area

Tombema, however, is used throughout this book to refer to both Upper and Lower Sau residents.[2]

Two major river systems dominate the Kompiama area: the Sau mentioned above, and the Lai, which flows into the region from the south and then joins the Sau at a low, eastern extremity of Tombema country. They then flow northward, joining the Yuat and eventually, the Sepik River.

The area as a whole is characterized by steep mountains and few large tracts of level ground. The flight into Kompiama from the flat, wide, Waghi or Baiyer valleys presents a striking contrast. The spacious valley floors through which those rivers flow are not found along the Sau and Lai Rivers. In Kompiama, gardens are planted mainly on mountain slopes at precarious angles. As elsewhere in the Highlands, homesteads are placed along mountain ridges – in times past for reasons of defense. Throughout Kompiama, dispersed homesteads dotted about the clan territory are the rule. There are no villages; rather, fellow subclansmen settle near a named locale which contains a *tee* ceremonial ground (*tee kamapi*). Each subclan has its own ground and makes the *tee* separately from other member subclans.

Males and females continue to maintain separate residences. Traditional men's houses, where several men of the same subclan slept, no longer exist. They have been replaced by private dwellings occupied often by only a man and his sons. Women's houses, also containing sleeping stalls for the pigs, are located nearby. In the case of polygyny, each wife has her own house. The taboos on women entering men's houses or even coming near them have ceased to be observed, but men and women still sleep separately. Men's houses (*akalyanda*) are easily distinguishable by their round shape, women's houses (*enda anda*) are long and rectangular, with internal pig stalls and small sleeping compartments at the back. These have the characteristic sloping ridgepole (*ima*) common throughout the Enga area (Meggitt 1957, 1964a:193; Ambelaum *et al.*, n.d.).[3]

The disbandment of men's houses and aspects of traditional Tombema religion and ritual (for example, *sandalu*[4] [see Meggitt 1964b, 1965b]) have been affected by the missions in the area. The Australian Baptist Mission (A.B.M.) has been present in Kompiama since the early 1950s; the Catholic and Adventists have more recently established bases. Many Tombema are nominal Christians and have been baptized. However, recourse to traditional divining techniques, belief in the power of the deceased and the efficacy of magic, continue. At least in Kompiama, missions have not affected participation in *tee* ceremonies. Meggitt (1964b, 1965b), Bulmer (1965), Westermann (1968), Feachem (1973), and Brennan (1977) as well as two volumes produced by the New Guinea Lutheran Mission (1968, 1970) discuss traditional Enga religious practice, much of which applies equally to Tombema.

As elsewhere in the Highlands, seasons in the Kompiama area are not well-defined by either rainfall or temperature. Still, they are significant for agricultural tasks geared to them. The "dry season" begins in April or May and lasts until September or October. The "wet season" then commences. Rainfall recorded at the patrol post for the years 1974 and 1975 confirms this seasonality. A total of 325.8 centimetres of rain fell in 1974, 96.7 centimetres during the dry season, 229.1 centimetres during the wet season. In 1975, 342.3 centimetres of rain fell, 114.5 centimetres in the dry season, 227.8 centimetres in the wet season. Temperatures are relatively constant throughout the year. At altitudes of habitation between 1,219 and 1,828 metres above sea level, day temperatures may reach 80 degrees Fahrenheit,

A local pastor preaches the evils of *tee*-making while a fellow subclansman makes his *tee*. The pastor, a rival of the *tee*-maker had, earlier in the week, given five pigs as *saandi pingi* himself.

night temperatures dropping to 40 degrees. Dry season temperatures are slightly cooler than wet season ones.

The agricultural cycle is geared, more or less, to these seasonal changes.[5] Thus, April and May are normally times to begin making gardens: bush is cleared, trees cut, and fences prepared. When the fences have been secured, dried plant material is heaped and burned and crops planted in the ash. All crops are planted at the same time, and all gardens are mixed. There are no gardens which contain only single crops such as sweet potatoes, as are found elsewhere in Enga country (see Waddell 1971, 1973). The timing of crops ready for harvest provides an easy calendric reference for planned activities. Crops are distinguished as "male" or "female", and this designation determines who plants and harvests them, and who is in charge of their weeding and care. Very small gardens may be planted near to one's house during the year, but these are subsidiary and not common. Within this timetable, spinach greens, a female or male crop depending on the variety, and cucumbers, a female crop, are ready for harvest first, in September and October. Corn, an introduced crop without gender, is ready next, in October and November. Varieties of beans, a female crop, should be ready for harvest by late November or so. Sweet potato (*mapu*), a female crop of more than thirty-five varieties, is ready usually by December or January, perhaps earlier. Taro (*maa*) also a female crop, of over twenty known varieties can be harvested between January and March of the following year. The taro is exhausted by May or June, but sweet potatoes can be harvested from original plantings for two or three years. Bananas and sugarcane, male crops of multiple varieties, may be ready a year after planting, often a bit longer. Yams of both male and female kinds, also take a year or more to mature. Edible pit-pit and peanuts are also important. Tobacco is grown by men under the eaves of their houses. There are a great variety of vegetables foods to supplement the staple diet of sweet potatoes. Even for European tastes, the diet is not a dull one.

Gardens are not well laid out or planned. The most unusual feature of agriculture in the Kompiama area is the absence of mounding, common throughout the rest of Enga. This fact probably reflects the lower population density and hence less need for more intensive agriculture in Kompiama. Even at higher altitudes, mounding is not practised: rather, gardens are rambling affairs, large and spread out, often encompassing half a hectare or more. Larger gardens are partly planted in one season, the remainder reserved for the next. There are still areas of primary forest on the eastern side of the station down near the Sau River, but most gardens are made in secondary growth. When the last of the sweet potatoes are taken, pigs are allowed into the garden to root for leftover tubers and to turn the soil. By this time, fences are becoming weak and are rotting. After the pigs have done their job, these gardens may be immediately replanted, or, more usually, they are allowed to lie fallow for ten years or more. Pig excrement is not used as fertilizer; casuarina trees known to regenerate depleted soil are much less common in Kompiama than in central Enga.

Garden plots are individually owned and passed on from father to son. Anyone, including closest agnatic kinsmen, who wishes to garden on land not his own, must seek permission. It will be shown later that permission is related to *tee* partner status. Specific trees are also individually owned, and provide important food and other material for their owners. Breadfruit ready in the early part of the dry season; red pandanus eaten regularly from the early weeks of the wet season; nut pandanus; sago; pawpaw; and black palm trees used in making spears and arrows, are owned by individual men and have been inherited from the original planter. These trees are often found in diverse locations – in other men's gardens or far away from home – but owners are well known and must be consulted if the produce is desired.

The Kompiama area presents a fairly typical New Guinea Highlands scene: steep mountains, difficult terrain, staple crop of sweet potatoes, and the yet to be mentioned pigs.

## The Tombema-Enga People

The Enga are the largest ethno-linguistic group in Papua New Guinea. The word "Enga" itself has no meaning in local language, and except for the educated few, the title has no significance, despite the fact that the Enga Province was established in 1973. The word "Enga" is first mentioned by Taylor (1930) in his report of the historic Hagen-Sepik patrol (1938-39), when he notes that "the people inhabiting the country west and northwest of Mount Hagen are known in the Mount Hagen language as Eng-a" (Taylor 1939-40:141). The Enga Province is now comprised of a number of populations speaking mutually intelligible dialects of the same language, further differentiated by minor cultural features. The total number of Enga speakers exceeds 160,000 persons. The most populous and densely settled areas are in "central" Enga around Wabaga and Wapenamanda. The subgroups identified with these locales are called Mai (Wabaga) and Laiapo/Raiapo (Wapenamanda). Near to Wapenamanda, on the southern side of the Lai River is another populous area, a valley system known as Tsaka (or written variously as Tchaga [Crotty 1951]; Syaka [Meggitt 1958, 1965a]; Saka [Bulmer n.d.a.]). The Kompiama area, subject of this study, with other parts of Enga is contrasted with "central" Enga, and has been termed "fringe" Enga (Meggitt 1965a:269; see also Dornstreich 1973). The population sizes and densities of fringe Enga societies are generally lower than those of central Enga.

Mai, Laiapo and Tsaka speakers refer to Kompiama area residents, without differentiation, as Saui (or Sauwi or Sauwa), after the Sau River. However, this name fails to make important cultural-linguistic distinctions which exist in the Kompiama region. Furthermore, Kompiama people do not refer to themselves by the name Saui (see map 2).

The most important local distinction is that between Mai and Tombema speakers. The Sau River is a natural boundary separating the Tombema speakers to the south (Upper Sau census division) from Mai speakers on the north side of the river (Lower Sau census division). The cultural-linguistic differences between them are noticeable if slight: Mai men wear round-shaped wigs, Tombema men wear long, straight ones as in Laiapo; there are minor dialect differences, and there is variation in the ritual of *sandalu* (Tombema-Laiapo) and *sangai* (Mai). These are just some of the more obvious differences. Tombema have more in common with Laiapo than with Mai. Part of two Mai-speaking clans are immigrants on the Tombema side of the Sau River, and part of one Tombema clan lives on the Mai side. Aside from these exceptions, Mai and Tombema speakers are separated by the river. However, Mai and Tombema speakers frequently intermarry, especially among those groups living near the river boundary. For the main topic of this book, the *tee* exchange system, I could discover no points of difference between the two areas. The *tee* system works identically among both Tombema and Mai. Although I refer throughout to Tombema society, my discussion, except where noted, applies equally to both Tombema and Mai areas.

Table 1 shows the populations of the census divisions administered from Kompiama in 1974–75.[6] Gross population densities and area sizes are also given. Areas are based on Westermann (1968) and the Village Directory (1973).

**Table 1**   Population of Kompiama Area Census Divisions

| Census Division | Population | Area (sq.kms) | Population Density (persons/sq.km) |
|---|---|---|---|
| Upper Sau (Tombema) | 8,583 | 388.5 | 22.1 |
| Lower Sau (Mai) | 4,274 | 259 | 16.5 |
| Wale-Tarua (Itapu) | 3,217 | 854.7 | 3.76 |
| Wapi (Lembena, Mai and Pinaye) | 2,345 | 828.8 | 2.8 |
| Totals | 18,419 | 2,331 | 7.94 |

There are 30 distinct clans represented in the Upper Sau, 22 in the Lower Sau. A less precise count shows 20 in the Wale-Tarua and 22 in the Wapi. Some clans represented in these figures have only a few members living in Kompiama. The average clan sizes for the combined Sau districts, Upper and Lower, is 247 persons per clan. This average is significantly higher than the 130 estimated by Meggitt for the Saui (1965a:270). Further information and a comparison with Mai and Laiapo clans is given in Table 2.

## Clanship

Throughout both Mai and Tombema areas of Kompiama, clans are generally the most inclusive structural unit. In both areas there are some named groupings which might be termed "phratries" but the majority of clans exist apart from any larger entity. And, even where "phratries" occur, one rarely hears their names mentioned,

**Table 2** Size of Kompiama Area Clans

| | Tombema | Mai (Kompiama) | Combined Kompiama (Mai and Tombema) | Mae[a] | Laiapo[b] |
|---|---|---|---|---|---|
| Number of clans in sample | 14 | 10 | 24 | 6 | 1 |
| Population in sample | 4,606 | 2,965 | 7,571 | 2,880 | 364 |
| Mean population per clan | 329 | 297 | 315 | 480 | — |
| Range of population per clan | 87-561 | 83-758 | 83-758 | 150-1,080 | — |
| Number of subclans in sample | 50 | 40 | 90 | 26 | 4 |
| Mean population per subclan | 87 | 74 | 84 | 110 | 91 |
| Range of subclans per clan | 2-8 | 2-11[c] | 2-11 | 3-6 | — |
| Mean number of subclans per clan | 3.8 | 4.0 | 3.8 | 4.3 | 4 |
| Number of lineages in sample | 69 | 76 | 145 | 60 | 13 |
| Mean lineages per clan[d] | 5.0 | 7.6 | 6 | 10 | 13 |
| Range of lineages per clan | 0-14 | 0-23 | 0-23 | 6-14 | — |
| Mean population per lineage | 67 | 39 | 52 | 48 | 28 |
| Mean lineages per subclan | 1.3 | 1.9 | 1.6 | 2.3 | 3.3 |
| Range of lineages per subclan[e] | 0-6 | 0-6 | 0-6 | 1-4 | — |

a Based on Meggitt (1965a:17; see also 1965a:14)

b Based on Westermann (1968:59)

c This clan contains as subclans, five immigrant groups which exist elsewhere as distinct clans. These five are added to the six resident subclans.

d The figures for Tombema are more precise than those for the Kompiama Mai. The fact that lineage names are not often used introduces some error into this calculation for the Kompiama Mai.

e Many subclans are not further subdivided, that is, they contain no lineages.

and their significance is difficult to assess. Clans in all cases are the territorial units, occupying named locales with distinct boundaries, and are the units whose members are said to co-operate in war-making. Clans are the units within which widows are redistributed. In most cases, clans are also the largest exogamous units, but in Tombema and Mai areas five cases of exogamous "great clans" were recorded: in the Mai area three (each of three clans), in the Tombema area two (one of three clans, one of four). Otherwise, all other clans form distinct exogamous groups.

If the larger groupings are to be called phratries, there are immediate difficulties in discovering their functional significance and meaning. Meggitt (1971:196-97) suggests that in Mae society, "brother" clans of one phratry may aid each other in defence or engage in "tournaments" against other phratries. There is no evidence of this in the Kompiama area, Mai or Tombema. In the Kompiama area, an ideology of common descent uniting clans in such groups is absent. They do not occupy a continuous tract of land, and in many cases, member clans of these larger groups are the most ferocious enemies. Kinship terms are not applied (for example "brother" or "father's brother", Meggitt 1964a, 1965a:51) to fellow members of these phratries. Member clans never come together for any common purpose. It is almost by accident that they came to my attention: the status of some clans as members or not is a point of dispute or ignorance. Within the Tombema area where my field site was located (with Mamagakini clan, see below), two supraclan groups were named: one called Aiamani, the other called Lyungini. Aiamani consists of the following clans with populations given in brackets:

| Sauli | (461) | Yalingani | (392) | Tangaipu | (257) |
|-------|-------|-----------|-------|----------|-------|
| Walumini | (171) | Yauwani | (367) | Sampe | (126) |
|  |  | Pinai | (561) |  |  |

Yalingani, Tangaipu, Walumini and Sampe believe they share a common male ancestor and do not intermarry. Lyungini has as member clans:

| Mamagakini | (535) | Kirapani | (506) | Wangini | (405) |
|------------|-------|----------|-------|---------|-------|
| Tinlapini | (439) | Wakenekoni | (165) | Malipio | (124) |

Kirapani, Wakenekoni and Malipio form an exogamous great-clan. All other clans of each phratry intermarry. Several other clans claim to be either Aiamani or Lyungini but the above groups are the only consistently named members. These two phratries contain 13 clans (of 30 represented on the Tombema side), but more than half of the Tombema population. The Mai side has at least four groupings of the phratry type. The fact remains however, that the majority of clans in both Tombema and Mai areas are "unattached" to larger groupings and exist as independent units. This is in sharp contrast to the Mai where no clans apart from larger phratry groups were found (Meggitt 1965a:8).

The idioms used to describe all levels of social groups are similar to those given for the Mae (Meggitt 1965a), and suggest a structure of patrilineal descent. The existence of groups based on an ideology of descent cannot be doubted; to describe them as corporate, or to assess their significance in shaping the behaviour of member individuals is, I would argue, a separate question. Decisions of residence and allegiance are not overly constrained by descent group membership. In this book in the context of the *tee* exchange system, I maintain that the importance of descent ideology is minimal. As in Kuma, descent groups in Tombema society are important mainly in the service of exogamy (Reay 1959:44).

The most basic Tombema expression to describe a descent unit is "line" (*tara*) or "line of men" (*akali tara*). Appropriate modifiers can be added to denote groups of greater or lesser inclusiveness. Clans are most often referred to as "line of men" (*akali tara*), "one line" (of men) (*tara mendei*), or "big line" (of men) (*tara andake* or *tara yale*). Subclans are referred to as "one men's house" (*akalyanda mendei,* or simply *akalyanda*) or "small line" (of men) (*tara koki*). Groups like Aiamani and Lyungini have no special name to distinguish them from clans, but when pressed, informants thought *tara andake* the most suitable. More will be said of subclans below. There are also smaller, named groups which are not often mentioned. These might be termed "lineages" (compare Meggitt 1965a:15). Members of these groups cannot, however, locate genealogically every other co-member. These units may be referred to as "families" (*palu*) or more descriptively as "the mark, or boundary of one penis" (*pongo lili* or *pongo lili mendei,* [compare Meggitt 1965a:15]). Sometimes the latter phrase is elaborated to *mendei pongo itange*. *Itange* adds the meaning of stem or trunk, that is, *pongo itange* is the "line of persons stemming or growing from the penis of one man". The usage suggested by Meggitt (1964a:192; 1965a:15) to apply to the patrilineage, "people of one blood" (*taeyoko mendei*) is not employed by Tombema and Mai speakers near to Kompiama. The substance of blood is passed to children through the mother and this links them indissolubly with their maternal kinsmen. It cannot therefore be a symbol of patrilineality. The Tombema have not, as far as could be determined, elaborated the idiom to one of cognation, linking descendants of a female ancestor for several generations as the Melpa appear to have done (A.J. Strathern 1972).

Genealogical knowledge in Tombema is weak. Many persons could not name their grandparents, very few could go beyond. Genealogies described as "typical" of the Mae (Meggitt 1965a) could not be elicited from Tombema informants (compare Bulmer n.d.a:5). Founders of the lowest, named groups called "lineages" above, where known, are placed in the generation of father's grandfathers of living adult men. Beyond this, groups and their founders exist as "just names" and their genealogical continuity is assumed not known. There is little in the way of firm ideological belief to substantiate the present structure of groups. Few individuals would hazard the view that subclan founders were all "brothers" of one clan father, for example. Segmentation does not occur in a predictable way or based on structural principles. Immigrant subclans exist in almost every clan, and it is commonplace for subclans to be founded by sister's sons rather than by pure patrilineal descendants. The Mamagakini clan is a good example and will be discussed below. Thus, the situation is typical of other societies in the Highlands: the idioms seem to express a patrilineal ideology, but the actual circumstances produce groups with a mixture of members based on diverse criteria. Individuals say they belong to their father's group and should reside there, but these statements carry little conviction when important decisions are made.

To review this brief section, the structural units of most importance in Tombema society are the clan and subclan. Phratries are rarely mentioned and no activities are organized around their exclusive membership. Aspects of clanship have already been mentioned, their most important role is in the regulation of exogamy and warfare. The former is clearly an aspect of clanship, the latter is thought to be a clan activity, but rarely, if ever, can be. For the subject of this book, however, subclans are the most important groups. These are the units whose members make their *tee* together at the same ceremonial ground. Waddell (1972:108) also notes that the *tee* is organized at the subclan level. Only in Mae-Enga (Meggitt 1974) does the clan appear to organize *tee* ceremonies. In Tombema, the *tee* progresses from subclan to subclan before going on to the next clan. Every subclan has its own *tee* ground and recognized bigmen. As shall be demonstrated, competition in exchange is most pervasive among fellow subclansmen of all statuses. It is not suggested that the *tee* is organized at the subclan level or that its members combine as a group to make it; rather when the *tee* arrives, each individual subclansman makes his personal display of pigs and valuables at the same time as other, close agnatic brothers.

## A History of Local Clans

All clans in the Kompiama area share one basic feature: they did not originate there, and they have no myths of origin linking them to specific places near Kompiama. While Lacey (1975) has discussed the "non-human progenitors" of clans and phratries in the Wabaga and Wapenamanda areas, my own attempts to find the same descent lines for Kompiama area clans were unsuccessful. Rather, narratives relate fairly recent immigration to Kompiama. With it, I presume, is a loss of knowledge or interest in tales of non-human ancestors giving rise to human populations in specific areas, areas which are no longer their own. The origin stories of Kompiama clans are adventures of fission and segmentation from parent groups caused by disputes and warfare, and subsequent journeys into the Sau area from Wapenamanda, Tsaka, Wabaga and Ambumu. My data support Meggitt's proposition that "peripheral peoples assert that their ancestors, of a few generations ago emigrated from the crowded central division to colonize the empty valleys" (1965a:269). The Sau valley was one of them. Thus, the Wapenamanda and Wabaga areas of central Enga appear to be the places of origin of all Enga populations, including even some Baiyer Valley groups. Central Enga clans possess origin myths to specific places which suggests a long period of residence and history in those areas.

The other common feature of clans throughout the Kompiama area is the typical Highlands phenomenon of the fission of clans, the incorporation of immigrant groups as subclans, for example, and to a lesser extent, the "disappearance" of clans through their absorption into other groups after death or dispersion in warfare has reduced their numbers. The evidence of these occurrences is often circumstantial. But, in general, fluidity is basic to clan composition. Individuals may shift their allegiance. Subgroups of all sizes have in the past used the ties of their individual members, based on exchange, affinity, and maternity to split from their parent groups and take up residence with different clans. With the passage of time, these groups have become "full" members of their "new" clans.

Within the Kompiama area, there have been at least three distinct waves of immigration. The first of these was led by clans of the Aiamani group. It is believed that Aiamani clans originated in the Tsaka valley. The second wave of immigration involves the Lyungini clans. It is unlikely that all Aiamani clans were in the area before Lyungini ones began to arrive. But the general belief is that Aiamani arrived first, Lyungini next. Lyungini clans place their origin on the Mai/Laiapo divide, between Wabaga and Wapenamanda.

The final wave of immigration involves the Mai clans on the north side of the Sau River. Generally, Mai clans followed Tombema ones, although some Mai clans entered the area at about the same time as Aiamani/Lyungini groups. The Mai clans living furthermost to the east on the lower Sau, trace their origins to the Wabaga area. They entered the Kompiama area probably just opposite the present station site, across the Sau River. Gradually as other clans arrived from the west, they were pushed, or moved voluntarily further east, to their present locations. These clans were probably barred from crossing the Sau because that area was already becoming occupied by Aiamani and Lyungini groups.

It is not always clear for what reasons these clans left their places of origin. The stated causes often seem too petty for the consequences. Yet Kompiama was one place to which disgruntled central Enga groups moved. During the past two generations, there have been some minor population movements from the Kompiama area towards the Wapi. When speaking of the *tee*, Tombema say that it goes on and on until there are no longer people. With the expanding populations, the *tee* system too could expand, as it continues to do today through the Wapi and beyond it. Kompiama, however, is the northern point of a triangle, of which Wabaga and Wapenamanda form the base points, in which most *tee* activity takes place.

## Patterns of Warfare

The first patrol to enter the "uncontrolled" Sau Valley after the war (in July 1948) noted that "many old houses were seen and most places were devoid of stockades and such devices . . . it is thought that fighting is not general" (Patrol report no. 1, 1948:4). Other, later reports say that the "best fortifications yet seen in Wabag were found on the divide between the Sau-Lai Rivers". Still others speak of the destruction caused by intertribal fighting between Sau groups. One of the most interesting comments from a patrol officer was that "fighting around the lower Sau is very rarely between two groups only; as mercenaries are often used, this tends to give everyone in the vicinity an interest in the battle" (Patrol report no. 3, 1950:8). While these remarks reflect varying opinions, Tombema speak as though warfare was a constant feature of their lives before enforced pacification. Homicide compensations, which continue to be made today, suggest the prevalence of warfare, death and destruction. Nevertheless, it is argued later in this book that the *tee* is a powerful mechanism of social control, containing aggression and inhibiting warfare, at least at times when a *tee* neared. In the patterns of warfare and the mobilization of a fighting force are many contradictions which control their spread and furore.

Warfare is always discussed as if clans were involved. Regardless of who participated in a given battle, enemies are allotted on a clan basis. A clan's enemies are known by two terms: "to fight with weapons" (*yanda pipi*), is the most common usage among Tombema speakers; and "war regalia ever-ready" (*kutipu kalya palenge*), a phrase more often used by Mai speakers. Allies are said simply "to be together" (*pakenge*). While enemies are traditional, well-defined, and never changing, allies are always *ad hoc*. In the past times of war, there were no permanent alliances between clans in the area. There were some clans with whom war was not made, but this does not mean that their members were automatic allies. The evidence of informants is that individual men from non-enemy clans, or even at times from enemy ones, joined in a battle for reasons of their own. Thus, while clans were the warring units, allies were recruited on an individual, not clan basis. One of the most important criteria of an ally was an existing *tee* relationship. But the death of an ally, a man not a member of one of the principal combatant groups, had to be compensated by men of the allied side, not by men of the killer's group. This rule alone would seem to place limits on the escalation of any given battle.

The most striking feature of warfare throughout the Kompiama and wider Enga area is the oft-quoted saying "we marry the people we fight" (Meggitt 1965a:101). In every case, a clan's fiercest enemies provide the majority of wives. It is not uncommon for a man's mother, his wife, and sister's husband, to be members of different clans, all of which are bitter enemies of his own. Clans which do not intermarry or do so only infrequently, are usually clans with whom war is not made. The social environment of Kompiama clans is narrowly circumscribed and restricted: marriage and warfare take place among contiguous groups. But equally important is the fact that a person's most important *tee* exchange partners also come from these same enemy groups. To marriage and warfare can be added exchange with members of the same groups. These features contribute to a basic paradox: enemy groups provide a person's closest exchange allies taken mainly from affinal and matrilateral categories.[7] Exchange partners do not fight for there seems little point in trying to kill a person who is essential to one's *tee* performance and on whom one depends for most of his wealth. There is good evidence to believe that *tee* concerns took precedence over hostility in the individual case: *tee* partners who met on the battlefield would move away from each other, or retire. Sometimes they would forewarn a close exchange partner of an impending attack. The important point is that these extra-clan ties and allegiances based on exchange can limit the extent of an individual's participation in clan wars. This fact compounded would seem to inhibit a clan's war-making potential.

These patterns of warfare, marriage and exchange apply to every Tombema and Mai clan. Clans who make war and inter-marry, are not only geographically contiguous, but also in most cases either precede or follow each other in *tee*-making order. A chain-like network exists in which members of warring groups depend on each other most of all for *tee* access and achievement through the flow of pigs and valuables. These facts certainly serve to mute and control intergroup hostilities.

Wars were fought for a multitude of reasons: theft, non-returned bridewealth, accusations of sorcery, past killings and disputed boundaries. Ostensible reasons for war are, however, little more than that; clans who are true enemies have a history of struggle and warfare, and any single incident is unlikely to have a "real" cause, but rather is part of a continual and continuing cycle of enmity. Individuals also fight wars for a variety of personal reasons. There is no evidence in Kompiama of clans living on land forcibly taken, or now claimed by an enemy group as formally theirs. In a number of instances, there are small patches of ground between neighbouring enemy clans which are still disputed, but gardens are not made there by either side. These areas seem more symbolic of enemy status than foci of root causes of hostility. In the Mamagakini clan, an example occurred in the past of the displacement of a population by amicable agreement rather than warfare. In general, Kompiama appears to have been a refuge for clans from central Enga. Populations continually displaced each other in the area. But with land readily available, minor confrontation led to moving away rather than war. Arriving groups pushed others to their present locations which have now been fixed for several generations.

## The Mamagakini Clan

Mamagakini, a Lyungini clan with a population of 535 persons, is the clan from which the most detailed information of this book was collected. The men in the samples used throughout this book are drawn from Mamagakini's various subclans. Mamagakini territory is located northeast of the patrol post, across two low ranges, and part of their boundary is the Sau River, running eastward to join the Lai. Mamagakini are a Tombema-speaking clan, yet due to their proximity to the Sau River, maintain extensive contacts of all kinds with Mai groups. Mamagakini territory comprises approximately ten square kilometres, yielding an overall population density of 54 persons per square kilometre, a figure high compared to the Sau average. Most homesteads were traditionally located along a ridge splitting their territory. A vehicle road completed in 1967-68 now runs through Mamagakini territory to the Sau River. Many people have moved down to the lower altitudes. The various Mamagakini subclans are dispersed throughout their territory, and have some residential discreteness. This is not strict, but depends more importantly on inherited garden sites and a desire to live near them.

Mamagakini is composed of eight subclans: Mapete (93 persons), Mupani (50), Munimi (79), Tareyane (108), Tayowe (135), Kopane (9), Yauwani (38) and Angaleyani (23). Mupani is an immigrant subclan, not a "true" (*tolae*, "straight") one. Mupani say they were once a clan the size of Mamagakini, but death through illness reduced their numbers. However, when Mamagakini was moving towards its present location, Mupani, who were living with the Pinai clan, split off. Some came with Mamagakini to their present home, some remained with Pinai as they do today.[8] Mupani have joined Mamagakini as a subclan, they have their own *tee* ground, and observe rules of clan exogamy.[9] Munimi too, is not a "true" Mamagakini subclan. Munimi means "woman's reed skirt", and this subclan was founded by a Mapete woman's son. Mapete means "men's loin covering". A Mapete woman married a man of another clan and after her husband died, she returned with her son, named Lakaiyala. This man is thought by some to be a patrilateral cross-cousin of the grandfathers of present adult men. Both Mapete and Munimi are not named after men, rather, they are descriptive titles.

Tayowe are thought to be "straight" Mamagakini, that is, patrilineal descendants, though there is some disagreement.[10] Tareyane contains a subgroup called Puli which are believed to be sister's sons to Tareyane. Yauwani and Angaleyani are both immigrant subclans, their parent clans living elsewhere in the Kompiama area. Yauwani and Angaleyani continue to intermarry with Mamagakini but yet consider themselves "part" of Mamagakini.

Thus, of eight Mamagakini subclans, three are immigrant groups: Mupani, Yauwani and Angaleyani. At least one other has known maternal connections to Mamagakini, Munimi. Only Yauwani and Angaleyani intermarry with other Mamagakini subclans. The others have become fully incorporated and observe the rule of clan exogamy.

Kopane and Angaleyani recognize no further divisions within the subclan. The other subclans do, but I reiterate that I could find no functional significance (for example, marriage payment responsibility, see Meggitt 1965a, 1974) attached to them, and indeed their names were very rarely mentioned. The following are named "lineages" (*pongo lili*) of Mamagakini subclans: Mapete-Ompo (78 members), Kendepo (15); Mupani-Kusi (29), Minjolene (21); Munimi-Paipu (47), Piyau (32); Tareyane-Maipe (19), Puli (54), Wambupena (35); Tayowe-Nandipa (107), Korale (28); and Yauwani-Neneyape (25), Kiwani (13). After some prodding, informants speculated that lineage founders were father's grandfathers of the current generation of adult men; men who had led these groups into the Kompiama area.

In addition to immigrant groups and assimilated nonagnatic ones living with Mamagakini, a large percentage of the resident population have remembered "nonagnatic" ancestors linking them to Mamagakini. Tombema distinguish agnates (*tolae* Mamagakini, "straight", "correct", "right" Mamagakini) from patrilateral cognates (*mandipae*, "to bear or produce"). Mother's brothers and maternal crosscousins are called "the owners of the children" (*wane tange*) of their sister. Male affines, whether co-resident or not, are referred to as "men of women" (*wanakali*). Persons who reside without kinship connections of any kind are called "other people" (*endakali waka*).

For the purpose of classification here, it is important to distinguish "etic" nonagnates from "emic" ones, a point emphasized by McArthur (1967) and A.J. Strathern (1972) among others. Etic nonagnates are those persons with a remembered nonagnatic ancestor providing access to group membership. In some sense, this is an "objective" classification, elicited from persons in genealogical questioning. It is an anthropological definition of "nonagnate". Some of these persons however, despite remembered nonagnatic connections are classified by co-residents as agnates, *"tolae* Mamagakini" in the present case. In contrast, emic nonagnates are those who have both remembered nonagnatic ancestry and are locally classified and understood to be nonagnates. In other words, some etic nonagnates have been "converted" to emic agnatic status. Meggitt (1965a) calls them "quasi agnates".[11] Etic and emic categories do not coincide, but short genealogical knowledge and rapid "terminological conversion", means there is some overlap.

Table 3 shows Mamagakini's resident, adult male, nonagnatic population: those persons with remembered nonagnatic connections present in their genealogies. These are etic nonagnates. They are listed according to their kinship link to Mamagakini. The "dependents" category, lists the children of these men. In-marrying women are here excluded.

**Table 3**  Mamagakini Nonagnates

| Mamagakini Link | Number | Dependents | Total |
|---|---|---|---|
| M (*mandipae*) | 21 | 43* | 64 |
| MH | 3 | 11 | 14 |
| WB/ZH (*wanakali*) | 18 | 21 | 39 |
| FM | 13 | 13 | 26 |
| FFM | 10 | 22 | 32 |
| no connection | 4 | 4 | 8 |
| Totals | 69 | 114 | 183 |

\* Of this total, two children whose mother has died, live with their mother's brother; two others live with their divorced mother, who has returned to Mamagakini. The remaining 39 are dependents of the 21 men.

Based on individual genealogies, 183 of 535 (34 per cent) Mamagakini residents, adults and children (excluding in-marrying women) are nonagnates. While all Yauwani and Angaleyani members are necessarily included in these figures, only those Munimi and Mupani residents with known nonagnatic connections are included. That is, although these subclans are believed to have nonagnatic founders, or to be immigrant groups, only individuals in them with other, stated, nonagnatic links are included in the above table. If all Munimi and Mupani were included, the percentage of nonagnates would almost double.

Men and their dependents whose father's mothers were Mamagakini, or men whose father's father's mothers were

Mamagakini, are genealogical nonagnates, but in kinship terminology, are not distinguished from actual agnates. Additionally, 39 of 43 dependents of men whose mothers were Mamagakini women are also terminologically agnatic (Meggitt's "quasi agnates"), although their fathers (*mandipaes*) are not. Thus, subtracting men with a father's mothers' link and their dependents (26), a father's father's mothers' link and their dependents (32), and dependents of men of Mamagakini mothers (39), only 86 Mamagakini residents (or 16 per cent) are emic nonagnates. As generations pass, nonagnatic ancestors are forgotten and their descendents become "straight" members of the clan. The "terminological conversion" process requires just two generations. But, terminological transformation does not necessarily signal total incorporation. A person assumes full membership by actively participating in clan affairs and by observing rules of exogamy.

Persons in other categories are nonagnates both emically and etically. Men whose mother's husbands are Mamagakini, and their dependents, become agnates gradually by maintaining residence and by observing rules of exogamy which might not ordinarily apply to them. If they observe these rules, they disclaim their own clan affiliation. Often, children whose mothers married Mamagakini men, will themselves marry inside Mamagakini and their children's children will then become *tolae* Mamagakini. Those in the *wanakali* (wife's brother/sister's husband) category and those who are *mandipae* (Mamagakini mothers) are emically nonagnates, but their descendents, if they maintain residence with Mamagakini, will not be. Obviously too, persons with no Mamagakini connections are emically not "straight" Mamagakini. These are persons who have been sponsored, in most cases, by other resident nonagnates.

There are 69 genealogical nonagnates among adult or nearly adult men resident with Mamagakini. The total number of men in this category is 149. Thus about half (46 per cent) of all adult men are nonagnatic. Subtracting those men whose father's mother or father's father's mother were Mamagakini, but retaining resident men whose mothers were Mamagakini women, reduces that percentage to 31 per cent (46 of 149). These figures are comparable with those of Meggitt, as reanalyzed and presented by McArthur (1967:284). If resident nonagnatic adult women (usually wives of Mamagakini men) are added to the 183 (etic) nonagnates, 56 per cent of those persons resident inside Mamagakini (301 of 535) are domiciled on the basis of linkages which are not etically agnatic.

I do not intend to analyze in detail the significance of non-agnates in Tombema society. The above discussion is intended to place my data in the context of an old theoretical debate. To discuss them further would create an impression that Tombema themselves are overly concerned with who is or is not agnatic. The fact is, they are not. The figures show that men with Mamagakini mothers and wives are readily and often admitted to membership. In most instances, widowed or divorced Mamagakini women brought their children back to their natal clan, and they become full members of it. In other cases, men decided to live with their wife's or sister's husband's group after disputes of one kind or another with their own clansmen. Although the terminological conversion to agnatic status takes two generations, I know of no cases where adult sister's sons or wife's brothers or sister's husbands have suffered at the hands of "full" Mamagakini members. There is no one point where "true" membership is achieved. Persons are members of a clan until they show they are not to be so considered, by breaking the rules of exogamy for example. The whole notion of "membership" in clan groups is somewhat vague.[12] Changes in residence can be sponsored by single members. In some cases, resident non-agnates sponsored other nonagnates. Nonagnates are not less wealthy than agnates; they are not more often unmarried; they have a higher number of exchange allies on average; and they do not have to tolerate smaller garden plots or limited access to cultivable land. Seven of 18 Mamagakini bigmen (39 per cent) are nonagnates, three have Mamagakini wives, four have Mama-gakini mothers. In sum, no status differences could be detected between agnatic and nonagnatic residents. And, it does not appear that Mamagakini is any different from other clans in the Kompiama area. In most cases, some kinship connection to Mamagakini is essential for taking up residence. Only four men without some Mamagakini tie were resident.

## Conclusion

Using one style of analysis, Tombema society could be viewed as if organized in groups, exogamous patrilineal clans. But the topic of this book, the *tee* system, demands a different focus, if only because the *tee* community and the important relationships validated by it, go beyond the narrow confines of a person's own clan. And too, it is an individual, not some other social entity, who organizes his *tee* relations and alone makes decisions relevant to *tee* performance. In the following chapters, the formal structure of Tombema society is given little prominence. Rather, the individual ties of exchange are given most attention. Throughout, the point is argued that exchange concerns are individual ones and not related to group, that is, clan motives. Rather, the *tee* is the locus of intragroup competition. My analytical preference for individuals and networks of linked individuals instead of groups, hinges on what I believe to be the bases for decisions and actions taken in the *tee*. The following chapter begins by discussing *tee* policy and practice.

## Notes

1. The Kompiama Local Government Council was established in 1966, partially uniting the four census districts. The Wale-Tarua and Wapi census divisions are only now becoming fully represented on the Council.
2. Lang (1973) records *tombeama* as meaning "down river". Waddell (1972:15) calls the area *tubiama*, a "Lai Valley division". My informants rejected the meaning given by Lang. They suggested that Tombema is a name, that is, a dialect, like Mai. They also wanted me to use that name in reference to them. I use Tombema in preference to the more established Saui.
3. Meggitt (1964a:193) says affines (*imangge*) are people "of one ridge pole". *Imangge* contains the root *ima* which means ridge-pole, but Tombema, at least, do not make the connection that Meggitt notes for the Mae.
4. *Sandalu* has decreased in frequency, but is still held occasionally. Tombema are adamant that *sandalu* is held for *tee* reasons as Waddell (1972:86) also notes. A *sandalu* occurred during my stay in which I participated. It occurred prior to *tee lyunguna* (see chapter six).
5. At the time of fieldwork, there was very little cash-cropping of coffee in the Kompiama area. I recorded no details, but I would estimate that about $2 per capita per annum is earned in coffee production. By comparison, Baiyer, Wapenamanda and Wabaga areas produce much more coffee. The *tee* has also been slow in coming from these areas.
6. Populations are taken from the tax records of the Kompiama Council. A comparison of their census for Mamagakini with mine suggests high

accuracy. Paying taxes in Kompiama is a mark of prestige and self-sufficiency, and few people try to avoid paying them.

7. Melpa (A.J. Strathern and A.M. Strathern 1969:139) tend to contract marriages in clans that are "minor enemies", with whom *moka* relationships are important. Kuma (Reay 1959:59) prefer to marry into friendly clans. "Hostility between clans" in Kuma is "strictly incompatible with inter-marriage . . . ". Enga alone seem to marry and exchange with acknowledged major enemies, a point of some importance later in this book.

8. A number of Mupani men have Pinai mothers. Pinai live near the Kompiama station and aside from these Mupani marriages, no other Mamagakini marriages with Pinai exist. Thus, the split of part of Mupani from Pinai appears to have taken place no more than two generations ago.

9. Recently however, a Mupani man married a woman whose mother is a Tayowe woman. Normally, this marriage would be prohibited. This suggests that at least some Mupani interpret exogamous rules less strictly than "true" Mamagakini members.

10. Some informants said that Tayowe was also founded by a Mapete woman's son, a Yauwani man. It is sometimes also said that Kopane are the "children of Tareyane".

11. In so doing, Meggitt (1965a) mixes the emic and etic notions of agnate. His clans thus appear more "agnatic" than they really are (see McArthur 1967; Barnes 1967).

12. The question of what defines membership in a clan has not been answered properly. Is participation in clan affairs the criterion? Many authors admit that affiliation may be uncertain in many cases. But is membership in a descent group, strictly defined, important? Anthropologists' preoccupation with groups has led to the view that the people studied are also preoccupied with them. A person's group affiliation is not worn as a tag nor is it constantly referred to, at least in Tombema society.

# TWO

# The *Tee* System:
# Policy and Practice

The *tee* grows on a person's skin

An Enga saying

In its essentials, the *tee* is an intricate economic situation involving credit, finance, and repayment, often with interest. Credit through loans in the form of pigs and other valuables are invested with partners during an initiatory period of transacting called *saandi pingi*. Men must give pigs to other men to satisfy obligations, including that of friendship, and pigs that cannot be provided from a person's own stock must be financed from other partners. These accumulated debts of *saandi* are then repaid during the *tee pingi* phase of the cycle. This is a time of great ceremony and prestige-seeking, as men line their pigs in rows and boast of their ability to repay. Men whose rows of pigs are the longest are acclaimed "bigmen", known in Enga as *kamongo*. They are famous for their skill in attracting pigs, and for their generosity in dispersing them. Sometimes, but not invariably, a further series of exchanges follow *tee pingi*. It is called *yae pingi*. *Tee*-makers return sides of pork to men who contributed live pigs to their *tees*. Each set of exchanges follows definite directions. A man takes *saandi* from certain partners only and invests them with other men. These man then make *tee* to him, repaying their debts. *Yae pingi* is made to the same partners to whom a man gave *saandi*. It is a return for their *tee pingi*. In any phase, contributors and recipients of valuables are discrete; a man cannot take and give to the same person in any of the *tee's* stages.

These are the barest "ground rules" of *tee*-making. I will elaborate on these phases and show how the rules are put into practice.

The terms *tee pingi* and *mena tee pingi* ("to make [pig]*tee*") refer both to the institution as a whole, and more specifically to the middle phase of *tee* cycle when the biggest displays of gifts and live pigs takes place. *Tee*, in the phrase *tee lenge,* means "to request", "to ask for" (*lenge* — "to speak"), and some informants insist that herein lies the meaning upon which the whole institution is based.[1] For after all, in the *tee*, a person is constantly asking others for pigs. As the intermediate phase in the cycle, *tee pingi* is essentially a time for requiting debts incurred during the preliminary phase, known as *saandi pingi*. *Saandi pingi* is made to exchange partners in the confident expectation of a return with interest when the *tee* is subsequently made. But while a profitable increase is always hoped for, a return based on Tombema equivalences is acceptable and sufficient to sustain the exchange relationship. The profit motive in *tee* transactions has, in my view, been over emphasized by previous writers (compare Westermann 1968; Meggitt 1974). Enga do, however, distinguish *saandi* from other categories of debt, called *yano*, when a more or less exact equivalence in repayment is due. Furthermore, while a man can repay a debt, *yano yukungi* (literally "to pull or lift it out") he cannot repay a debt of *saandi* (*saandi yukingi* is not used) except by making the *tee*.

In sum *saandi* transactions take place between *tee* partners within the *tee* context, while other debts are created between men who may share no *tee* status and in theory require a different sort of repayment. An analysis of specific *saandi* transactions between individual *tee* partners is made in chapter five. It will become clear that *saandi* are not, in a strict sense, "gifts" at all, and Enga assured me that they do not give valuables as *saandi* "without cause or reason", that is, unless a specific request is made. Although there are variations to this rule, *saandi* are requested by those with a specific need, and a man does not give a payment to another man unless he has "asked for it", (*saandi tee lenge*). Thus *saandi pingi* and *tee pingi* are best glossed as "debt incurring payment" and "debt requiting payment" rather than begging the question by calling them initiatory of main "gifts" (compare Meggitt 1974).

In any *tee* cycle, these two phases are clearly demarcated and essential parts. The third phase, called *mena yae pingi* (*mena yae* − cooked pork), in which a return payment is given to those who made *tee pingi* is sometimes, though not invariably, part of a *tee* cycle. Tombema, apparently in contrast to other Enga (Meggitt 1974:171) maintain that this stage of the *tee* is negotiable and does not follow automatically from the *tee pingi* phase. Ethnohistorical accounts of *tee* sequences lend evidence to this proposition. If the *yae* phase is omitted, a new sequence of *saandi pingi* is begun by partners in the opposite direction from the previous *saandi*, thereby inducing a reciprocating *tee* from partners in the opposite direction from the previous one. While a simple diagram belies its inherent complexity, the following is an ideal cycle of three *tee* (see Meggitt 1974).

**Figure 1**   An Ideal Cycle of *Tee*

| Tee | | individuals in clans | | | | |
|---|---|---|---|---|---|---|
| | a | b | c | d | e | f |

| | | | | | | saandi pingi |
| --- → → → → → → → → → → → → → → → → → → → → → → → → → → |
| **I** | tee pingi | | | | | |
| ← ← ← ← ← ← ← ← ← ← ← ← ← ← ← ← ← ← ← ← ← ← ← ← ← ← ← |
| | | | | | | yae pingi |
| → → → → → → → → → → → → → → → → → → → → → → → → → → → |

| | saandi pingi | | | | | |
| ← ← ← ← ← ← ← ← ← ← ← ← ← ← ← ← ← ← ← ← ← ← ← ← ← ← ← |
| **II** | | | | | | tee pingi |
| → → → → → → → → → → → → → → → → → → → → → → → → → → → |

| | | | | | | saandi pingi |
| → → → → → → → → → → → → → → → → → → → → → → → → → → → |
| **III** | tee pingi | | | | | |
| ← ← ← ← ← ← ← ← ← ← ← ← ← ← ← ← ← ← ← ← ← ← ← ← ← ← ← |

Any Enga can present such a picture, but anyone can also speak of exceptions and irregularities: several *tee* flowing in the same direction, *yae pingi* not being made, *tee* of opposing factions, *tee* moving in opposite directions, and so on. The duration and direction of each phase is not strictly set by custom, so an inherent aspect of *tee* procedure is its negotiability deriving from the political context in which it takes place.

Although the separate phases can be described as if they are discrete, there is in fact, a single continuum of giving and receiving between individual exchange partners and it is thought of as such. It is not simply that debts are incurred during *saandi pingi* and reciprocated during *tee pingi*, and then a new cycle begins. If a *yae pingi* phase follows, this creates new debts in the next round of *saandi. Yae pingi* payments become "debt incurring" ones. If no such phase follows, the *tee pingi* payments themselves create debts for the following *saandi* period. Pigs are in constant movement between partners, and to view *tee* phases as sharply discrete and bounded is to misrepresent ideas of *tee* giving. All phases affect future ones. Debts incurred in one *tee* can be held over and returned in another. Pigs may be given against the main flow to gain credits in a later *tee* before the present cycle has been completed. Each individual tallies his own transactions with other partners, and each transaction feeds into a single ongoing relationship. Clearly, the complexities are great and many more will emerge in the course of this book.

Having presented this general sketch of the *tee*, I will now discuss each phase of it in greater detail.

## Tee **Phases and Processes**

### saandi pingi

Enga say "*saandi* pulls pigs", noting further that men who do not give *saandi* do not find pigs in the *tee*. They also say that "men do not give *saandi* without reason", that is, unless requested. The first statement is a simple truism in Kompiama: it is obvious to all that those men who do not give pigs do not receive them. The second, however, is not so obvious and here the theme of shame intrudes into *tee* giving as a powerful sanction to enforce the eventual repayment of debts.

Although Tombema–Enga do not themselves make the contrast, there are two types of *saandi* transactions: one which follows the stated rule and another, which while not explicitly requested, is the result of the actions of the potential recipient of the *saandi* payment. Both types are solicited, one explicitly, the other implicitly. I will not deal at present with the reasons individuals give for seeking *saandi*. The person who gives *saandi* is not entitled to ask the recipient what he intends to do with it. Although the information might be volunteered, if the valuable is being passed on, the immediate recipient may not know its ultimate purpose himself. The real point at issue is the relationship between two individuals dealing in the *tee*. Where the pig has come from is not the concern of the recipient; where it is going is less important to the donor than his relationship with the immediate recipient, for ultimately, he alone guarantees the return regardless of its destination.[2]

The mechanics of this process are diagrammed below:

**Figure 2**   A *Tee* Transaction

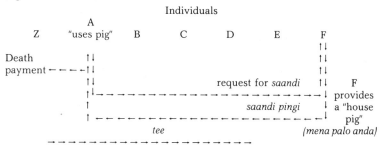

The seven letters above represent individuals in a *tee* chain. Most likely, they are members of separate clans, but they may be fellow clansmen.

Individual A needs a pig, perhaps to make a death payment (*laita pingi*) for his child to his wife's kinsmen. Such needs, when *saandi* may be required, are as numerous and varied as Tombema contexts for giving. Man A, not wishing to use a pig of his own, or having none to give, asks B for one, but this man also has none suitable to give him. So, B in turn asks C who asks D, who also has no pig to give, until the sequence of requests reaches F. B may simply refuse A and for various reasons, decides not to ask further, in which case A solicits someone else. By the time F has received the request for *saandi*, great distances and numbers of clans may have been bridged and it is highly unlikely that F knows A and the reasons for his request of a pig. Person B probably knows, and perhaps C, but that knowledge quickly fades with distance, and if it is not volunteered, it remains unknown. If it turns out that F has a pig he will give (whether "house-raised" or not), he agrees to give it as *saandi* to E. Man E may say to whom he is giving it (that is, to D), but he may not, and E may or may not know where the pig F gives him has come from.

The pig is given to E, then to D, to C, to B and finally to A, who with due ceremony makes the death payment to his in-law in clan Z. The links in this chain are pairs of men who may be close neighbors, but the total chain (Z to F) may span a considerable geographical distance. Based on A's request, a debt of *saandi* has been incurred to B, B to C, C to D, and so on. Only F has incurred no debt, for he has supplied the pig from his own house. Man A has "spent" a pig but clan Z will make a subsequent *tee* before he does. The recipient of A's (really F's) pig in his wife's clan may decide to reciprocate this pig, which will allow A, and in turn B, C, D, and E to requite their earlier debt of *saandi* in order. In this way, lines of debt and credit build in the *tee*. Chains may be shorter or longer than this: A might ask B, who furnishes a pig of his own; in other cases the chain may carry on well beyond F. However, following this one request for a pig by A, many separate individuals are paired as links in a chain, simultaneously taking credit and becoming indebted.

The basic structure of *saandi pingi* is always the same. Pigs from individuals' houses move up the *tee* line step by step between pairs of partners until they are withdrawn and used for specific purposes. The return will originate from the user. The person who makes use of the *saandi* payment must be prudent, for he is responsible for providing the return: hence the basic Tombema rule of not giving *saandi* unless specifically asked. One does not frivolously squander assets nor take undue risks.

Men solicit *saandi* in order to take brides and make other payments that are obligatory or desired, and in this way, all other exchange spheres become incorporated into *tee* prestations and procedure. As long as *saandi* payments flow in the proper direction, that is, in the direction for building credits, it does not matter how they are actually invested or used.

Within this general framework, there is much scope for variation and individual strategy. In this way, *saandi pingi* becomes more than just a mechanical process. There are two distinct strategies in *saandi*-making. One is for a man to supply as many pigs as possible from his own house, which of course, presupposes that he has the pigs to do so. If he follows this course, the returns in the *tee*, including any attached profit, come to him and he can distribute them to whomever he chooses. The alternative strategy is for a man to finance by *saandi* from others (as, in Figure 2, B, C, D, and E did) and take the added risk of proper return, so that he himself can fulfil his own debts. In practice, bigmen and aspiring men employ both strategies, financing through *saandi* to the hilt, and often leaving themselves short of pigs at home too. These are the financial and production risks which if successful can lead to greater prestige.

*Saandi* may also take a different form. This type is not requested but rather is an inducement to attract the unpromised house-raised pigs of a *tee* partner. This process is again initiated by the potential *saandi* recipient who has a house-raised pig. Consider the following typical example. A man and his wife have finished clearing and planting a garden and decide to reward themselves by eating pork. They have also been looking after pigs of their own, raised at home which belong to them.[3] The *tee* is still some time off. The man goes to a *tee* partner in the direction that *saandi* is asked (and in the direction that the *tee* will eventually be given) and tells him that he and his wife have a very large pig that they have been looking after and would like to give him when the *tee* comes. He makes his intention known quite informally and may even refer to it only obliquely by saying "my wife and I are tired of feeding pigs" or "a pig of mine always strays from home and needs to be given away" (but without mentioning to whom). However the message is phrased, the meaning is clear enough: "If you would like this pig, send *saandi*". With this type of veiled request, the kind of *saandi* payment to be given, for example live pig or pork, is left for the contributor to decide. As will be pointed out later, the person who provides *saandi* has the chance to manipulate these requests to his own advantage. In more explicit *saandi* requests the would-be recipient can specify the type of *saandi* he needs; this information is passed with the original request. After the implicit overture, it is up to the potential *tee* recipient, if he wants the pig, to find one as *saandi* to offer as inducement for it. *Saandi* approaches our conception of a gift only in this form. A person has made no specific request for a *saandi* payment, but has implicitly sought *saandi* for a pig he and his wife have raised. My early query was, "Why don't you kill your own pig and eat it, rather than incur a debt by seeking *saandi* for it?" But it is obvious that such an act would be foolish in *tee* reasoning. If a man is going to give a pig away, he might as well take *saandi* for it. When the *tee* comes, he is able to present the pig and gain prestige by giving it away.

A person may send out such messages for many of his own pigs. A couple rarely kill and eat their own pigs. Why should they, when they can eat those of others and later gain renown by presenting their own pigs to him? (See Rubel and Rosman 1978.)[4]

Furthermore, house pigs that are not promised (by taking *saandi* for them) are still susceptible to being taken "for nothing" in the *tee*. A close, important partner may "cry" for them and the owner then be obliged to give it, without having gained the benefit of *saandi* for it.

Some other strategic aspects of *saandi*-making can be briefly mentioned. *Saandi* requests that are implicit do not necessarily require immediate action. A man, though, may wait too long, until another fills the request and the pig is promised to someone else. However, the *saandi* contributor tries to wait until he has received two such offers. Since he can specify the kind of *saandi* to be given, he may kill one pig, send sides of pork to two different partners, and rightfully expect to receive two pigs in the *tee* for the one of his own he has killed.[5] By making *saandi* in this fashion, he may be able to double his initial investment. A man may also give pigs in advance of the *tee* in the direction it will follow, a practice known as "taking out a pig" (*mena yukupae*). A person may take such a pig without giving *saandi* for it, but vaguely promising to do so later. When he subsequently gives *saandi* the person who gave the *yukupae* may invest it with another man and gain the return of another pig. When the *tee* is made, the *saandi* contributor may make a strong appeal for this additional pig, even though his *saandi* was intended for a pig he had already received as *yukupae*. Tombema-Enga say that a man should not seek *saandi* for a pig that is not his own to dispose of, either one received as *yukupae*, or, more importantly, one whose rightful owner is further down the *tee* chain.

It should now be apparent that the *saandi pingi* process is highly complex and the potential exists for numerous snags and deceptions. I have merely touched the surface of its intricacies. However, the bonds of friendship and trust, and the accepted responsibility for fulfilling one's obligations make the system work with much less trouble than might be expected.

### tee pingi

The first phase of the *tee* cycle has been characterized as the time for incurring debts. Throughout the Enga area, along its various *tee* roads, individuals have established credits with some partners, and have become indebted in the process to others. Pigs, pork, and other valuables have not simply flowed to one

A *tee* ground (*tee kamapi*) in the Tsaka Valley, the day before and the day of the presentation of pigs in *tee mamaku*.

end of the *tee* chain from the other, but have been taken out and put in by individuals all along the way. This point has not been sufficiently noted by Meggitt (1958, 1972, 1974). All debts have accrued in one direction, towards the *tee*. A hard and fast rule is that one cannot incur debts in the direction which the following *tee* will not cover. A man does not ask *saandi* from partners who will make the next *tee* to him. The *tee* will reciprocate their debts to him. No person in a *tee*-giving position would listen to a request for *saandi* from a man in a *tee*-receiving position. Givers and takers in any sequence are absolutely separate.

The *tee pingi* phase of the cycle is the time during which all debts incurred in the *saandi* phase should be reciprocated, at least theoretically. In contrast to the often private *saandi* contributions, *tees* are public, festive occasions, which in Tombema at least occur on a subclan basis. Each subclan has its own ceremonial ground (*tee kamapi*) and each of its members has placed his individual row of pig stakes (*mena limando*) across the ground, indicating the number of pigs he will give away.[6] These may be pigs he has already received from *saandi* investments, pigs a new partner may have given him without prior *saandi*, pigs partners have returned to him so that he can present them publicly (*mena yukupae*), and pigs his wife has raised at home (*mena palo anda*) and are now being injected into the *tee* flow by him.

Using figure 2, the hypothetical example can be followed through the *tee* phase.

It has been shown how a pig of F's was passed to A and was used to make a death payment to a partner in clan Z. The person in clan Z who took the pig, might well have invested it too, but we will suppose he has held the pig, that is, it is at his house. When his subclan (of clan Z) makes its *tee*, he makes a decision. Suppose that he and A are brothers-in-law, and A is a valued exchange partner. The man in clan Z finds two pigs (of his own or from other *tee* transactions) and gives them to A, usually making it clear that he is making this return in reciprocation for the earlier death (*saandi*) payment. If instead, he has reinvested the pig, and only one "replacement" has been returned for it, this pig will be passed on to A.[7] When A makes his *tee* next, he passes these two pigs on to B. There is no thought of stepping over B to give directly to C, or to F; the immediate transaction involves only A and B, and to whom the pigs are given concerns A only as far as B. B then takes the two pigs, ties them to stakes, and publicly gives them to C when he makes his *tee*.

B's place in this chain (like those of C, D, and E) is simply as a middle-man, known in Tombema as a "rope-holding man" (*kende tombo nyingi akali*). B has helped A secure a pig to make the death compensation and he is therefore entitled to take these pigs (and thereby extend his own row of pig stakes) and pass them onward to C. He is recognized for his ability as a *tee* maker, as an agent for others: a man with a high credit rating and financial reputation. He does not "own" these pigs in any sense, he controls them, and has had a hand in bringing off the transaction for A. Most importantly, the exact pigs that A receives from Z must be given to B, for, according to *tee* rule, no substitutions of any kind are permitted. B at his *tee* gives them to C, who likewise ties them to stakes, and gives them in due course to D, and so on down the line, reaching F. Ability to finance and a high credit rating are as important, if not more so, than actual assets in live pigs. F started this process with a *saandi* payment of a pig from his own house. He takes the pigs from E and is now faced with a decision of his own. He can remove these pigs from the *tee* if he wishes. If one or both are good breeding sows he may do so. He can substitute and send them on. He may decide to send them both onward in the *tee* he is soon to make, begin new partnerships with his "profit" or gain further credits down the line with established partners. The choice is his, in short, to hold or to dispose of these pigs as he wishes.

Just as in *saandi pingi*, when payments were put in and taken out along *tee* chains, in *tee pingi* too, house-raised pigs and other valuables are put in and taken out in reciprocation for house-pigs contributed during *saandi*. In neither phase therefore, do pigs become over-concentrated in any one part of the network; rather the flow of pigs continually evens out.

Each *saandi* payment linking two individuals follows its own prescribed course. The *saandi* contributor does not usually know where his payment has ended, but he may know two or three of the men along the chain who have handled the pig. When these individuals make their *tee*, he is present to see what his investment is likely to bring in return, and follows carefully the steps to his most immediate partner, from whom he will directly receive. If, as frequently happens, bigmen have a hand in a hundred or more transactions in a single *tee* sequence, the difficulty and complexity of keeping track of where one's investments have gone beyond immediate partners, means a formidable task.[8]

Depending on a person's productive and financial ability, and the reliability of his partners, and that of partners of partners up the *tee* chain in meeting their obligations, a man can essentially reciprocate, although not perfectly, his outstanding debts in a *tee*. Of course, the longer the *saandi* chains, the more precarious and uncertain one's control over the return. Again it is worth noting that *tee* chains are made up of dyads of men and their success depends on each in turn fulfilling their obligations. Most pigs are passed onward, though some are taken out of the *tee* to replenish a person's home herd. Most individual herds are diminished following a major *tee* but not to the extent one might expect. From one point of view, in *saandi* and *tee*, Tombema are simply exchanging pigs *quid pro quo*. However, in the next phase, the "return pork payment" (*mena yae pingi*), pigs are killed as a beginning to the next cycle of exchanges.

*mena yae pingi*

I have already mentioned the Tombema view that *yae pingi* is a negotiable and not invariable part of the overall *tee* system. A *yae pingi* does not follow every *tee*, even every major one. Some are planned and never eventuate, and sometimes only certain individuals participate. If a *yae pingi* does not follow a major *tee*, the pigs given in the *tee* itself become a sort of *saandi* for the next *tee* which flows back in the opposite direction to the previous one.

Just as individuals as members of clans have made the *tee* in

*Mena yae pingi*: Sauli men prepare to present pork sides as a return payment for *tee lyunguna*.

serial fashion, the *yae pingi* duplicates the procedure in precisely the reverse order. Clans make *tee* in an exact sequence, and *yae pingi* mirrors that order in the opposite direction. Just as in *saandi* and *tee*, when pigs are taken out of the flow to be used and to replace one's own, pigs are taken out of the *yae* phase too, and consumed. *Yae* is the time for killing pigs and for eating them. Tombema say that when a *yae* occurs, not only men, women and children eat pork, but even dogs have a feast, and the "ground finds a share", that is, the meat rots and is thrown away in the bush. Enga have no method of preserving pork and the length of *tee* chains in distance and in number of links, make for considerable difficulties in the orderly performance of this phase. People are fully aware of this dilemma, and more *tee* partnerships dissolve at the time of *yae pingi* than at any other. But, it is also a time when, due to the surfeit of pork, gifts can be made to create new partnerships between men. If however, a man has passed a pig in the *tee* and it is killed, and he receives no return for it, the material basis of the *tee* relationship, the pig, has vanished. Failure to return pork threatens the relationship and unless it is a strong one, it cannot be smoothed over.

Every person who made the *tee* of live pigs also kills pigs in *yae*.[9] *Yae pingi* procedure can be illustrated by returning to figure 2 (p. 42).

A *saandi* payment has been followed from A to a clan Z member and two pigs have been returned in the *tee* to the original source, F. For the purposes of this example, assume that F took both pigs out of the *tee* and decided to keep them, as he is entitled to do. If however, he had passed them down to another person, these pigs (if still alive) would be in another person's possession, leaving the present holder responsible for making the return. F holds these pigs, having taken them from E to whom he gave the initial *saandi* payment. Clans prior to F's have made their *yae* prestation of killed pigs and the time comes for F's subclan to do so. He knows he has taken two live pigs from E and has not passed them on. *Yae* is the time to reciprocate them, at a rate of one pork side (*mena sapya*) for each live pig given in the *tee*. F thus owes E two sides of pork in this transaction.

F may choose to kill one of the actual pigs E has given him. If however, one or both are sows, he may substitute a pig of his own, although in such circumstances, the actual pigs given in the original *tee* remain, and this may entitle E to make further claims on them later. When they are killed, or if one has a litter, E may ask for a share of it. Additionally, should F receive a side of pork from an earlier clan's *yae pingi*, he may try to use it as repayment to E, rather than kill an actual pig E gave him. This too is not strictly legitimate. Tombema say that as long as the actual pigs remain alive, E (and also the individuals in the chain to clan Z) have an interest in them, and any other payments (aside from the actual pigs) create new chains of debt.

One cannot so easily convert pigs and pork from one debt-chain into debt-reciprocating payments of another. Each pig has its own history of movement from partner to partner. Tombema say that only when it dies do the obligations attached to it cease, and then ideally, a side of pork from that same pig should be returned to its original source.

> To simplify again, F decides to kill one of the actual pigs E gave to him. He does so and sends two pork sides to E. E, remembering his obligations, sends them on to D, then to C, B, and A who gives them once again to his brother-in-law in clan Z. This man is entitled to eat both of them if he desires, since he originally provided them in reciprocation for the death payment. He may eat only one of them, and send the other onward, thus creating a new debt for the next *tee* cycle. At this point, *yae pingi* becomes a prelude for the next *tee* series. A's brother-in-law in clan Z eats one of the sides. When the *saandi* period begins anew, a request of F to E may follow the same path back to Z and he is obliged to give *saandi* along the same path that eventually returns to F. The cycle and the chain of relationships are thus perpetuated through time and *tees*. The person to whom Z passed the additional side of pork is obliged in a similar way.

In this manner, *yae pingi* creates *saandi* obligations for the next *tee*; *saandi* in this sequence going in the opposite direction to the previous one. The process has come full circle, and is ready to begin again. "Big *tee* roads", important, continuing chains of men, become established and prosper in *tee* after *tee*.

A person does not kill in *yae pingi* only those pigs that he has previously taken out of the *tee* as F did. A man may decide to kill expendable, relatively smaller pigs of his own in *yae*, in the hope of acquiring bigger pigs in the *saandi* phase of the following *tee* cycle. With long *tee* chains and as pork begins to rot, individuals who receive sides of pork may actually try to avoid eating or holding sides due to them and instead, quickly reinvest them. Sides of pork that one eats demand a return payment later. However, if a man gives sides of pork that have not been solicited, or if he simply dumps pork sides on someone's door, he will not necessarily find a return at the proper rate. There is thus a check on the indiscriminate slaughtering of pigs. Pork sides given with-

A recipient of *mena yae pingi* takes his sides of pork away. The man, Uu of Mamagakini, received 17 sides that day, all but one of which was passed onward.

out prior request are, nevertheless, often used to initiate new partnerships and may serve as the beginning of a fruitful relationship. All pigs given in the *tee* are not killed; indeed, according to the prescribed rate of return, only half of those given would be needed to satisfy all claims. There is thus a net increase of live pigs in the direction the *tee* has moved. The pigs and valuables comprising this increase become the objects toward which *saandi* is made in the next cycle.

The example I have used throughout this exposition is but one transaction of a hypothesized, notational individual. To appreciate the true complexity of a man's participation in the system, this one transaction must be multiplied by his total number of transactions. An idealized picture of the *tee* has been presented: it is essential to know how it should work, and sometimes does, before examining its political and competitive aspects. These will emerge in the following chapters.

## *Tee* Valuables, Equivalents, and Increments

The *tee* is more properly called "pig *tee*" (*mena tee*), but the transactions between partners involve more than pigs. In Tombema, there is no separate category of persons labelled "trade partners", nor any commodities labelled "trade items". All valuables and commodities that are not produced or available locally, come into the area through the *tee* chains that have been discussed above. Individual *tee* partners supply the scarce resources in Tombema society.[10] Specific areas within the Enga *tee* sphere "produce" these commodities and they are distributed throughout Enga by the *tee* network. All of these valuables are readily convertible into only one other, pigs. Some traditional Tombema valuables have passed out of *tee* currency, others are now disappearing, and still others are coming into the *tee* as conditions and values change. But pigs remain the focus of the entire *tee* system and so far as I was able to discover, they have always been so. They are the single most important valuable in all of Enga. Table 4 gives as complete a summation as possible of Tombema valuables, both past and present, distinguishing those wealth items appropriate to various stages of the *tee*. There is a clear pattern. I shall then discuss their equivalents and the potential increments that "good" and valued *tee* partners can expect for *saandi* payments they make.

In this scheme of valuables, only pigs are appropriate exchange items in every *tee* phase. In the *saandi* phase, pearlshells and cassowaries are only infrequently used to incur debts while live pigs and sides of pork are the most often used currency items. Other items make their entry only in the *tee pingi* phase. The overall picture is that payments of pigs and pork are sent outwards along *tee*-linked pairs of individuals from Tombema in *saandi*, and in the *tee*, they receive in reciprocation, valued items not locally available. Throughout the Enga area, Kompiama is known for its pig production. In the Wapenamanda area, Kompiama is referred to as the "homeland of the pig" (*mena yuu tange*). Tombema convert their pig reserves during *saandi* into other commodities returned in the *tee*. Once in the area, these items circulate against standards of pig and pearlshell, but never pass out of the area in the same direction in which they have come. All items belong to a single "sphere of conveyance" (Rappaport 1967:106–107). But as in the *moka* (A.J. Strathern 1971:112–13) there is no clear demarcation between "utilitarian" and "ceremonial" goods. Furthermore, the "social relationships" and "mode of reciprocity" appropriate to these valuables are the same (see Salisbury 1962; A.J. Strathern 1971:113–14).

The major *tee* items, pigs and pearlshells, are also the essential valuables in every other context of exchange including bridewealth. One cannot distinguish Tombema spheres of exchange on the simple basis of which items are appropriate to each. For this reason and others, the *tee* is best viewed as an exchange forum encompassing all others. The various types of exchanges can be distinguished according to occasion and range of likely

**Table 4**   Tombema–Enga *Tee* Valuables

| Item | Appropriate *Tee* phase | Used in *Tee* | |
|---|---|---|---|
| | | presently | traditionally |
| Pigs (*mena*) | | | |
| Cooked side of pork (*mena sapya*) | *saandi pingi* *yae pingi* | ✓ | ✓ |
| Two cooked sides of pork (*mena ita*) | *saandi pingi* *yae pingi* | ✓ | ✓ |
| Live pig (*mena saka*) | *saandi pingi* *tee pingi* *yae pingi* also *mena yukupae kendesa maingi* | ✓ | ✓ |
| Uncooked side of pork (*mena saka sapya*) | *saandi pingi* *yae pingi* | ✓ | ✓ |
| Cassowaries (*laima*) | | | |
| Baby cassowary chicks (*laima, laima yakane*) | *saandi pingi* *tee pingi* also *laima yukupae* | ✓ | ✓ |
| Shells | | | |
| Mother-of-pearl, *Pinctada maxima* (*mamaku*) | *saandi pingi* *tee pingi* | ✓a | ✓ |
| Baler, *Melo amphora* (*powange, tamenge*) | *tee pingi* | ✓a | ✓ |
| Nassa or dog-whelk shell, *Nassa* (*kakapu*) | *tee pingi* | | ✓ |
| Cowrie necklace, *Cypraea* (*lyange*) | *tee pingi* | | ✓ |
| Conus, *Conus litteratus* (*kaleta*) | *tee pingi* | | ✓ |
| Green snail, *Turbo marmoratus* (*bilyo*) | *tee pingi* | | ✓ |
| Other items | | | |
| Ash salt (*aipi*) | *tee pingi* | ✓b | ✓ |
| Tree oil (*topa*) | *tee pingi* | ✓b | ✓ |

participants, but in the end, all exchanges are connected to the *tee* and particular contexts are only arbitrarily defined.

Table 5 presents the rates of exchange, the return equivalents "expected" by Tombema in reciprocation for their initiatory *saandi* investments. These equivalents represent the lower limits of what is needed to sustain a partnership. If a man returns less than this standard rate, he jeopardizes the relationship. However, he may be able to deter a defection with the promise of later, greater rewards, while temporarily offering only a token gift.

The rates of exchange are only approximations, what is normally expected in reciprocation. For illustration, I return yet

**Table 4** (cont'd) Tombema-Enga *Tee* Valuables

| Item | Appropriate *Tee* phase | Used in *Tee* | |
|---|---|---|---|
| | | presently | traditionally |
| Stone axes *(pyakambyo)*; white/green *(koka/kundina)*; black *(puputi)* | *tee pingi* | ✓b | ✓ |
| Cassowary feather headdress *(laima iti)* | *tee pingi* | ✓b | ✓ |
| Bird of Paradise feathers *(yaka iti)* | *tee pingi* | ✓b | ✓ |
| Black palm: for spears, bows, arrows *(bona)* | *tee pingi* | | ✓c |
| Spinning yarns *(elyoko)* | *tee pingi* | | ✓c |
| Tree fruit *(itatu, musa)* | *tee pingi* | | ✓c |
| Steel axes, spades, shovels | *tee pingi* *saandi pingi* | ✓d | |
| Money | *saandi pingi* *tee pingi* | ✓e | |

a Tombema say that both *mamaku* and *powange* are on their way out of the *tee* as valuables, *powange* rather more quickly.

b These items are presently given only occasionally in the *tee*, but are in no immediate danger of going out of currency. They were more important in past times.

c Tombema locally produce these valuables, but only *bona* was ever used in the *tee*. All of these items are used as *tee* valuables by people of the Wale-Tarua (called Itapu by Tombema). They are, however, not sent towards Kompiama where they are available.

d These items were used in the *tee* immediately after the arrival of Europeans, but have since disappeared from it.

e I have not seen money handed over in the *tee* in the Kompiama area except for one instance when a pig died, was cut and sold for cash. The total sum explicitly representing the pig, was handed to the intended recipient. Mai and Laiapo appear to use money more frequently in the *tee*.

Pigs, pearl shells and cassowaries are the most important Enga *tee* valuables, but pigs the most important of all.

again to figure 2. The first crucial decision rests with A's brother-in-law in clan Z who decides to make a return of two pigs for the one pig *saandi* he received from A. Tombema say he has "added on" or "joined a pig" to the original one (*mena kamba pisingi*) to make the return. This expression is the only one known to me

**Table 5**  Some Tombema *Tee* Exchange Equivalents

| *Saandi* Payment | | *Tee* Return | | |
|---|---|---|---|---|
| Side of pork (*mena sapya*) | = | live pig | (*mena saka*) | or |
| | | pearlshell | (*mamaku*) | or |
| | | salt pack | (*aipi*) | or |
| | | tree oil | (*topa*) | or |
| | | stone axe | (*pyakambyo*) | or |
| | | feathers | (*yaka/laima iti*) | |
| Two sides of pork given to same person (*mena ita*) | = | live pig or two pearlshells | | |
| Live pig | = | live pig plus pearlshell | | or |
| | | two live pigs (if *saandi* pig was large) | | or |
| | | cassowary | (*laima*) | or |
| | | stone axe (if *saandi* pig was small) | | or |
| | | tree oil  or | | |
| | | salt | | |
| Pearlshell | = | pearlshell or live pig (small) | | |
| Cassowary | = | cassowary or live pig (large) | | or |
| | | live pig (small) plus pearlshell | | |

which suggests the notion of "profit". There is no rule in *tee* dealings which require a person to make an incremental return; rather, he chooses to do so as an expression of his valuation of the partnership. "A man with a good heart adds a pig and gives", Tombema say.

> In the early example, A is bound to give these same pigs onward towards F; F's *saandi* has "found" this return plus addition, and Tombema are adamant that these exact pigs, no substitutions, must be passed on. Other valuables may be added to them by B, C, D, or E, but they, not A or his brother-in-law, receive that portion of the return in the *yae pingi* or a later transaction. This adds yet further complexity. If A's brother-in-law decides not to return at all for some reason, all other members of this *tee* chain are in jeopardy of losing their immediate partners. If A defaults to B, C may also lose out, and D has no recourse expect through C. When *tee* is made, such situations inevitably occur. If A does default to B, B may decide to contribute a pig of his own to satisfy his debt to C, thus preserving the partnership (see chapter seven). The option on the return during *yae* then rest with B, not with A or his relation in clan Z. It is possible that only one pig finds its way to F. Thus, while there are standard rates of return, they become practically meaningless because of uncontrollable circumstances inherent in the *tee*.

Bargaining and negotiating between individuals and the private decisions which must be made, are more fundamental factors affecting return than any standard rate of exchange. Persons constantly make statements about how they value a *tee* partner by what they are prepared to add on, or subtract from a payment. These are personal decisions which confront "ordinary" and bigmen alike.

The essential point is that in the Tombema view, each valuable given secures a return eventually; this return and whatever else the giver wishes to add influence the next transaction. If a person gives another a pig as *saandi*, and a return of one pig is made, these two partners are not necessarily equal in Tombema way of thinking; rather the person who received last is indebted anew, and whatever that pig "finds" should be returned to the original *saandi* recipient. However, if the recipient "feels" that the return merely equals his original *saandi*, he may leave it at that. The two men are, strictly speaking, equal, and no further *tee* relations or transactions may be forthcoming. This notion is also important in the return of bridewealth (see Feil 1981). Equality implies a moribund relationship.

Estimations of equality do not stem from a simple consideration of the exchanged valuables themselves: for example,
whether the returned pig was the right size matching the *saandi*,
or whether the *tee* payment was made according to the proper
rate of return. Rather, a recipient chooses to feel indebted, and
unequal, and hence desires to keep the relationship in the *tee*
active and alive. The continuation of a partnership is tested at
each transaction. Tombema themselves try to judge the motiva-
tions of their partners to determine the spirit in which the payment was made. Was the return merely meant to adequately
cover the debt? Was there some indication, material or otherwise, that the contributor was giving more, so as to create a new
debt and induce a further return, and to sustain the partnership
beyond this technically "equal" stage? The value of Tombema
wealth items themselves is not fixed. There is negotiated and
exchange value only. Objectively, individuals recognize and can
evaluate the size and sex of pigs for example, or the size, cut,
shine and "redness" of pearlshells. However, when debts are
reciprocated in the *tee*, equivalents may not be so easily
weighed. With almost every valuable, there is a way by applying
different or varying standards, to shift the burden of debt, to
make it greater than the initial payment, with the suggestion of a
new return. *Tee* friendship means indebtedness, but it is a
shifting indebtedness, depending on the direction the *tee* is
moving.

## *Tee* Roads and Directions

Before the ban on warfare in the middle 1950s travel within the
Kompiama area was severely restricted. Men knew of distant
places only by name, and a person's knowledge of his *tee* connections and their extent was correspondingly narrow. A man
generally dealt with *tee* partners in contiguous clans only. There
was little conception of an overall *tee* system, and ties between
individuals were highly insular. Marriages are highly concentrated in near clans, and this fact reflects the concentration of *tee*
partnerships between individuals in proximate clans. The *tee*
flows "step-by-step". With increased mobility and security of
travel, Tombema have recently been able to gain some glimpse

of the ramifications of their more localized contacts and some notion of the geographical extent of the *tee*. These discoveries have had some harmful organizational effects on the maintenance of the *tee*. These will be briefly mentioned later.

Tombema Enga, situated as they are in the northeastern section of the *tee*'s ambit, understand their relationship to the overall system only imperfectly. Their complaints about the slowness of *tee* movement reflect their geographical position in it. Due north of them live people called Wapi with whom they have made *tee*, following intervening steps, for as long as they can remember.[11] A *tee* that begins there comes to Tombema quickly, a fact which Tombema only partly understand as attributable to few clans and low population. To the southeast are Kyaka Enga, who again furnish Tombema with pigs, but only "after lots of talk and threat".[12] However, the two major sources of pigs for Kompiama people are due south, in the direction of Wapenamanda, and southwest from Wabaga. The *tee* roads from Laiapo (Wapenamanda and the Tsaka Valley) are "heavy" according to Tombema, both because of the large number of pigs and other valuables that come from there, but also because of the *tee*'s slow plodding movement along these roads. Tombema men who have travelled there for the first time have been amazed at the number of people and clans through which pigs must pass before the *tee* reaches the Kompiama area. Tombema attribute to Laiapo area men, and those in between, the peculiar characteristic of "sleeping with both ears open", listening to rumours of *tees* in either direction, thereby heightening their indecision and lack of resolve in sending *tees* quickly towards Kompiama. For the Wabaga side, however, *tees* come quickly. "Mai people listen, and their talk travels like a rushing stream", while that of Laiapo men "circulates slowly like a stagnant pond". These are the characterizations Tombema make of the *tee* roads which affect them.[13]

Tombema orient themselves in the geography of *tee* along roughly a north-south axis, describing the directions as "down" and "up". North towards the Wapi is "down"; the area lies at a lower altitude than Kompiama. South is "up", towards Wapenamanda and Wabaga (southwest), both of which lie at higher altitudes than Kompiama. For Kompiama residents, when a *tee* is "on top", it is coming from a roughly southern direction, from

Wapenamanda and Wabaga. When a *tee* is "down below" it is coming from the Wapi, the area to the north of Kompiama (compare Lacey 1975:159).[14] An individual also has *tee* partnerships both "on top" and "down below". Since the *tee* flows in one direction, he takes exclusively from one set of partners, either those "above" or "below" him and gives to the other set.

Individuals distinguish their partnerships in terms of giving and taking because clans and their subclans make *tee* in a rigidly prescribed sequence. The clans of people who have given pigs in the *tee* are "clans at the back" (*tee maita*), while people in clans who receive valuables are "clans at the head of the *tee*" (*tee ayomba*). This distinction applies to both individuals and groups. For Tombema, the progress of a *tee* involves turning to look in the direction from which pigs are to come, and when they have arrived, gradually turning one's back in that direction and sending them ahead.

Whenever individuals from two or more clans are gathered for *tee* discussions, one group or the other is always referred to as the "owners of the *tee*" (*tee tange*). The "owners" are the people who will receive the *tee* from members of other clans present. Any clan may be *tee tange*, depending on who else is present. On *tee* discussion expeditions to places from which the *tee* will come, complaints and public accusations are made by the assembled "*tee* owners". But they may return home and find members of clans who will receive the *tee* from them, present and making similar complaints, for they in their turn are the "owners" of a further segment of this *tee*. "Owners" of the *tee* are men to whom a person is indebted, men from whom he has taken *saandi* and to whom he will reciprocate in the *tee*.

Individuals, as members of clans which are arranged in a fixed order, give pigs and other valuables to partners who are members of several different clans. The cumulative effect of a subclan's *tee* is that partners in the clan that will make the *tee* next receive the largest portion of the pigs and other gifts. The remainder are given to partners in clans further along the *tee* route. Thus, there is not a single unitary flow of valuables from clan to clan (see Meggitt 1974:173 for a useful diagram illustrating this point). Rather, there is overlap in giving along the peripheries of the main clan-to-clan flow. Valuables then feed back into the system further on. The simple rule that applies is that

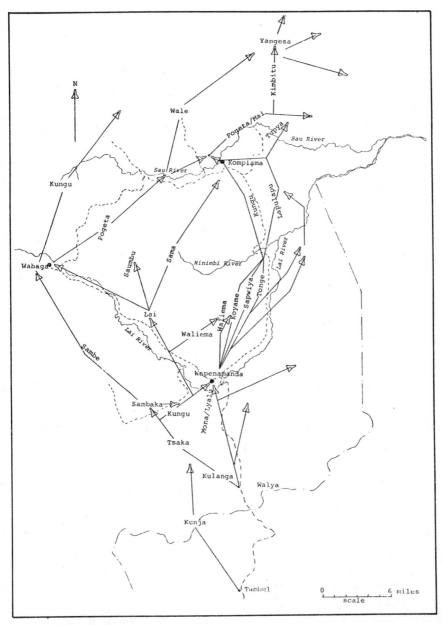

**Map 4** 'Major *Tee* Roads' (*Tee Kaita*)

"pigs follow *tee* friends" wherever they may be in the general, *tee*-determined direction.

The main named *tee* routes tend to follow major valleys and river courses. However, there is much criss-crossing over valleys and rivers. To sketch the overall geography of the *tee* is a difficult task. Meggitt (1972, 1974) and Lacey (1975) have discussed *tee* routes in the Mai-Enga area around Wabaga. For convenience, the brief outline of *tee* routes given below uses as an example, a downward moving *tee*, one coming into the Kompiama area from the Wapenamanda and Wabaga areas to the south and southwest. Map 4 gives the names and directions of important *tee* roads.

The *tee* at its southeastern extremity begins around Walya, in the Minyampu valley, southeast of Wapenamanda and roughly midway between Mt Hagen and Wapenamanda (compare A.J. Strathern 1969, 1971).[15] Beyond Walya, individuals may have specific ties with other men (for example in Tambul, called Kola by Tombema, or towards Melpa, called Simbai by Tombema) from whom they take pigs and inject them into onward-moving *tees*. But all members of a clan do not make *tee* until the majority of their exchange ties are with men of clans who also make *tee*, that is, until there is a concentration of ties.[16] Bowers (1968:98) points out that the Kokoli of Tambul are not intricately involved in *tee* cycles, but rather specific individuals continually send pigs towards eastern Enga. She remarks further that Kakoli are "happy just to have cross-cousins and affinal partners who have Enga affines" (Bowers 1968:97), and can therefore benefit from *tee* cycles, if only indirectly.

From Walya, *tee* roads run north and northwest into the Tsaka valley and into the Wapenamanda area. When the *tee* reaches Wapenamanda, it begins to have a bearing on Tombema. Also at Wapenamanda, the *tee* bifurcates, one set of roads heading west towards Wabaga and Mai–Enga populations, the other set heading north into Kompiama. Items are also sent into the Baiyer–Lumusa area from Wapenamanda, but Baiyer men send many of these valuables to Tombema partners across the Lai River later on. When the *tee* reaches Wabaga, it starts to circle back towards Kompiama and the Wale–Tarua. Allowing for numerous offshoots, several *tee* roads converge on Kompiama. Map 5 shows the set order of *tee*-making in the Kompiama area.

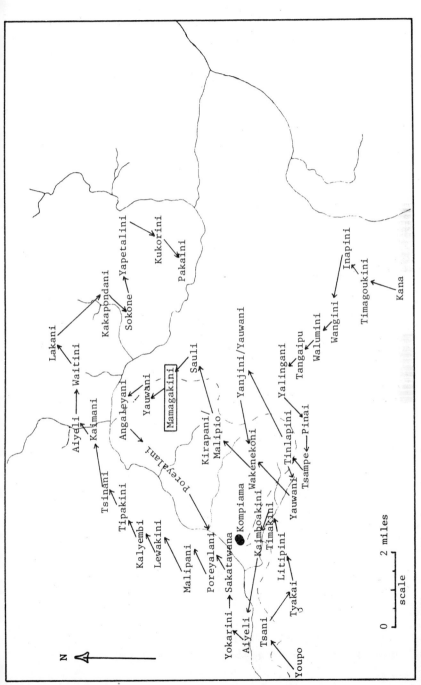

**Map 5** *Tee*-Making Sequence of Kompiama Area Clans

All men in the Kompiama area make *tee*. However, men on the north-eastern edge of Kompiama (in the clans Pakaini, Kukorini, Yapetalini, Yanjini and Sauli) have individual *tee* ties with men further east (to Melpa and Kyaka Enga) whose clans do not take part in the *tee* cycle. Pigs are passed to these men and are returned according to the requirements of the *tee*, as the Kakoli do with eastern Enga men. Elkin (1953:184), Westermann (1968:45), and Meggitt (1974:175), have commented similarly on the giving of *tee* valuables along the peripheries of *tee* routes. Meggitt (1974:174) especially gives this process great importance in acting

> . . . both as transducers and as homeostatic mechanisms, that is, as devices which, by injecting particular valuables into, or extracting them from, the *Te* network as required, help to maintain the volume of commodities at a given time at a level (or, better, within a range) more or less appropriate to the number of *Te* debts and credits being generated by the current number of participants, and their transactions.

This may be the case in Mai areas, but in Kompiama peripheral out-flow/in-flow is negligible. Rather the vast majority of exchanges occur among individuals in *tee*-making clans. This difference correlates well with the fact that the *tee* (although it has expanded) does not nearly reach the western boundaries of Enga (see Bus 1951:818). There is more individual, *ad hoc* exchanging along the *tee*'s peripheries there. In eastern Enga (Kompiama included), *tee*-making is an activity in which all men (and their clans) participate. There is less outflow of valuables from the major *tee* routes.

From Kompiama, the *tee* moves north into the Wapi. It is an area of very low population and therefore, the volume of pigs sent there is correspondingly low. When I visited the Wapi, there was evidence that members of clans at the end of these roads were making *tee* with men in the Schrader Mountains, across the Lai/Yuat River, in the Madang Province. *Tee* transactions with affines and maternal kin were occurring in areas where people had traditional marriage ties. Men in these areas, at the extreme ends of *tee* roads agist *tee* pigs with individuals and recall them when a *tee* is made. Tombema Enga say that the *tee* travels "until there is no longer people, only bush" and in this branch of the *tee*'s ambit, it appears to be true.[17]

Despite the converging roads and the outflow of valuables along the periphery of the *tee*, there is an overall unity in the flow of valuables in any one *tee*. The major branches move northwest from Wapenamanda to Wabaga, and north to Kompiama. The *tee* roads from Wabaga to Kompiama make the geographical area of the *tee* a triangle. Within it are the biggest populations and the most vigorous *tee*-making.

## *Tee* Timing

All *tee*-makers realize, however imperfectly, that they and their transactions are parts of a wider cycle system. Individual spheres of influence often do not extend beyond two or three clans in either direction in *tee*-making order from a man's own. And the majority of a man's *tee* gifts and those of his fellow clansmen are not given directly to individuals in clans very far removed from his own, at least in the first instance. The activities of *tee* partners are of a very narrow range, so the organizational problems posed by such an immense exchange cycle, lacking formal leadership and based solely on the extension of dyadic, insular ties, would seem to be staggering. The successful completion of a *tee* is a feat of endurance and persistance. It is an all-consuming focus of attention when it is coming, but Tombema are also relieved when it has passed and, for a very short period, ordinary life can resume.

As well as waiting for *tees* to reach them, Tombema often initiate *tee*-like activities of their own, a kind of miniature *tee* within the wider cycle. Such activities do not usually extend beyond several adjacent and proximate clans. These modest local cycles follow the same formal procedures as a major *tee*, but on a smaller scale. Death compensations or homicide payments provide a pretext for holding these smaller "*tees*", and individuals who participate in them need have no part in the specific compensation arrangements. A person's exchange partners may draw him in, or a man participates for other reasons of his own. In the past, Tombema have initiated *tees* from their own houses, or broke away and "cut the *tee*" from larger cycles when they were dissatisfied with its slow progress. Although Tombema place the greatest value on bringing and participating in the grand *tee*, there are smaller, continual activities of a *tee*-like character between major *tee* events. Such miniature *tees* occur throughout the Enga area.

Past *tees* are clearly negotiated happenings, and are not performed automatically according to any hard and fast set of rules, or to any fixed timetable. The difficulties of communication from one end of the *tee* chain to the other are obvious. The evidence of *tee* history leads to the overwhelming conclusion that the three-phase, alternating sequence of the *tee* is only an ideal characterization of it. Even well before European entry into Enga, the *tee*, as a forum of competition, was beset by personal manipulation and strategy as individual men sought renown for themselves and to deny it to their rivals.

All writers on the *tee* have suggested that it takes from three to five years to complete a full *tee* cycle, from the *saandi pingi* phase through to *yae pingi* (see Meggitt 1974:176 and the references cited there). My dating of past *tees* in the Kompiama area would seem to support this general time scale, but I think that *tee* periodicity is only indirectly related to the "time required to build up herds" (A.J. Strathern 1969a:60) following the previous *tee*. Tombema do not explicitly correlate pig breeding cycles and *tee*-making. Bulmer (1960b:7) and Meggitt (1958a:298; 1974:178) present a more determined view. Bulmer states that a "majority" of pigs are killed in the third *yae pingi* phase of the *tee*. Meggitt (1958a:298) estimates that "at least half" of the pigs in the *tee* (or 40 per cent of the total pig population, see Waddell 1972:118) are killed in the *yae pingi* phase.[18] Here it would seem important to make the distinction Tombema use concerning pigs that are suitable for the *tee*, and those which are not. The essential criterion is that of size, for only mature, or "big" pigs should be given in a *tee*. To some extent, a person's *tee* is judged by others not simply on the length of his row of pig stakes, but on the size of the pigs tethered to them. Small pigs are derisively called "rats" or "kittens", while big pigs are "like houses". In practice, small, immature, mostly male pigs (barrows) are sometimes given away too, while mature sows (with the potential for more litters) and some boars are held back. Generally, however, a person gives away mature pigs from his own herd.[19] If he takes pigs out of the *tee* in anticipation of killing them in *yae pingi*, he may then decide to substitute smaller animals from his own house and kill them instead. In discussing the dynamics of *tees* and pig killing in them, it must be rememberd that only a certain proportion of an individual's pigs (his mature boars, some barrows, and infertile sows) are involved. On the basis of evidence presented below, I estimate that on average an individual does not commit more than about one-quarter of his own herd to any given *tee* and accordingly about half of these might be killed if a *yae pingi* is held. Of course, a man gives away many more pigs, but these have come to him through his credit and financial dealings in which he has acted as an agent. The need to "replenish" the herd after *yae pingi* refers to the time allotted for immature pigs to grow large enough for inclusion in the next *tee*, not the time needed to "breed" a completely new herd. There is probably some minimum amount of time necessary, but it is not a decisive factor in the periodicity of *tee* cycles. A man's pig herd is at all stages of development at all times, and *tees* result in only his mature beasts being given away and being killed in *yae pingi*.

As a mnemonic device, Tombema Enga often cut the ear of a small house-bred pig soon after a *tee* has passed. When the animal has grown to full size, the next *tee* should be approaching. The practice, performed by women, is useful in planning the allocation of the herd.

Just what initially sets a *tee* into motion is something of a mystery. People who live well away from the beginning point like to believe that their demands for repayment of *saandi* have been conveyed step-by-step to individuals in the clans who start the *tee*. These days, bigmen set out on long and often solitary *tee* excursions, picking up their close partner and partner's partners, to discuss *tee* planning and urge men situated towards the *tee* origin to begin making it. Formerly, person did not travel beyond his nearest partner (usually in a neighbouring clan) to "talk *tee*". It would seem that individuals in clans closest to the *tee*'s starting point, men linked directly with members of these groups, would begin the movement to start the *tee* in motion. A similar level of *tee*-related activities would have been taking place at the same time throughout the *tee* area. Therefore, individuals close to the *tee* source, by seeking the return of their own *saandi* investments and urging the start of the *tee*, are reflecting the desires of those men further down the line with whom they have no direct communication. Credits have been established in the direction from which the *tee* is coming. A minimum amount of time is needed for enough credits and debts to build up, thereby making reciprocation worthwhile in a *tee*. A person does not wish to give away his "house-raised" pigs without at least having enjoyed some benefit, in the form of pork, for the labours of himself and his wife in having raised them. There is also a maximum time period, when too many debts have accumulated to be adequately reciprocated. Tombema do not measure this time in months or years, but make personal assessments and evaluations of the resources on hand and what a man may be able to take from elsewhere without having made an initiatory payment of some kind.

The actual start of the *tee* may be signalled by events which may be occurring throughout the *tee* community at roughly the same time, but which members of clans closest to the originating point use to get the *tee* moving. Firstly, a person's own stock of house-raised pigs may be dwindling. He has given killed and live pigs of his own, in addition to those secured elsewhere, as *saandi* towards the *tee*. If so, it is time to begin seeking repayment. Secondly, he may be having trouble financing from other sources. This is simply another indication of the shortage of suitable pigs all along the chain. Thirdly, if no *mena yukupae* have been sent as a sign that pigs will come from those invested, people may be unwilling to send any more pigs to increase their credits. They are thus implicitly demanding evidence that their investments have not simply gone astray. As these conditions worsen, more and more creditors along the chain grow impatient for repayment until those who are close to the beginning point of the *tee* are making urgent demands on their partners. Each partner tugs on the next to reciprocate.

Members of the clans that begin the *tee* have to obtain pigs individually from exchange partners who are outside the *tee* network. But once the *tee* has begun, although there may be minor delays, the *tee* moves as if under its own momentum, drawn by the cumulative desire and demands of those waiting to receive. Since there is a set order in *tee*-making, by the time it reaches a man, all of his potential contributors will already have made their payments. He may try to extract more pigs, and his efforts might yield some results, but the basic size of a person's *tee* will have been decided. Individuals still seeking gifts from men who have already made the *tee*, may wait and make their *tee* apart from their own subclansmen. Thus, although a subclan reaches some vague agreement about the precise timing of its *tee*, an individual may choose to ignore it and wait until he is satisfied that every last payment has been pried from men before him.

There is no overall organization to the timing of a sub-clan's *tee*: it is not determined by an individual bigman, nor does such a man direct any pigs other than his own to their recipients. However, the decision by one or several members of a subclan to make their *tee* and reciprocate their debts at a given time spurs other men to demonstrate that they too can muster their resources then. This bringing together of individual subclansmen to make a *tee*, on the same ceremonial ground and at the same time, is where the essentially "political" nexus of the *tee* rests.[20] A challenge is made by a man to hold the *tee* on a fixed day, and other men must take it up or suffer loss of prestige.

The timing of the *tee* is not so important as it appears to be in the *moka* (A.J. Strathern 1971). Delays in the *tee* are not as significant politically, for it does little good to seek further payments from individuals who have already made their *tee*. They have probably given as much as they can spare, and there is little point anyway in their giving privately. After the *tee* arrives, a man has little chance of radically altering his position in it by delaying. His procrastination might lead to decreased prestige.

While there may be an overall pattern to the periodicity of the *tee*, of say four to six years, it defies more precise predictability, and its performance relies on a number of factors, pig breeding cycles being only one. Deaths of prominent *tee* makers, or minor ones, along the *tee* chain slow its movements, as do wars (see below) and in times past, pig epidemics and garden failures (Meggitt 1974:179). Missionaries and government officials have tried, from time to time, to halt *tee* activity, but never with much lasting success. Nowadays, such things as national and local elections, and increasingly, (in areas more so than Kompiama) concern for business and local development have distracted some Enga from the *tee* and have affected its timing. Kompiama residents, as recipients at the end of the chain, are reluctantly recognizing their precarious position in it. A growing regionalism in *tee*-making might be predicted with further fragmentation of the overall *tee* community.

## The *Tee* and Other Spheres of Exchange

It was mentioned above that regardless of the ostensible, particular context in which a gift of a pig or pearlshell is given, the transaction is significant and somehow related to the *tee* system. The Enga recognize as much themselves. In discussing this point, they will often remark, matter of fact, that "a man can call a gift anything he chooses, but it is still the *tee*". In this perspective, the *tee* is best understood to be a "general", all-encompassing exchange institution, within which all kinds of debts are both incurred and reciprocated. The *tee* is the only occasion when outstanding debts of all types can be repaid.[21] It is a time of general accounting when overdue debts are made right. But, as has been shown earlier, certain types of transactions between *tee* partners are also, more specifically, *tee* ones: a side of pork is given to a man to "pull" a live pig later when he makes his *tee*. This transaction is strictly a *tee* one: *saandi pingi* is made and a return in the *tee* follows. At other times though, a person needs a pig to satisfy an obligation to give in a "non-*tee*" sphere, to give bridewealth or make a death payment for example. In these situations, the same procedures and practices that operate in the *tee* regulate these payments. The individual transactions are called by different names, but their repayment comes when the *tee* is made.[22] The distinction between *tee* and non-*tee* is an arbitrary one.

There is no gift made in Tombema society, for any reason, which is not thought to entail a similar return. All transactions are, in theory, binding on the recipient to make a suitable repayment, whether made for bridewealth, homicide, or whatever. The *tee* regulates the timing of the return and the direction in which debts accrue. Debts accumulated prior to the *tee* are reciprocated in it.

When a person makes payments under a different name than *tee*, he gives them primarily to already existing *tee* partners. Such partners have a history of transacting and these specific payments must be placed within the total framework of their *tee* dealings, rather than as separate events in themselves. When a gift or payment is made to a person who is not already a *tee* partner, it is a solicitous offer to become one. The valuables and expressed equivalents used in all spheres of giving, whether *tee* or on other occasions, are the same. This fact adds to the convertibility of non-*tee* transactions into *tee* ones. Again, I emphasize, the flow of valuables between *tee* partners is seen as a unity; although specific transactions can be named, in accounting of debts and repayment, they are all part of the one system, the *tee*.

The strategy of incorporating non-*tee* payments into the *tee* system is well recognized by Tombema. There is little public value in giving pigs as private affairs when attendance is low and only those persons hoping to receive are present. Maximum value is gained by presenting as many pigs as possible before large audiences. *Tees* provide the venues for widest acclaim.

Meggitt (1974:169–70; 1977:122) has attempted to link the hierarchy of Mae–Enga groups with the ceremonial prestation in which each engages. Furthermore, he suggests that clans have priorities for giving in one sphere or another.

> Because a clan has access at any time to a limited number of pigs to use in exchanges and compensations, its members have to agree on some order of priorities for prestations. Thus, transactions are ranked in terms of the hierarchical structure of the social units involved, so that the payment of homicide compensations takes precedence, for incidence, over the giving of brideprice. (1977:140)

In another context, Meggitt writes of how individuals are "constrained" in exchange contexts by their obligations to descent groups (1977:121). This view, I believe, puts the emphasis in the wrong place. At least in Tombema, clans are not "responsible" (Meggitt 1974:169) for making *tee* and homicide payments, subclans for death compensation, lineages for bridewealth, and so on. All Tombema transactions are individual ones, without overall planning, and without group concerns or co-ordination in mind. It is true though, that a man makes *tee* at the same time and place as fellow subclansmen. *Tee* transactions are, however, strictly individual ones; only the venue is common to the subclan as a whole. Aside from this, no group of any kind is thought, or held responsible for making any prestation. Individual *tee* partners alone agree that a payment is appropriate, and thus make it. When a man decides to make a death payment for example, he gathers together his payment of pigs, those he has financed and those from his own herd, and gives them. He does not check with others in his subclan to ask permission, or seek their help or encouragement. There is, however, nothing to prohibit another clansman or subclansman from using the occasion to make some payment of his own. This sometimes occurs. Who the recipients are in these instances makes it clear that they are in no sense a part of the other person's presentation. A man simply takes advantage of a public gathering to make payments for his own personal reasons.

Individual strategies and considerations take precedence over any group ones, and Tombema do not even speak as if groups are responsible. Events such as death, homicide, and marriage oblige specific individuals to give to others. Existing *tee* relations (or partnerships sought) define to whom payments are made. The *tee* itself provides the occasion, the timing, and the overall framework in which they are given.

## Notes

1. Meggitt (1974:174) suggests that the *tee* institution is partly derivative of homicide compensation, apparently also known in Mae-Enga as *te-pinggi* (Meggitt's orthography). He claims therefore that both the ceremonial system and homicide compensation bear the same name. Homicide compensation is defined by Meggitt as "cause or origin-settling" (1974:174). Tombema (and Mai informants questioned) were emphatic that *tee pingi* (however spelled) is not the term for homicide compensation. However, there exists in Enga the phrase *tee pingi* which means "to begin" or "to start" (Meggitt's origin-settling). But the *tee* ceremonial institution is *tee pingi* and has a different tonal stress. Thus, *tee* (to begin and homicide payment) and *tee* (ceremonial exchange) are not the same word at all. As a result, Meggitt may be mistaken in suggesting that one institution grew from the other which had the same name. With a different tonal stress, the word *tee* also means "ant" in the Enga language.
2. Some Tombema say that a request for *saandi* might be refused on the basis of the intended destination, for example, if the ultimate user of the valuable was considered a bad risk. But this knowledge is not often available and less often used.
3. An important aspect of *saandi* is to spread pork through the *tee* community to eat. "House-raised pigs" are those which have been produced at home and on which there are no claims. They are natural increase. Thus, gifts of pork are made to the owners of house-raised pigs to secure them in the *tee*.
4. The giver of *saandi* also benefits from his payment if it is made in pork, for he may eat all but the "sides" (*mena sapya*) which are the units of *saandi*-making. The pig's head, backbone and chest, all choice portions, can be eaten by the *saandi* giver and if he can deploy a side of pork to two different partners, he can expect the return of two pigs. He both eats pork and doubles his investment. There is no taboo on a couple which prevents them from eating a pig they have raised. People feel that pigs are too valuable to eat and should be given away, although pork is the favourite food. This basic contradiction is resolved by eating pork supplied by others as *saandi* and giving the pig, secured by *saandi*, in the *tee*. Both giver and receiver benefit.

This is the kind of investment that Tombema relish, but the majority of them are not of this kind.

One pig is attached to each stick; sticks are spaced three to four feet apart and all rows of sticks begin at the same point. A comparison of the length of rows of pigs is thereby easily made and the man with the longest row is the biggest man.

The man in clan Z may though add on another pig to what the investment has netted, to show how much he values the partnership (see Elkin 1953:198).

Tombema have no device for keeping tallies of where investments have gone and in what number. They also wear no pendants or badges like the Melpa *omak* (A.J. Strathern 1971) which signify to others the number of transactions in which they have engaged.

A man who did not take pigs out of the *tee* does not, in theory, have to kill any in *yae pingi*; pork will be returned from men who have taken his pigs, and he passes these sides on. In practice even these men kill pigs if only to establish credit for the next *saandi* phase. I also recorded no examples in which men failed to take pigs from a *tee*. Men also kill pigs of their own to cover debts which have not been returned to them.

Meggitt (1974:168) presents a different picture for the Mae; he suggests that trade, as "contigent, finite, private transactions" exist apart from the *tee* system.

I have no evidence that the Wapi have only recently been brought into the *tee* sphere. The Wapi population is small but Tombema assert that they have always made *tee* (compare Bus 1951; Meggitt 1974).

Coffee production and missions appear to have eclipsed the *tee* in importance in the Baiyer area.

The size of populations in Laiapo and Wabaga partly reflect these characteristics. The *tee* begins south of Wapenamanda and most, if not all, Laiapo (including Tsaka valley inhabitants) participate in the *tee*. To the west, the *tee* does not reach far beyond Wabaga and *tees* from there come more quickly (see Bus 1951).

According to Lacey (1975:159) who worked around Wabaga, *lanao* and *lalyo* have east/west bearings for central Enga; a *lanao tee* moves easterly, a *lalyo tee* moves westward. These designations appear also to conform to the altitudinal lie of the land.

Around Walya is the *tee/moka* interface. Men are bilingual and are involved in both exchange systems. But the *moka* is less systematic than the *tee* which allows men to participate in both and perhaps to manipulate obligations and valuables for greater reward (see A.J. Strathern 1969a, 1971 and Meggitt 1974 for some details).

At this point, the *tee* becomes a system with all members of clans participating in set order. Prior to this point exchange ties between individuals are *ad hoc* and not regularized by an overall structure which prescribes patterns of loans and investments and the method and timing of repayment.

The need to send pigs onward as investment is an essential aspect of the *tee* and contributes to its expansion.

Meggitt (1958a:288, 298) assumes a ratio of one pig per person, a population of 40,000 persons and 30,000 pigs (75 per cent) involved in a *tee*. Half of these (roughly 40 per cent), he argues, are killed.

Feachem (1973b) does not recognize this point when he argues that two pigs per head are necessary for a group to start the *tee*. The part that "financed pigs" play in the *tee* is also obscured by his analysis.

20. A man may announce that he intends to make the *tee* on a certain day, only to change his mind in order to confuse others. He may show up at the *tee* ground late to make a big impact, he may try to make the *tee* alone, before his rivals are ready or after they have given pigs and when he knows his distribution will outshine theirs. Thus the informal decision to hold a *tee* on a given day is always subject to manoeuvering and personal strategy as subclansmen try to upset each other's plans and boost their own performance. But most subclansmen meet at the given time to show others that they are good and ready.

21. Not only pig debts are repaid at a *tee*. A man repays personal debts with pigs. For example, if a man has been sick and a *tee* partner has cared for him during the illness, he may specifically give him a pig in reciprocation for his care. This fact may be announced when the distribution is made.

22. This point escaped the attention of colonial administrators who, in the past banned the *tee*, but allowed homicide and other transactions to continue without realizing they are essentially part of the same system (see Feil 1979). This point is not made clear by other writers on the *tee*.

# THREE

# Pigs, Pearlshells, and Production

Also, there is no society similar to that of the *moka* existing among the Enga.

Wirz (1952b)

The *tee* is unquestionably an old institution. The fact that much of the Enga area is linked in one such overarching system, and that the complex processes and practices mentioned in the previous chapter have developed, is perhaps ample proof of its old age. While Tombema–Enga do not have myths and stories of its inception, no one can remember a time when the *tee* did not exist. Tombema say they have always had the *tee*, and always will. Kleinig (1955:4) writes that as far as old men can recall, "there has been *Te* made in this area, and their fathers told them the same thing. They became highly indignant when I hinted that the *Te* may be of comparatively recent origin". There is no evidence which suggests that the *tee* is a recent introduction into the Kompiama area (compare Meggitt 1974:175, 195).

Lacey (1975:161) postulated that at some places in the Wabaga area, west of Kompiama, the *tee* may have begun in the latter half of the nineteenth century. He also relates some oral traditions, which describe how the *tee* originated. However, in the two traditions cited (Lacey 1975:175–76), the focus of the story is the source of pigs, not the origin of the *tee*. In one, for example, a man agitates the water in a pond, and a pig comes out. "It is with the pigs that came from this lake that men made the *tee*" (Lacey 1975:176). My reading of these oral traditions is that the *tee* and pigs originate together; pigs and *tee*-making are inextricably intertwined in the Enga past.

Both Meggitt (1974) and Lacey (1975) posit the diffusion of the *tee* through various clans and regions, perhaps from east to west; I suggest that people may have simply brought the *tee* with them as they migrated, in most cases away from central Enga. Some of these migrations into the Kompiama and Wapi areas have been discussed earlier. *Tee* or *tee*-like institutions or, more generally, reciprocal obligations in which valuables are exchanged characterize ever Enga society, indeed, nearly every Highlands society. While there have certainly been changes, modifications and elaborations to the *tee*, there is no evidence which points to its introduction by a few well-placed men who initiated and controlled it to their own advantage (Meggitt 1974:87). A record of *tee* of the past fifty years or so is given in Appendix 2.

Throughout the Highlands of Papua New Guinea, pigs are the dominant, most highly valued items of exchange. Shells of all types and perhaps cassowaries, are the only other items which, in some societies, approach the value of pigs. Other commodities are also exchanged and traded along with these prominent items, but when this occurs, it is possible to determine which of the several items has the highest value. Obviously, the people themselves are usually clear on this point: they may aim to convert less valued goods into those of higher value; scarcity may determine highest value; the volume of things exchanged may reflect their importance; the labour-time necessary to produce an item may signal its value, or there may be "cultural" value placed on an object because of its pedigree, size, texture, myth of ancestral association or so forth. Despite the number and variety of exchange items used, it is possible to characterize systems on the basis of the dominant, most highly valued items of exchange.

Pigs have this unquestioned status in a majority of societies. The antiquity of pigs in the Highlands, perhaps up to 9,000 or 10,000 years old (White and Allen 1980) suggests their fundamental role and importance in the historical exchange economies of the region. With the later introduction of sweet potatoes, and the potential of the "Jones Effect" (Watson 1977), the value of pigs as items of exchange grew, until in some societies, every exchange context demanded pigs. A person's prestige depended on his standing in pig exchanges, and the need to acquire and produce them expanded as exchange encounters widened and proliferated. Pigs were also the major protein source and every decision to consume pork had to be weighed against the political effect of giving it. The Enga for example, note this ambivalence with the maxim that "good people send pigs and take them back; bad people think only of eating them". It could be argued on firm ground that pigs, as dominant items of value, are historically prior to any others, at least in the Highlands. Therefore, exchange systems which rely heavily on pigs are likely to offer some sort of baseline upon which further developments of exchange systems are predicated.

The Enga *tee* is, more properly called, *mena tee*, "pig *tee*". In the New Guinea Highlands, it is the outstanding example of an exchange system which gives pigs the highest, almost sole, exchange value. I have described how pigs are needed for every prestation: to gain wives and promote peace, to compensate enemies and allies, and to achieve personal power and prestige. All scarce social goods and benefits derive from the exchange of pigs. The relationship and interdependence of pigs and people is basic in Enga society (Feil 1976). Other items change hands in the *tee*, but pigs have by far the greatest value. Cassowaries, for example, are valued *tee* items, but not as valuable as pigs, for as Enga say, they do not bear litters like pigs. The same applies to shells. In terms of volume and acknowledged value, pigs are dominant in the *tee*. Enga often speak scornfully of the neighbouring Melpa *moka* saying, "they have no pigs to exchange only pearlshells". I will discuss aspects of the *moka* system below and compare it to the Enga *tee*.

## The Production of Pigs

It is a truism that the production process is prior to exchange. As the dominant item of exchange in the *tee*, how are pigs produced in Tombema society, who produces them, and what relations do people enter into to produce them, and what are the implications?

To produce pigs, a person needs a breeding sow, land to cultivate crops in order to feed them, and labour for a variety of tasks, the most important being to plant and harvest food, and to care for pigs' daily needs and maintenance. The single most important fact relating these productive forces in Tombema society is that all of these requirements were everywhere locally available, and were not restricted nor controlled in any way. The character of the Tombema *tee* is a direct reflection of this situation. In Enga society, the production of pigs holds no mysteries; only mundane hard work and effort lead to success in pig production, for the means are open to all. Of course, some men and women are more successful than others, but the means to raise a herd, even a large one can be acquired by anyone regardless of marital status, descent line, residence, or community standing, a point Tombema defend fiercely. As will be pointed out, this has profound implications for relations between men, and between men and women.

Many mechanisms exist for acquiring a breeding sow to start a herd. Sons and daughters are often given a gilt (young sow) to look after. For a man, it becomes the basis of his future herd; for a woman, it and the litters it bears go along with her as the return bridal payment made by her father to her new husband (Feil 1981). In addition, young female pigs are often "loaned" for a fee of two or three piglets from the first litter. Thereafter, the person who took the loan owns the sow outright and can build a herd of his own from it. Only young sows can be loaned in this way. If a sow dies and has a dependent litter, the piglets are "adopted out" and a gilt can be acquired in this way. Again, some fee is paid later. In short, sows needed to produce herds can easily be obtained if, as is rare, a person is without one.

Land and labour too are not restricted or in short supply, and do not pose barriers to pig production for anyone. In the Kompiama area at least, land is plentiful. Specific plots within a clan's estate are inherited from father to son, or in the case of a co-resident sister's son, from a mother's brother. Gardening rights are often granted to outsiders virtually without restriction; residence is fluid. Pigs are let out to forage during the day and return at night to be fed sweet potatoes. Waddell (1972) suggests that about 80 per cent of a pig's diet in Laiapu–Enga consists of cultivated food. It would seem that among Tombema this figure is lower, due to more extensive foraging opportunities. However, the necessary land to cultivate crops for a pig's dietary needs is abundant and available without hindrance.

The labour necessary to produce pigs is normally handled jointly by husband and wife, but in a number of cases, bachelors on their own have been able to produce sizeable herds. They alone cultivate the crops and supply the necessary labour to look after a herd. Bachelors too are often vigorous in *tee* proceedings. Monogamous households successfully compete with polygamous ones in pig production. One husband/wife pair had the second largest pig herd, 47 animals, at the time of my pig census in 1976. Others were nearly as productive. The pig population for all of Mamagakini clan is given in Appendix 1. Specialized labour, a complex division of labour, or even restricted knowledge, is not a prerequisite for pig production. The means are open to all, and through hard work success can be achieved.

A basic equality among men stemmed from open access to the means of pig production. This point is of crucial significance for an analysis of the character of the *tee* system (see below). In the production of the highest valued items of exchange, pigs, men did not need to enter into relations with other men to produce them. The success of bachelors is ample proof of that. A married couple was usually the basic unit in which decisions relating to the production of pigs were undertaken. The equality of access to means of pig production meant that exploitative relations among men were less likely to develop and that the *tee* exchange system would involve competition between essentially equal men. This point will be returned to below.

But what of the relations between the sexes in the production of pigs. If exploitation between men did not occur, what were the resultant relations between the sexes stemming from the production of pigs? It has been argued before (Feil 1978a, 1978b) that the production of pigs is a complementary effort involving both men and women. In Tombema society, women have a vital, acknowledged share and interest in producing the items of highest exchange value, pigs. Garden work requires the skill of both sexes: men do the heavy work of clearing and fencing while women plant and harvest. Joint decisions are taken in allocating small plots of land to others, and prestige comes to both husband and wife for their industry and success in making a garden. Women bear the brunt of pig care and maintenance and provide them their food. But men are not far off and often help in their provisioning. Men must also track stray animals and keep watch over unruly ones. In the *tee*, both men and women have a say in the exchange of pigs, a near-equal say, I would argue. Their combined decision to exchange further reflects the complementary side of the production process. These points will be expanded upon in the following chapter.

Whether or not exploitation in pig production between the sexes occurs in Tombema–Enga society is a difficult question. The concept of "exploitation" itself is fraught with difficulties. How does one measure it, discover it, or indeed define it? Recent Marxist economic anthropology (for example, Clammer ed. 1978) seems to suggest that "exploitative relationships" exist in any socio-economic formation, not just in capitalism; one must simply find them. With these issues in mind, I would argue that in Enga pig production and ultimately in their exchange, men do not exploit women and that for example, the labour time necessary to produce pigs is equally shared by both men and women. I will show however, that men and women do have complementary views of the *tee* process. The verdict on exploitation hinges on what the total production process is thought to entail, and whether or not labour time is taken to be the sole measure of exploitation.

The production of pigs for their own sake has no value at all in Tombema society. Only by exchanging them, by giving them away, does "social value" accrue to the producer of a pig. Thus, the production and ultimate exchange of pigs should be regarded as a single process (Frankenberg 1967:84). The social concomitants of this combined process offer the key to understanding the workings of the *tee*. If production and exchange are linked together, then the complementary aspect of a woman's and a man's effort is further made manifest. Women are the more prominent producers of pigs, even though they often privately and publicly exchange them; men are the more prominent exchangers of pigs though they help to produce them too. Their joint, mutual decisions in these two facets of the total production of pigs mean that intersexual exploitation is also less likely to occur. The following chapter will return to the issue of women in the *tee* system and their role in the production process will again be highlighted.

A suitable comparison can be drawn between the equality of access to the means of pig production in Tombema society with that of pearlshell production and exchange in the *moka* of the neighbouring Melpa of Mount Hagen, well-known in the writings of A.J. Strathern (for example, 1971). This analysis will set the stage for a further comparison of their social and political organizations.

## Pearlshells

Shells, and in Melpa society, pearlshells, are the other dominant item of exchange value in the Highlands.[1] Although there is some archaeological evidence of cowrie shells in other parts of the Highlands as early as 9500 years ago (White and Allen 1980), the entry of pearlshells into the Mount Hagen area further west, is much more recent. Hughes (1977:193) cites old informants who claim that pearlshells were unknown to them when they were children in the 1920s. A.J. Strathern (1971:236) mentions an old bigman's view that the arrival of pearlshells and the intro-duction of *moka*-making were historical events belonging to the time of his father. Strathern, however believes that this account significantly foreshortens the time scale. It may also be that the valleys to the south of Mount Hagen were uninhabited or only sparsely settled a few generations ago. Recent migrations into the area from the south, due to warfare or other reasons, meant that the new immigrants could become more frequent and inten-sive exchange partners, linking southern pearlshell sources and the Melpa people to the north (Hughes 1977:198).

Despite the apparent late entry of pearlshells into the Melpa area, they rapidly assumed ascendancy as the most valuable *moka* items. Pearlshells became more valuable than pigs (Meggitt 1974:194), the "supreme object of personal wealth" (Williams 1937:92) and shell *moka* was considered the "most prestigious" (A.J. Strathern 1979:534). Data of Strathern's on *moka* payments during his fieldwork in the 1960s also confirm pearlshells as the most numerous valuables exchanged. Thus, the Enga *tee* and Melpa *moka* provide a significant contrast between an exchange system using and valuing pigs above all else, and one in which pearlshells predominate.

It is clear that Enga have always known of pearlshells and used them in the *tee* as they do today, yet they never came to be as highly valued as pigs. The earliest ethnographic sources from the Enga area described a situation in which pearlshells were scarce, but even so, less important than pigs (Leahy and Crain

1937:254). Wirz (1952a, 1952b) in two early papers, said that unlike the *moka*, in the *tee*, pearlshells had a decidedly secondary importance, and that a man's wealth was measured by his pigs, not his shells (1952b:71). The inescapable point is that the Melpa, for whatever reason prior to European contact, seized on pearlshells as a new standard of exchange value.² Pearlshells replaced pigs, while the *tee* remained firmly, pig *tee*. A transformation which had wide-ranging implications occurred in the exchange economy of the Melpa. The Enga say that the *tee* has always existed, much as in its present form. In contrast, perhaps what Strathern's old informant was really saying, is that *moka*-making with pearlshells *is* relatively recent, it is a new kind of exchange, not involving pigs, the "traditional" items of value. With the adoption of pearlshells, the *moka* represents a profound historical transformation of an exchange system like the *tee*, based on pigs.³

With pig production the means were open to all. What of pearlshell production in Melpa society? Obviously, pearlshells are not "produced" as such in Mount Hagen at all. They come into the area from coastal Papuan sources. What is "produced" however, are the *exchange links* made up of interpersonal ties which facilitate the entry of pearlshells into the Melpa region. Furthermore, Strathern leaves no doubt that these exchange chains were made up of allied bigmen, and that their control over pearlshell valuables in the past at least, approached a monopoly (for example, A.J. Strathern 1979:532). Perhaps through propitious marriages, or merely because of their renown, influential men could range further afield than ordinary men, and establish the connections which brought the most highly valued exchange objects into the area. The supply of pearlshell wealth was therefore regulated by bigmen and control kept firmly in their grasp. Pearlshells were foreign imports, but through manipulation and alliance, bigmen "produced" them locally through their exchange ties.

While Tombema more conventionally produced their items of exchange value, pigs, and the means of production were available to all, the same does not apply to Melpa pearlshell exchanges. As A.J. Strathern has noted,

> The possibility of claiming the highest prestige for the manipulation of shell valuables explains, in a sense, why the *moka* system involves

both pigs and shells. Everyone could **rear pigs** and everyone had access to rights of land use. The overall scarcity of shells by contrast enabled a "purer" version of prestige economy to be built on them . . . Control over these gave them [bigmen] an extra edge over other [ordinary] men who had similar resources in terms of land and pigs (1979:532-33).

To signify their achievements in the most prestigious of exchanges, Melpa bigmen wore tallies of cane (*omak*) around their necks to proclaim publicly the size of their pearlshell holdings. Wealth in pig exchanges meanwhile go unrecorded in Mount Hagen as they do in Enga; there are no personal, visible markers of success in the pig *tee*. This "new" exchange of pearlshells demanded a novel expression of a man's rank.

The adoption of pearlshells as dominant exchange items and the concomitant relations of production it brought about, represents a further significant alteration to the relations applying to pig production. Relations between men, and those between men and women were profoundly transformed. When the Melpa adopted pearlshell as the most prestigious standard of value, and owing to their controlled scarcity, men had to enter into relations with other men to acquire them. Bigmen had a near-monopoly and relations of dependence, and perhaps exploitation followed, in which bigmen would give the sought-after shells in return for political allegiance, patronage, labour, or simply for prestige. As well as controlling the production and circulation of shells, bigmen could also control the reproduction of others by contributing or withholding pearlshells from younger men, who needed them for bridewealth to acquire wives (see Meillassoux 1978). These processes in turn accentuated the political and economic gulf between powerful and influential men, and ordinary ones. The basic equality which stemmed from open access to the means of pig production was undermined in the conversion to pearlshell exchange. These features of the production process are also reflected in the overall functional character of the *tee* and *moka*. While it is not suggested that relations of exploitation could not exist in an exchange system of pigs like the *tee*, I am asserting that pearlshell exchanges offered far wider possibility for some men to exploit others, to control more completely the means of producing vital exchange items, and to create a system of rank.[4] Productive relations between men were transformed: men needed other (big) men to obtain pearlshells.

In a broader perspective however, relations between the sexes were also transformed.

With the adoption of pearlshells, relations of potential exploitation between the sexes were heightened and extended. The complementary side of pig production in Tombema society has been argued. But with the exchange of pearlshells, the role of women in the production of valued objects is totally absent.[5] In Melpa society, a woman through her part in their production can exert moral coercion over the disposal only of pigs. She has no say whatsoever over the allotment of shells. Men can rightly claim that as transactors in pearlshells, they alone have produced the items of both highest value and greatest number. The value and role of women is thereby diminished and a lessened political involvement is the result (Feil 1978b). As sole producers of pearlshells, Melpa men claim complete ownership and hence total control of their exchange (A.J. Strathern 1979:535). The devalued status of women as mere producers of pigs (A.M. Strathern 1972) contrasts to the higher value given to the transactors in shells, that is, men. The contrast with Tombema women is striking.

The fact too that pearlshells are foreign imports, the method of production of which is unknown or obscure, furthermore allows a greater mystification to be put on them, especially by men who controlled them and who would benefit from their mysteries.[6] Leahy (Leahy and Crain 1937:195) tells how some Melpa thought pearlshells grew on trees. A.J. Strathern (1971:235) reports that an informant told him that "sky people, pictured as cannibals, . . . dropped valuables at the place where the "legs of the sky" reached the earth i.e. at the end of the earth. . . . Alternatively, he said, people thought that perhaps people in distant places obtained them like stone axes, from quarries." While Melpa women and ordinary men knew of pig procreation magic, "only big-men were thought of as having access to magic by which to draw in shell valuables . . . " (A.J. Strathern 1979:534). Men, especially bigmen, were the beneficiaries of the mystifications surrounding pearlshells. No doubt they propagated this ideology. It was a further prop in their position of power, and a reinforcement of their indispensibility to the community, for "producing" pearlshells and exchanging them at a price with lesser men. The mundane nature of pig production offers another striking contrast. Women, more than men, know the spells and magic to increase their herds.

What I suggest, then, is that the adoption of pearlshells by the Melpa, (or more precisely perhaps, the adoption of pearlshells by Melpa bigmen and their ability to coerce others into accepting them as more valuable than any other exchange objects) led to relations of dependence and exploitation between men and between men and women, relations which were less possible as long as pigs were the recognized items of highest exchange value. Pearlshells were scarce and controlled, whereas the means of pig production much less so. The sociopolitical implications of pearlshells versus pigs are profound and are reflected in the ethnographic evidence, both past and present. As well as attempting to unravel these contentious threads, some more formal features of the *tee* and *moka*, relating to pigs and pearlshells will be discussed next.

## The Sociopolitical Implications – Pigs versus Pearlshells

It was the control over the production of exchange valuables, pearlshells, and the accompanying transformed social relations of production of them, which perceptibly, but radically, altered the social and political life of the Melpa. Intrinsically of course, pigs and pearlshells are very different kinds of exchange items, which also affects the character of the *tee* and *moka* systems. Pigs are mortal in a way that pearlshells are not. Pearlshells represented a new form of durable wealth. It is probable that Melpa bigmen who were prominent in pig exchanges seized on pearlshells as a way to consolidate their power and position and make them permanent and reproducible. A person's future standing in pigs is often highly precarious. Epidemics, deaths, and illnesses can quickly deplete a herd and lead to financial ruin, while pearlshells, aside from breakages and loss, are immune to such calamities.[7] The reproduction of pigs is an extremely arduous and continuous proposition; success from generation to generation cannot be guaranteed. Pigs have therefore, inherent limitations if a man's power and prestige, as it is in Tombema, are based on them alone. Thus, Melpa exchange routes along which pigs travelled were converted into avenues of pearlshells in the *moka* (A.J. Strathern 1979:532). Shells, durable and controllable, were adopted as wealth by bigmen intent on establishing less temporary superiority. But pearlshells had their limitations too, for they became highly inflationary as I will point out below. Melpa bigmen could not yet, however, have foreseen what lay ahead.

Pigs must also be fed whereas pearlshells eat very little. The agricultural and labour requirements for supporting a large pig herd are immense and in a system like the *tee*, based on pigs, very long interpersonal exchange chains are necessary to relieve and balance the pressure on local resources. Thus an Enga man who finds his pig herd to be temporarily too burdensome can finance some pigs or give them in advance of the next major *tee* (*mena yukupae*).[8] He knows that partners, or partners of partners, along the chain will be able to accommodate them, depending on their own current situation. As I showed in the last chapter, complex financial and redistributive procedures exist in the *tee*, while as A.J. Strathern reports, in Mount Hagen, "explicit chain arrangements are restricted to sets of a few tribes at the most" (1969a:62). *Moka* exchange chains are short by comparison, while Enga *tee* chains are "vastly greater" (A.J. Strathern 1969a:62), a feature which can be partially explained by the nature of the items exchanged. The *tee* as a total system involves a much larger, interlocking population than the *moka* and, in terms of formal requirements is more complex.[9] A *tee* cycle often ends in the mass killing of many pigs (*mena yae pingi*) which en- sures that resources are not stretched beyond tolerable limits, and that pigs maintain their value as a scarce, though locally pro- duced item, not subject to inflation. The fact too that Tombema love to eat pigs means that political gain is sometimes sacrificed in order to consume pork.

If, as I maintain, the adoption of pearlshells had profound con- sequences for Melpa society, while with pigs the Enga continued an older exchange pattern, we must look to the ethnographic evidence for clues of confirmation. Information on the *moka* prior to the introduction of pearlshells is scanty at best. Instead, I take (with reservations) the Enga *tee* to represent an approxima- tion of pre-pearlshell *moka*. In the next chapter I examine the processes and structures which differentiate Tombema–Enga from Melpa, and work to prevent a similar transformation of

Tombema sociopolitical organization. With pearlshells, the *moka* was transformed, a transformation stemming from the production process. The *tee*, I argue, more fully retains its links with the past, even to this day. There should be then, significant contrasts between the *moka* and *tee* deriving from the processes mentioned.

In the *moka*, the political significance of exchange broadens beyond what the *tee* is capable of. Bigmen controlled pearlshell valuables and as such were able to more closely coordinate group activities in exchange. Bigmen could strike more expedient alliances, for their own good and their groups, invest more widely and further afield, and manoeuver more freely, largely because they monopolized shells and were seen as the essential links between their communities and pearlshell sources. The individual transactions of pigs that distinguish the Enga *tee* (see chapter six) are devalued in the *moka*. The emphasis on groups as the exchange units in *The Rope of Moka* (A.J. Strathern 1971) can be contrasted to the emphasis on individual transactions in the *tee* (see also Feil 1980). This differing emphasis has an ethnographic, not merely an epistemological basis. There is little or no coordination of a group's exchange activities in pig *tee*. Enga bigmen give and receive more pigs than others, but they have no say whatsoever over the transactions of others. Thus, the functional significance of the two ceremonial systems of exchange is different: the *moka* concerns competitive intergroup relations headed by bigmen;[10] the *tee* concerns interpersonal relations and intragroup competition stemming from equal access to the production of exchange valuables. The *moka* is seen as a surrogate for warfare, the *tee* as a reflection of ties of personal friendship. Both systems promote social control: the *tee* through cross-cutting ties of personal loyalty, the *moka* through political alliances contracted through the medium of large gifts. A.J. Strathern writes that around Hagen one hears, " 'Before we fought and killed each other now . . . we can pay for killings and make *moka*.' Although such statements are *post hoc* evaluations, they do reflect the fact that *moka* and warfare are seen as two different ways of asserting group and individual prowess." (1971:54) Thus the *moka* allows for a political impact based on the power and coordination of bigmen leaders which the *tee* does not have. I will elaborate these points of the *tee* below. This fact is further reflected in the kinship status of *moka* and *tee* partners. A significant percentage of *moka* partners are described by Melpa informants as unrelated.

Further evidence of increased politicization of *moka* exchanges is that increments, in return *moka* payments, were clearly an inherent and expected part of the system. A.J. Strathern notes that "it is the increment, strictly, which can be referred to as *'moka'*, the rest is there simply to meet *'debt'* " (1971:10). This too suggests a more competitive relationship between givers and receivers of valuables, providing a context and measure for relations of superiority and inferiority, certainly more so than is present in the *tee*. Most *tee* transactions are simply *quid pro quo*. A person receives back in pigs about the same as he earlier gave, and, is so considered a good *tee* man. Competitive gift-giving between partners, basic to the *moka*, does not exist in the *tee*. This fact is consistent with the view that *tee* partners, regardless of their clan affiliations are allies, not enemies. Recent ethnographic studies of the *moka* and *tee* thus reveal considerable contrasts: a more political and powerful role for Melpa bigmen, a greater political content to *moka* dealings which the *tee* does not possess, and intergroup political relations headed and coordinated by dominant Melpa bigmen. Enga bigmen, aside from making larger prestations, have little or no say over their groups or another individual's exchange dealings.

Earlier ethnographic information dating from the 1930s is also very useful, and further substantiates the existence and evolution of rank and exploitative relations in Hagen society which I have explored above. These sources must however be treated with caution. While the missionaries and others whose accounts are used lived for long periods in Mount Hagen, their interpretations of Melpa social structure and economic life may be overrigid or miscast. The intent here is not to decide the truth or falsity of their characterizations (if indeed it were possible), but merely to argue that their studies provide important support for the propositions this chapter has put forward. It may be moreover that more contemporary accounts have failed to come to grips with profound changes in the exchange economy which have greatly affected Melpa society during the past forty to fifty years. This case will also be advanced below.

A number of early accounts speak of the greater importance in

Mount Hagen of place rather than tribe. The earliest is that of Reverend Ross (Ross 1936) whose views were supported and elaborated upon by the economist Gitlow who visited the area in 1945 (Gitlow 1947).[11] It is worth quoting them at some length here:

> The *tribes* have no outstanding chiefs, but *each place* has its own headman or headmen. The headman is usually the richest, and most powerful person in the "place". His power and influence descend to his son when he dies. . . . Men are known not so much by their tribe as by their place. (Ross 1936:354, emphasis added)

Gitlow, further, writes that

> The Kona, or Place, is the basic local grouping of the Mount Hagen natives. . . . The Kona is truly the basic grouping. . . . Between the tribe and the Kona, there are groupings of several Kona, each of which submit to the *limited* authority of a paramount chieftain. . . . The paramount chieftain exerts authority . . . (over such matters as) warfare, *moga* ceremonies. . . . (Gitlow 1947:25, emphasis in original)

Each author points out that a headman's "word is law" in his place only and has no meaning elsewhere. These references to place rather than tribal affiliation are striking. There has been much debate about the relative importance of descent versus locale in the New Guinea Highlands, as well as the relationship between the two groupings.[12] On the basis of the above sources, it appears that Hageners at that time stressed place, and that each was headed by a powerful man. Furthermore, a headman's name was prefixed by his place name, not his tribal name (Gitlow 1947:25).[13] While both authors state that a headman's political muscle emanated initially from a large family following, it seems that isolated domestic units were brought together to form "sovereign and independent" places (Fortune 1947), under the control of a dominant man. Whether or not the "economic defects" of the domestic mode of production (Sahlins 1972) were finally overcome, it seems clear that political-economic ties of place assumed greater importance in Hagen than has been reported elsewhere in Highlands ethnography. This is a necessary first step in the movement towards established rank, and Hageners in these early reports seem to have taken it. The controlling interest of Melpa bigmen in *moka* ceremonies and all that this entails, was the basis of their authority.

The references above to the passage of power between generations of leaders are also significant. This information obviously does not fit the stereotyped "bigman" model much used by Highland anthropologists. This model based on Sahlins' (1963) early paradigm stressed *inter alia* the temporariness and lack of consolidation of a bigman's political power. Phrases like "chiefly lineage", "chiefly blood" and "chiefly class" abound in the work of Ross and Gitlow, and the other sources to be mentioned below. In addition, more recent ethnographers have also noted claims of hereditary leadership in the Highlands. Reay (1959:114) wrote that the Kuma, western neighbours of the Melpa, "asserted that when the acknowledged leader . . . dies his eldest son succeeds him". A.J. Strathern himself mentions, while downplaying hereditary aspects of Melpa leadership, that "major big-men have a 3:1 chance of being the sons of big-men". (A.J. Strathern 1971:210). Conversely, only one-half of contemporary Tombema-Enga bigmen had fathers who were themselves so considered (Feil 1978a). Furthermore, no early Enga sources cite evidence of ascription to leadership, nor are there any current beliefs or ideology of the sort Reay noted for the Kuma. Standish (1978) has reviewed much of the evidence and believes strongly that hereditary elements in Highlands leadership in pre-European times have been severely overlooked. Included in his survey of earlier writings is the view of Vicedom, a missionary among the Melpa, who described Hagen leadership as "ascribed" (Vicedom and Tischner 1943–48, Vol. 2). Whether or not Highland leaders were "despots" or "directors" (A.J. Strathern 1966) may also depend on the time period in which the anthropological analyses took place. The evidence from the early Melpa sources indicates a greater degree of ascription and more power and authority attaching to leaders than Strathern's more recent work suggests. I will return to this point below, but clearly, the first Melpa accounts stress the interconnection of wealth, power, family and political authority over place by "chiefs".

Much more information concerning rank and stratification in early Hagen society comes from the work of Vicedom, a missionary, who arrived in the area in 1934 and lived there for five years. His observations are thus among the earliest for the period of early European contact. He describes an indigenous system of class stratification. Allen (1967:41) finds eight named classes in Vicedom's account, A.J. Strathern (1971:205) interprets four, while Gitlow (1947:34) distinguishes five. All are based on either the work of Vicedom or Ross.[14] Regardless of the discrepancies in the number of classes, such a well-formulated system of stratification is nowhere else in evidence in the Highlands in either past or present sources. Men of the top class are those of chiefly blood, according to Gitlow (1947:35) numbering about 100 men in a tribe of 1700 men (less than 6 per cent). These men alone participate in *moka* exchanges according to all accounts, and they alone possess and control its magic (Allen 1967:41–42). These men are polygnists and support members of the lower classes. Next, there is a sort of "middle class" (perhaps about 80 per cent of the population, Gitlow 1947:35), who are "freemen", who have land rights and some independence from the chiefly class. Below freemen are at least two other classes of "rubbishmen" and "serfs", perhaps 14 per cent of the population (Gitlow 1947:35), who are totally dependent on the upper class for their needs. They support the chieftains, work for them, and are in all ways their minions. Vicedom called them "slaves". They own no land or other property, and live in rough shelters. Gitlow gives a further, vivid description. "They must carry out their master's orders, which often involves performing missions of a violent nature. As a consequence, they tend to become a dangerous element in the area. Since they have nothing to lose in the way of property, they are said to become ruthless in carrying out raids for their chief." (1947:36) Serfs are unmarried and they often perform the work of women, caring for pigs. Some are war refugees who have been granted political security by a chief in return for labour. While Gitlow suggests that the serf-master relationship is voluntary, quite the opposite is clearly the case. For protection and maintenance, serfs must enter into an exploitative relationship; in return for labour and military service they receive the requirements for their existence. Finally, to quote Gitlow, "Each chief will have at least one [serf]. Ninki, the most influential local chieftain . . . has five serfs. Father Ross has estimated . . . that in the Hagen area one-tenth of the entire population belong to this class." (1947:37)

Obviously, there are all kinds of interpretative problems stemming from these ethnographic descriptions. A.J. Strathern (1971:204, 208) points out many of the difficulties, including whether these were "true classes", what part marriage might have played in crossing class boundaries, and he further questions many translations of terms which Vicedom supplies. He then defends his categories of "big-men", "ordinary men" and "men of low status" and all but dismisses Vicedom's and Ross's picture of a bounded class society. As correct as his criticisms may be, the overwhelming evidence from that time is of a system of rank or stratification, dominated by a group of power-ful, wealthy *moka*-makers who enjoyed some measure of ascribed status and exploited some if not all lower status members of society. If we grant any credence whatsoever to those early accounts, and the weight of evidence makes them difficult to ignore totally, there is a problem to explore here. Why do the descriptions of past and present Melpa society differ so much? What of the basically consensual view of Melpa society, as well as the received view of Highland societies in general?

To summarize: prior to European contact, Melpa bigmen seized on pearlshells as the standard of exchange value. By so doing they sought to devalue the role of pigs in the prestige system. This process was perhaps slow and cumulative, perhaps not. Monopolizing the means of production of exchange valuables, pearlshells, and transforming thereby productive relations between men, and between men and women, bigmen established at least an incipiently stratified society. This system was based on control of a durable wealth, containing the features of dependence mentioned above. The Enga meanwhile, con-tinued to produce pigs for *tee* exchanges and their ties to a more "historical" exchange economy remained unbroken. Wirz (1952b) neatly summed up the comparative point: men involved in *moka* were "grouped in one society" of exclusive membership, and that membership in a clan "has nothing to do with membership in a *moka* group" (see also Golson 1982:112). Wirz goes on to suggest, but not develop, a contrast with the Enga and the resulting character of the *tee* which has no similar type of "exclusive" organization. The missionaries and others were, I believe, witnessing the culmination of a transformed exchange economy, one which had inexorably substituted pearlshells for pigs. Importantly, it had been an internal transformation with bigmen, whose power was hitherto impermanent, the prime movers. The remainder of this chapter briefly examines the external circumstances which radically and quickly altered the picture given by these first Mount Hagen residents. It occurred as a result of European intrusion into the area.

## Pearlshells and Inflation

Durable, easily transportable, scarce, and capable of being rigidly controlled, pearlshells were the basis of rank and exploitation by "bigmen" in Hagen society at first European contact. From about the early 1930s, Europeans first began to enter the Mount Hagen region. Prospectors led by the Leahy brothers were first, followed closely by the Australian Administration led by J.L. Taylor which established airfields and an administrative post. Then came the missionaries, Catholic and Lutheran, in the mid-1930s. Mount Hagen became a centre for administration and population in the Western Highlands, a position it holds to the present day. The influx of Europeans meant, of course, that a large, foreign population's daily needs had to be met; food and labour had to be purchased from the local people. Australian money had no value at the time, so Europeans turned naturally instead, to a locally scarce, but to them easily transportable, durable, and abundant item of currency: pearlshells. Europeans began to use pearlshells, the highest valued local wealth item, not as objects of ceremonial exchange, encumbered by cultural rules, and handled by the privileged few, but as money, to buy local food and work from all. With this attitude and the ability to secure vast numbers of pearlshells, the basis of the hegemony of bigmen in the Hagen area was soon to collapse.

What is more, Europeans seem to have known what they were doing. The first prospectors, the Leahys, record in their account of the time:

> Dan (Leahy) readjusted himself to the new order of things with considerable promptness, being as Jim had always maintained "a very solid lad with a ton of savvy". . . . He found that Ewunga Creek could be made to yield moderate returns in gold though we had considerably inflated the shell currency and thereby raised the cost of food and labour. "When shells get too cheap" said he, "I'll introduce knives, mirrors and coloured cloth". (Leahy and Crain 1937:271, 272)

The Melpa were of course eager to obtain the treasured pearl-shells. They had been scarce, and in the hands of bigmen only prior to this time. Melpa of all kinds began to bring their pigs and other garden produce to the Europeans in exchange for the highest valued objects, pearlshells. By 1938, Europeans in the Mount Hagen area numbered between 700 and 800 men (Hughes 1978:315), purchasing several tons of pigs and food per day. Food supplies, including pigs, in the Hagen area became scarce (Hughes 1978) but wealth among the people, at least in pearlshells, grew out of all proportion to times past.

Hughes (1978) has documented well the airlift of pearl and other shells into the Mount Hagen area by European miners and missionaries. Pearlshells were obtained from Manus Island and Thursday Island in the Torres Strait, "a chartered DC3 aircraft brought supplies from Thursday Island, a £1000 load fetching ten times the price in Mt. Hagen" (Hughes 1978:313). But still, the intense desire to obtain shells outstripped the supply. Millions of shells were requested from European residents in Mount Hagen to be used as currency. Perhaps five to ten million were distributed by them (Hughes 1978:315). The result was that Hageners close to European settlements became very wealthy, very quickly, in pearlshells. Ross (cited in Gitlow 1947:71–72) reported:

> Thousands of these shells were passed around the area in the ten years of white occupation. The result was that the native of the Hagen area became the millionaire. He could go out to the fringe of the area and buy wives with the shells he was gradually hoarding. Where a chief would formerly be a great man with 3 wives, now he could buy 8 or 10. Young men who formerly had no standing could now raise their status by working for the white man, receiving payment in shells.

The result of this mass importation of pearlshells was to devalue them and with it, the control of bigmen over the exchange economy. All men, regardless of status, could now acquire pearlshells through their labour, and "purchase" with them, wives and other scarce commodities, including prestige, formerly held only by bigmen. It must also have been that the *moka* system underwent a profound democratic change (A.J. Strathern 1966) or at least a change in which a bigman's power was severely curtailed.

European intrusion into the region also had a pacifying effect. Even before *Pax Australiana* years later, the massive airlift of

pearlshells brought peace to the area. Leahy (1937:272) wrote that the increased trade in pearlshells has "pacified the neighbourhood. Since pigs are getting scarce and the Mogei's [a local tribe] are loaded down with the shell money, they've made peace with all their old enemies in order to buy pigs." It seems therefore that the other avenue of power for Melpa bigmen, the organization of war, was likewise beginning to be undermined (see above Gitlow 1947:36). Peace partially came to the area with the local need to expand the pearlshell trade. Thus, starting with the entry of Europeans into Mount Hagen, the traditional exchange economy and the power of leaders based on it started to collapse. Out west, the Enga were essentially immune from these occurrences. Pearlshells had never, in pre-European times, assumed great importance. Pigs could not be mass-produced and airlifted in, and the Enga area was still too remote to attract a very large European population. The Pacific War brought a decreased involvement of Europeans with Hageners and slowed the import of pearlshells. The exchange economy and exchange relations had however been affected and transformed yet again, this time beyond recognition, and the sociopolitical effects must have been tremendous.

It is impossible to say whether bigmen lost all of their control of Melpa society immediately and totally. The evidence seems to suggest a lessening of their power with a gradual turning back towards pigs as the standard of exchange value. This would have given, overall, an egalitarian aspect to Melpa social relations. This, I think, approximates the current ethnographic view of that society (see A.J. Strathern 1971). As well, a bigman's power was not absolutely a reflection of his control of pearlshells and he may have held on to some power through magic, healing, oratory, and other means. The total and historical legacy of bigmen and their position could not have been so quickly and totally demolished. I would argue that the bigman paradigm, the competitive aspects of the *moka*, the pattern of war, and other aspects of Melpa social structure (including male–female relations) as described by current writers, are the result of the historical processes I have outlined. Bigmen for example no longer have the power they once held, they no longer so completely control the items of exchange value as they once did. Their power is less ascribed and reproducible; they must attract followers, for they can less easily compel them. The ban on war-fare meant that refugees have not gone searching for protection. Groups, clans or tribes, have re-emerged over "places" as the basis of bigmen's more limited and temporary authority. Or-dinary men have more chance to become big, and bigmen can bequeath less to their offspring. These are the ethnographic descriptions which the first generation of anthropologists in the Highlands first made, but I suggest they stem from a situation very much changed from that of the early and middle 1930s (see also Hughes 1978:316). Our current views of "traditional" leader-ship, social structure and ceremonial exchange may need to be revamped if the argument put forward here has any merit.

And this historical process continues. Cash cropping has taken off in the Hagen area, and money has become an important *moka* valuable, supplanting pearlshells as items of value. The recent work of A.J. Strathern (1979) shows how bigmen, through an adept and adaptive ideology, have sought to control cash by, among other means, comparing it to their traditional control over pearlshells. It has, they say, the same properties, women are disallowed from owning it, and ordinary men are encourag-ed to channel it through bigmen for the *moka* exchanges.[15] Bigmen are trying, with some success, to become "capitalist entrepreneurs" perhaps as they did in the past replacing pearlshells with money. But money is as inflationary as pearl-shells, and women and men of lower status can earn it by selling their labour too. Thus any immediate consolidation or attempted recouping of power by bigmen is likely to be shortlived. In contrast, the Enga *tee* has failed to incorporate money (Feil 1978a), pigs are still "more valuable than money" and cannot be easily bought in the area. When money is given, which is seldom, it is symbolic of a pig that has died along the *tee* road. Mount Hagen bigmen have a tradition and history of political control and their switch to money must be analyzed in that context. The recent upsurge in Highlands fighting may also be a further indication of an attempt by bigmen to regain their authority in a banned institution by promoting violence (see Standish 1978).

Hagen society and more widely, much of the Highlands, has undergone profound changes since European contact. These changes can largely be traced to the effects of a transformed exchange economy which has had concomitant, far-reaching social and political ramifications. For the Melpa, it was the second transformation, an imposed exogenous one which accentuated and then destroyed an indigenous movement towards rank fostered by bigmen. The "ethnographic present" should consider and reflect these historical processes.

In a provocative paper, Brunton (1975) asks "Why do the Trobriands have Chiefs" and finds an explanation in the ability of Omarakana chiefs to close off the exchange system and limit the circulation of exchange items. The Highlanders however, provide him with a negative case, for "Highland societies have not developed a system of hereditary social stratification and chieftainship" because "nowhere was it possible to monopolize and close-up the trade and exchange system" (Brunton 1975:556). Control over scarce exchange items is here given much less emphasis than exchange connections themselves and the convertibility of exchange items. The Trobriands and a few other societies in Papua New Guinea have always been viewed by anthropologists as anomalous cases of stratification. The more important questions however, are not whether one society or another was stratified, but what the conditions for the development of stratification are, did they exist widely throughout Papua New Guinea, and what are the historical processes in which one society realized stratification and another not. Cultures are very creative in their bases and methods for establishing rank and stratification and fostering relations of exploitation and control. In Hagen society as opposed to Enga, I suggest that bigmen by controlling the production and ultimate exchange of pearlshells rather than pigs, created the circumstances for the development of rank.

On the basis of the available evidence, it is nearly impossible to answer the question of why did pearlshells come to be valued in Mount Hagen while in Tombema–Enga pigs remained the most highly valued exchange items even though pearlshells were known and scarce. I would argue however, that this question is less important than an analysis of the implications for Hagen society of the adoption of pearlshell exchange. For the Melpa, a political answer seems most likely: some influential men saw pearlshells as a way to extend and consolidate their power and position. One must still explain the acceptance by the wider population of pearlshells as a standard of value and wealth. When pearlshells became the objects of supreme value, thereby decreasing the value of pigs and their production, Melpa women lost their crucial role in and partial control of the exchange system. They no longer helped produce the items of highest exchange value, pigs. In the following chapter, I turn to the involvement of Tombema women in the production and *tee* exchange process. Tombema women provide a partial answer to why the *tee* withstood the changes that affected the Melpa *moka*, and more widely, Hagen society. I also examine further some structural aspects of the *tee* which help explain its continuity.

## Notes

1. Pearlshells (*pinctada maxima*) known in Enga as *mamaku,* in Melpa as *kokla kin* are important throughout the Highlands. Salt, stone axes, plumes, and a variety of locally produced items are also important, but are secondary to pearlshells and pigs, at least in Hagen and Enga. These are the only two items which enjoy complete convertibility and circulation, while other, less valued items can usually be exchanged only away from their sources, never towards them.
2. The view advanced here is that exploitation occurs when access to the means of valued resources is restricted in any way by an individual or group of individuals. This restriction is used for political advantage, and to the detriment of others who do not have open access to these valued resources. Such, I argue, was clearly the case with the exchange of pearlshells.
3. But see Golson (1982:133–34) who argues that pearlshells as markers of inequality were taken up or converted by already powerful families whose dominance originated much earlier, based on differential access to preferred wet-taro agricultural land and hence more prolific pig production opportunities. Golson's paper extends back into prehistory aspects raised in my analysis, first published in 1982 (Feil 1982). It also answers some questions first raised in that paper.
4. By rank and stratification, I mean a hierarchy of political-economic statuses which may be recognized by the members of society themselves. There are clear-cut political and economic differentials between the strata and the members of each may recognize their status as opposed to others. Status differentials are likely to continue across the generations.
5. In fact, very little rancour between the sexes occurs over *tee* exchanges. Women also own pigs and give them away.
6. Pig epidemics mark the history of the *tee*. Meggitt (1974) notes an outbreak of pleuro-pneumonia in the late 1940s which wiped out Enga pigs and led to the reorganization of some *tee* phases (see also Feil 1978a).
7. Modjeska (1982) has argued the related point that with pearlshells, exchanged for pigs, Melpa men mystified further the value of women's labour, by creating a system in which pearlshell exchange was seen to exist independently of women's part in the production of pigs. Pearlshell

exchange was purely a male activity. Pearlshells are abstract mystifications of women's labour converted by men from the pigs women produce.

8. *Mena yukupae* literally means to "lift out a pig". If pigs are unruly, too numerous, or a person is tired of looking after many, he can choose to send pigs onward in the *tee* chain in return for credits in the forthcoming *tee* cycle. These pigs may be returned before he makes his major prestation in order to demonstrate to all that they are his, although earlier given.

9. Complexity is difficult to measure, but the fact that there is a single *tee* which links all Enga communities, that all clans are arranged in a set order of *tee*-making, and that all Enga make *tee*, seem to suggest a greater overall organizational complexity than the Melpa *moka* possesses.

10. The subtitle of A.J. Strathern's (1971) work on the *moka*, is "Big-Men and Ceremonial Exchange in Mount Hagen, New Guinea". Bigmen are the only prominent individuals whose exchange activities are noted by Strathern. Bigmen and the groups they head are given the overwhelming, predominant place in his analysis (compare Feil 1978a).

11. Reverend Ross lived for twelve years in the Mount Hagen area. Gitlow used much of his information in his account of the economic life of the region.

12. There is a voluminous literature, too massive to mention here. Watson (1964), Langness (1964) and Lepervanche (1967-68) were the first to discuss the issue of descent versus residence in the New Guinea Highlands. To my knowledge, nowhere in the ethnographic literature is "place" so stressed as in these early Melpa accounts.

13. Bulmer (1960) has noted that the Kyaka-Enga of the Baiyer Valley "tag" individuals with clan or sub-clan names. I did not find that this occurred among Tombema-Enga however.

14. Gitlow (1947) does not cite Vicedom so his views on the class structure of Mount Hagen society undoubtedly come from Ross.

15. A.J. Strathern (1979) presents an elaborate argument focussing on among other things, the role of ideology used by bigmen in attempting to control cash as they once controlled pearlshells.

# FOUR

# Women and Exchange

The *tee* belongs to this woman. It is made for her.
Ngoo, a Mamaġakini bigman,
speaking of his wife before making his *tee*.

Women have a vital, acknowledged role in the *tee*. I have argued
that this importance arises, in part, from their contribution of
labour in the production of pigs, the most highly valued items of
exchange in the *tee*. But pigs are exchanged in the *tee*, exchange
is the culmination of production, and I will point out that women
also have a critical part to play in the allotment of pigs within the
*tee* system (see also Feil 1978a, 1978c). In the transformation of
exchange economies, from pigs to pearlshells, the position and
influence of Melpa women were eroded, and Melpa society profoundly changed. In Tombema–Enga society, women continue
to be the fulcra of the *tee*, in both the production and exchange of
pigs.

In Tombema society, women are essential for the production
not only of *tee* pigs, but *also* for the creation of *tee* exchange
partners. The Melpa preoccupation with pearlshells excludes
women from a share in the production of society's most highly
valued items, and women, likewise, appear much less important
for the formation and daily functioning of *moka* partnerships.
These "production" aspects involving Tombema women as key
participants, highlights their greater value for the workings of
the *tee* in comparison to their feminine Melpa counterparts.
These facts also partially explain why Enga society withstood the
changes which occurred in Mount Hagen, stemming from a
transformed exchange economy.

## "Roads" of Women

Tombema men declare quite openly that "only women can create *tee* roads". This is a clearly stated principle for the formation of a partnership. Men say that "where our women go in marriage is where our pigs go later in the *tee*" and that "we send our women out, and pigs follow them". Each of a man's *tee* partners focuses on a woman who makes the partnership possible and serves as sanction and guarantor of the partnership.

Tombema constantly invoke metaphors of paths, ways, and roads (*kaita*) to describe the *tee*'s movements and geographical extensions. In many uses, *kaita* is a synonym for the *tee* itself. In this metaphorical usage, the *tee* is viewed as a "pathway" between men linked by women. Pigs and other valuables find their way along this path. While *kaita* has these general applications in *tee* matters, an individual often uses the word, with appropriate modifiers, to explain the basis of his connection to others with whom he makes *tee*. A man's pool of affinal partners, made possible by his marriage, belong to the "road of my wife" and the partners made possible by a man's mother belong to that road.

But women are not merely forgotten symbols of exchange roads. A large majority of partners are linked by living women (see below). For intraclan partnerships which usually rely on extended kinship, the man seeking a partnership must approach the linking woman (with whom he is distantly related) and seek some guarantee, explicit or implicit, that she is willing to act as go-between. A pig may be given which, if accepted, means that the woman is willing to safeguard and buffer the relationship. Men often do not discuss individual, private, *tee* matters if the linking woman is not present. Exchange partners whose links to a woman's husband are other than through her (for example his mother or his sister) may also approach her and seek her "house-raised pigs". She may enter into a "special" relationship with these men, characterized by name taboos, which are a mark of friendship and mutual interest in exchange matters. Requests for house pigs are, then, male to female transactions, rather than male to male ones. Women are the fulcra, in principle and in fact, of *tee* relations.

Thus, men not related by a woman cannot be *tee* partners.

Virtually all *tee* partners, known in Enga as *kaita miningi*, "holders of the way", are linked by a woman. Even men of the same clan, related principally by agnatic dogma, stress and prefer to emphasize a distant, non-agnatic tie in order to initiate a partnership of exchange (Feil 1978a). Intraclan partnerships are, however, few in number in comparison with interclan ones, and insignificant in importance. Members of different clans can become linked by women only through marriage. When discussing how the *tee* works in abstract, people frequently used marriage payments as the archetypal *tee* transaction: "an initial gift of a pig was given to a brother-in-law at marriage, *tee* relations began from this; we have followed in the same way". I surmise that in its beginnings, the *tee* was solely an exchange institution involving persons from different clans linked by women. That too is its essential character today. Women's part in influencing and directing *tee* transactions has been explored in detail elsewhere (Feil 1978b, 1978c).

Here it is important to note that while all *tee* partners are related through a woman, such is clearly not the case among the Melpa. A.J. Strathern (1971:144) notes for the Melpa that "there is often a possibility of choosing to regard a partner as a distantly related kinsman/affine, or as unrelated". In the analysis of partners participating in the *moka* given by A.J. Strathern (1971:144–45), 43 per cent of all recipients of valuables were unrelated. As expected, bigmen had more unrelated partners than others. In a sample of more than 2,100 *tee* partnerships described in the following chapter, not one was considered unrelated, even those of all bigmen questioned.

*Tee* partnerships are often based on the most tenuous kinship connections (Feil 1978a), yet they are still thought to possess some partial kinship content. *Moka* partnerships on the other hand, appear to have a more political side, a "radicalization of the kinship function" (Sahlins 1972:132) has taken place, in contrast to Enga *kaita miningi*. While women are essential to create *tee* partnerships, and are crucial to their everyday working and maintenance, Melpa men, especially bigmen with their control over pearlshell transactions, could create partnerships of their own with unrelated men, thereby circumventing any feminine influence and downplaying even more the role of women in the exchange economy. Melpa women were unnecessary for producing not only items of value, but also the very relationships on which the exchange system rests. The crucial role of linking women in the *tee* is further explored when we consider what happens to partnerships when a linking woman disappears through death or divorce.

## Dissolution of *Tee* Partners

Tombema say that two men "come together" or are "joined" in the *tee* by a woman, that they base their relationship on a female link, and that when it no longer exists, the incentive to maintain the relationship disappears. This view is, I think, a recognition that women alone can guarantee the integrity of men in *tee* dealings, and without that guarantee, the relationship may flounder. Women are in a unique structural position, and their loyalties in *tee* matters are not fixed with regard to a particular place or person.

A woman may tell a linked man when he is not being treated fairly in the *tee*, and her presence and willingness to reveal improprieties acts to prevent and safeguard the interests of men linked to her, who are located elsewhere. During marital separation, *tee* relations are suspended between the partners she links; after divorce, those partnerships cannot continue. In sum, women provide the ultimate sanctions of *tee* partnerships. This being so, it is easy enough to understand how a death or a divorce – the loss of a link – results in the collapse of a *tee* partnership.

Tombema men reluctantly accept these occurrences, but they do not consider the ending of a partnership through a woman's death in the same way they do a collapse due for example to non-reciprocation (see chapter seven). The latter results in anger, the former in regretful resignation, especially if a major partner has been lost and his debts from the last *tee* not returned. A good partner may sometimes reciprocate accumulated debts even after a woman's death has occurred, but this is not a certainty. Rather, a partner who has many credits owing to him when the linking woman of the partnership dies, tries to create a situation in which some equalization can occur. For example, a man was owed many pigs from a previous *tee* by his sister's husband.

Suddenly his sister died. During the mourning period, the brother killed several pigs and presented them to his brother-in-law. This pork was distributed by the deceased's husband to the assembled mourners. The payment was an inducement for the brother-in-law to make a death payment for his wife. By making the preliminary payment, the woman's brother hoped to receive a large part of it. A death payment is always greater (and often very much greater) than the preliminary payment; it is made in live pigs, and it may reduce the balance of payments between the partners. If a death payment is made, the partnership may continue for some time further, but its termination is inevitable. The husband of the dead woman, especially if the marriage has been a long one, makes the payment in part to acknowledge his debt to her for her service and companionship, and the payment is usually made from the pigs she has raised herself. These pigs, had she lived, would probably have gone in the *tee* to her brother or her other relations anyway. Even after death, the pigs a woman has raised may find their way to her relations.

When a linking woman dies, some partners are in a position to redefine their relationship and perhaps shift some of the burden of responsibility on to another woman whose importance as a link was not hitherto recognized. They may seek her help by offering a small gift and call each other by a new kin term recognizing their tie through her. Such redefinitions of relationships are not always possible and partnerships lacking another female link often cease if a death occurs. When two links through different women are possible, however, the living link is stressed and takes precedence over the other which will be forgotten in time.[1]

Whatever the type of relationship, when a linking female dies, *tee* relations are fragile and subject to dilution or dissolution. But some types of relationships are more fragile than others. By far the most unstable partnerships at the death of a linking woman are affinal ones. Brother-in-law (*palingi*) partnerships are the most liable to dissolve. This dissolution may occur automatically unless a man's sister has children, preferably male, with whom he can eventually make *tee*. The incentive is absent to continue *tee* involvement with a sister's husband who has no children to take his place. If a sister's husband has only daughters the partnership is more precarious, but may continue. The mother's brother may hope eventually to make *tee* with his sister's daughter's husband. Waipape, a Mamagakini bigman was in this situation: his wife had died and he has two daughters but no sons; his sister died but her two sons are alive. He made the point to me by saying, "If I had no daughters, I wouldn't make *tee* with Poreyalani (his deceased wife's clan). If my sister's sons were not alive, I wouldn't make *tee* with Yapetalini (the clan into which his deceased sister had married). My daughters and sister's sons protect my *tee* roads."

After the death of a linking woman, partners individually reassess the value of the partnership. In a number of recorded instances, a man wished to continue to make *tee* payments to his sister's children after his sister had died. Their father, his former brother-in-law, had found a new wife, however, and was beginning to make payments to his affines through her, curtailing those to his former wife's brother. When this happens, the mother's brother-sister's son connection loses force and *tee* payments between them are unlikely to be taken up again.[2] When a linking woman dies, the chances of prolonging a *tee* partnership are possible. When a female linkage disappears through divorce, however, there is no hope of continuing *tee* relations.

Divorce not only means the break-up of a couple, it also leads to dissolution among all *tee* partners who use that woman as the basis for their relationship. Men without linking women cannot transact, and divorce means the immediate cessation of *tee* relations between men sharing that tie. This is so regardless of whether the wife or the husband initiates the divorce action. Tombema terminologically distinguish the two types of divorce, depending on whether the husband or wife brings the suit. When men seek the divorce, the proceedings are called "woman thrown away" or "woman told to go". In instances of this kind, the bridal payment is not returned, it "dies" with the recipients on the bride's side. When a woman seeks and secures divorce by leaving her husband, and failing to return after many promptings, the divorce is called simply "wife leaves husband" or "wife abandons husband". In these instances, depending on the length of marriage, the number of children, and other factors, the bride-wealth or a portion of it must be returned to the groom's side; it must be "lifted out".

Of 569 recorded marriages by Mamagakini men and women, I

recorded 48 divorces, a rate of 8.4 per cent (compare Mae–Enga rate of 5.3 per cent [29 of 540] recorded by Meggitt 1965a:150). In 21 of these divorces more detailed information was obtained. Briefly, these cases show that divorced couples were married an average of just over three years, but eight couples were married less than two. The 21 couples had only 13 children but 11 of them were childless. These figures support the general proposition that divorce occurs more usually among couples who have been married only a short time and have few or no children. With one or more children, marriages become more stable. The reasons given for divorce in these cases are set out in table 6.

**Table 6**  Ostensible Reasons for Divorce in 21 Cases

| Cause | Number of cases |
|---|---|
| Adultery | 7 |
| *Tee*-related infractions, for example, husband fails to fulfil obligations to wife's relations | 5 |
| Failure of husband to make death payments for deceased children | 4 |
| Husband takes second wife without compensating first wife; or attempting to use her pigs as bridewealth for second wife | 3 |
| Husband fails to look after wife properly, for example, to plant gardens or chop firewood | 2 |
| Total | 21 |

Physical abuse is cited as a cause of divorce, but no instances of it occurred in these cases. Twelve of 21 divorces were caused by *tee*-related issues. Death payments and marriage payments are a part of the overall *tee* system.

Women mainly initiate divorce. In the above 21 cases of recent divorce, women initiated 19 of them, men only two. The reasons are clear enough: if men seek divorce or in any way suggest that they favour a divorce, marriage payments are not returned. All of the pigs, pearlshells, and money remain with the wife's group. If, however, she decides to leave, and makes the decision public and final, all of the outstanding bridewealth must be returned. As with temporary separation, *tee* transactions between linked partners cannot take place when a divorce is pending. If it becomes final, all *tee* partnerships using that female tie cease. Men rarely divorce their wives, for to do so would not only mean the forfeiture of a large marriage payment, but all *tee* connections through her as well. If the marriage has lasted for any length of time, outstanding *tee* debts will also be lost.[3] To my knowledge, there are no actions by a wife which are considered "due cause" for divorce, allowing a husband to divorce her and still reclaim part of the bridal payment. A husband often tolerates wayward acts by the wife, such as adultery, rather than seek a divorce.[4] Tombema say that it is easy for a man to divorce his wife, but difficult for a woman to divorce her husband: "difficulty" here implies tortuous and painful negotiations with the inevitable loss of *tee* partners. Even if the bridewealth is returned, the pigs and pearlshells are never the same quality as those given earlier at the time of marriage. The husband is always the loser in divorce. Tombema also say that men are serious about marriage while women are capricious, and that wives and their mothers-in-law (who are never satisfied with the size of any marriage payment, no matter how big, and harbour malice against their sons-in-law for years) plot divorce while husbands and fathers-in-law try to prevent them. Whether or not this is the case, it is some indication that men believe they have more to lose in divorce than women. The *tee* is the primary consideration, for divorce can deal a serious blow to the standing of men who depend on the link provided by the wife to make and carry out exchanges.

Divorce disrupts the flow of pigs, not only between the principals to a divorce, but to other partners as well. Beginning with bridewealth payments, a flurry of *tee* transactions usually occur immediately following a marriage. Even if the marriage lasts only a year or two, partners created by it have probably transacted many times during the period. Due to the linking aspect of partners in the *tee* sequence, a divorce can have reverberations in many directions along *tee* chains. It is impossible to state accurately how many men depend on a single marriage as the basis for their *tee* partnerships. The groom has most at stake. Other clansmen cannot use his marriage to transact with his wife's kinsmen. However, in an example below, I show how intraclan affines are affected by a divorce. In one case that I recorded, a man lost 12 partners, (of a total *tee* network of 42 partnerships) including his major ones, following his own divorce. The marriage lasted nearly eight years. A multitude of transactions had occurred between these partners during that time, and the collapsed marriage had a profound effect on the *tee*-standing of the husband.[5] It is estimated that 20 to 40 partnerships may depend on a single marriage and, to these must be added the *tee* partners of *tee* partners (see Bulmer 1960b:11).

There are no examples of major or minor *tee* partners who have continued to transact after a divorce of a linking woman. This is true both for immediate relations (for example, actual sister's husband/wife's brother) and for more distant ones (for example, classificatory wife's sister's husband). However, as with the death of a linking female, men sharing more than one connection through a woman may transfer the focus of their relationship on to the other following a divorce. The character and importance of their relationship may, though, change as a result. Men of the same clan who use an in-marrying woman as the basis of their *tee* partnerships are subject to the same constraints resulting from divorce. In one case which occurred, a man took a second wife from the Tinlapini clan. Four members of his own clan with whom he had never before made *tee*, became his partners by making appropriate payments. These men shared connections to Tinlapini clan: two of the men had Tinlapini mothers, one was married to a woman whose mother was Tinlapini, the fourth was married to a Tinlapini woman. The marriage made these relationships possible for the husband when before they were not. Divorce took place after about two years however, brought on by constant bickering between the co-wives. The second wife left and the four new partnerships dissolved immediately. The outstanding *tee* payments made by these four men to the husband were lost; they were not reciprocated. Intraclan partnerships as much as interclan ones collapse due to divorce.

Divorce is the most disruptive event which can occur between *tee* allies. When a person fails to reciprocate properly, the possibility exists, however remote, for the partnership to be taken up again if the breach is subsequently mended. But with divorce, it is not possible. When a wife leaves her husband, other partners in his *tee* network may also lessen their commitments to him, for he is potentially a bad risk. Tombema say that "if a man is married he can always find pigs from his affines", even if he has none of his own. The converse is also true: a man who has lost a wife, whether through death or divorce, becomes a man whose credit rating is no longer certain and his *tee* exchange status may thereby suffer. Women are pivotal for the *tee* system, for there can be no exchange partnerships without them.

## Marriage and Warfare

The patterns of Tombema–Enga marriage and warfare further reflects the greater importance and potential control of the *tee* that Tombema women possess in contrast to Melpa women. Enga have gained notoriety (among anthropologists) in the Highlands for proclaiming "we marry the people we fight" (Meggitt 1965a:101). While Meggitt was writing of the Mae-Enga, western neighbours of the Tombema, the pattern of intermarriage and warfare holds throughout the Kompiama area as well. Of the six clans that are contiguous and marry most with Mamagakini and more importantly are most closely bound up with Mamagakini's *tee* interests, four of them – the clans, Sauli, Kirapani, Wakenekoni and Malipani – were their most feared and hated enemies. About half of all recorded marriages took place with members of these clans. Two other clans, Yauwani and Poreyalani, were considered lesser enemies, although I recorded numerous incidents which show that killings between these groups did indeed take place.

The structure and process of Tombema marriage arrangements have been described in detail elsewhere (Feil 1980, 1981). Here I would simply note that the order of clan *tee* prestations directly mirrors the concentration of marriages and equally the concentration of *tee* exchange partnerships.

**Figure 3** Recorded Intermarriages and *Tee*-making Order of Mamagakini and Near Neighbours.

Wakenekoni → Kirapani → Sauli → Mamagakini → Yauwani/Angaleyani →
(37)           (74)        (93)                        (68)
              Poreyalani              →            Malipani
              (48)                                 (42)

These closest clans in the *tee* sequence to Mamagakini provide the most valuables to its members, and also provide the most numerous and significant *tee* partners. Thus, warfare, affinity and *tee*-making take place most vigorously between the same groups. Moreover, the order of *tee*-giving between clans is fixed and does not change from *tee* to *tee* or from generation to generation. This suggests that the relative frequencies of intermarriage remains more or less the same through time. I have shown (Feil 1980) that marriage rules allow for and produce the concentrations shown above, rather than disperse marriages widely as others have argued for Highlands societies (for example Barnes 1962).

While Meggitt (1964b) has argued that the fear of Enga women by men stems from the fact that women, both wives and mothers, invariably come from enemy groups, it is equally true that women are the essential and vital links between exchange partners whose groups are perpetually at war. The majority of *tee* partners are linked by living women. During especially hostile encounters, Tombema tell how women were charged with making *tee* transactions themselves, substituting for linked men whose clans were fighting. At these times, women appear to have had safe, free access to "enemy" territory and clans, clans of which in most cases, they were natal members. Women took pigs back and forth from partners they linked. Pigs could then be passed on without formal ceremony. The *tee's* progress would not be impeded and the wars continued unabated. Thus Tombema women not only produced the vital exchange roads between men, they also were called upon at times, to carry out the transactional side of the *tee* as well. The pattern of intermarriage between groups at war give women a further prominence in the exchange system that Melpa women could not and did not have.

The Melpa preference is to contract marriages with "known and relatively friendly groups" (A.M. Strathern 1972:65), a situation which occurs elsewhere in the Waghi valley (for example Reay 1959). It has been pointed out previously that Melpa women are not necessary as links in *moka* partnerships, nor do they produce pearlshells, the most highly valued *moka* items. It can be added here that Melpa women were not needed as go-betweens of partners, members of hostile clans. The Melpa *moka* was not bound up with marriage, nor was Melpa marriage bound up with warfare. These patterns point to the general conclusion that Tombema women had considerably greater and more widespread influence and control of the exchange system than Melpa women could have. These structures of inter-connection: *tee*, warfare, and marriage had a conservative effect on Tombema society. They "prevented" historically the increasing tendency toward rank and stratification marking pre-colonial Melpa society, and exemplified by the Melpa adoption of pearl-shells as the principal exchange items.

## Ownership of Pigs

Tombema women not only produce pigs, but they "own" the pigs they produce, and house production forms a critical contribution to a man's overall *tee* prestation.

If one walks around a Tombema settlement and enquires who owns the pigs that happen by, he is told by knowledgeable informants that a certain pig belongs to a young boy or a young girl, or to the wife of so-and-so. It appears to make little difference that the boy or girl is only two or three years old and in some cases, still in the mother's dependent care and could not look after the needs of a pig. Here, attention is focused on young daughters and wives. Do they really "own" pigs? Or is the statement just a short-hand way of saying who is responsible for the pig? A man often explicitly allots a gift of other pigs to a young daughter and when she reaches the age of seven or eight she begins to tend and feed them under the supervision of her mother. A father may use these pigs in the *tee*, but in theory, the return (plus any additions) should remain in the "daughter's name".[6] Any offspring further accrue to the girl's herd. Pigs that a father invests in her name may lead to a *tee* partnership between the recipient and the daughter's husband when she marries. Any disputes that involve the daughter while she is growing up and require compensation in pigs, are settled from her herd (Feil 1981). When the daughter marries, these accumulated pigs usually go with her to her new home as initial *tee* investments from her father to the new son-in-law. Some pigs go with the bride as her own. Several cases were recorded in which teenage girls killed pigs from their own herd and consumed them with relatives other than their father or mother. Ownership of pigs by a daughter is a serious and accepted fact in Tombema society.[7] A wife, however, is not allotted pigs in the same way. A herd belongs to her by virtue of the labour she has given to produce it.

Tombema make a clear distinction between pigs produced at home and those received via exchange channels. Home-grown pigs are called "pigs of the house-sleeping stall" (*mena palo anda*), while those coming from *tee* partners are called "pigs of *tee* roads" (*tee kaita mena*).[8] Pigs that come from other sources have often been financed earlier from elsewhere, so that while they may be in transit at a given place, or in a person's temporary possession, their ultimate destination is to another place. They are being held, not owned. But pigs raised at home are "owned" by the woman whose labour produced them. She, not her husband, has final jurisdiction over their placement.

The breadth of female ownership is reflected in several other ways. In polygamous marriages, the pig holdings of each wife are kept absolutely separate. The pigs that each raises are given to *tee* partners linked through her; it is her decision, and her husband would not attempt to take pigs raised by one wife and send them to partners linked through another wife. Similarly, pigs coming from elsewhere on their way to relatives of one wife are looked after by her, not a co-wife, until they are given. She thus ensures a proper return for her investments made earlier by her own relatives or linked partners.

In the settlement of disputes, further aspects of ownership and responsibility become clear. If for example, in a dispute between husband and wife, the wife is adjudged the guilty party, she must find a pig to compensate her husband. She either relinquishes a pig she has reared or one she is tending that was to have gone to her relations in the *tee*. In other cases she may seek a pig from a clansman or finance one from a relative in her husband's clan to meet the debt and settle the issue. The husband is free to dispose of a pig gained in this way without regard to his wife's wishes. When the husband is required to find compensation, a similar process occurs: the wife gains a pig from him that she is free to dispose of, invest with a friend, or look after without interference from him.

A woman also gains pigs of her own in other ways: through fines involving the destruction of her garden by the pigs of another woman or man; in repayment by an unmarried man for pig tending; or in exchange for making string bags or woven aprons. To some extent, a man and wife own pigs of their own. These facts make sense of incidents like the following. A man gained a pig as compensation in a court case. After some weeks he decided to kill it to entertain visitors. When he went to get the pig, which he had tethered in a small cave near his house, he found it dead. Outraged, he picked up his spear and went off "to kill one of Yambame's (his wife) pigs". He shouted that since she had not looked after a pig of his, and it had died, he would "now kill one of hers". In the end, he did not, but his wife and the assembled spectators did not doubt his intentions. He threatened to kill a pig raised by her and intended for one of her brothers or fathers in the *tee*.[9] Pigs that a woman owns individually, gained in compensation or through return for services or goods are, in some cases, invested in the *tee* with men who are not existing exchange partners of her husband, thus creating informal exchange ties of her own, independent of and apart from her husband's *tee* network.

A large majority of pigs and other valuables that a person gives in the *tee* and *saandi pingi* come, of course, from other sources. A man acts simply as an agent for others a good share of the time, rather than just supplying items from his own house for investment. From a sample of Mamagakini men, table 7 shows the number of pigs and other valuables given in the last major *tee* of the late 1960s and the percentage of "house"-provided items in it.[10] Table 8 gives similar figures for the period of *saandi pingi* from 1969 to 1974. Table 9 summarizes the data. The tables further distinguish four status categories discussed more fully in the following chapters. If, as is claimed, women control house-raised pigs, these tables immediately give some indication of an individual woman's power over the total size of the transactions her husband publicly makes.

About one-quarter of the pigs given in *tee saandi* were "house-raised".[11] So-called rubbish men (*tipyakali*) show the highest percentage of house-raised to financed pigs in this *tee*; they are men who lack financial means and investment opportunities as bad risks. Bigmen (*kamongo*) and minor bigmen have contributed the most pigs from their houses.[12] The large investment of their own capital plus their considerable financial dealings, produce *tees* which are much larger than those of ordinary men (*mee akali*).

These tables also show that in the years 1969 to 1975, of 2,679 valuables given in the *tee* by this sample of men, 2,267 (85 per cent) of them were pigs or parts of pigs. Thus, in terms of value and volume, pigs are dominant in the *tee*. Data of A.J. Strathern's on *moka* payments during his fieldwork in the 1960s, shows pearlshells as the most numerous valuables exchanged. In one *moka* distribution (A.J. Strathern 1971:147), 1,608 valuables were given, of which 1,249 (78 per cent) were pearlshells and only 358 were pigs. Thus the Enga *tee* and Melpa *moka* provide a further significant contrast as I have maintained.

The point of these tables is less to highlight the transactional frequency of men of a certain status than to demonstrate the important "production" side of *tee* contributions. About one-third of all pig payments originate from a person's own stock. The significance of women, as producers and directors of "house-raised" pigs is obvious. While pigs "financed" from others greatly outnumber those produced at home for inclusion in the *tee*, the number of "house pigs" could certainly alter the "political" outcome of a man's *tee* should they be withheld or reduced. They make up the "balance of power" in many cases between a man's claiming bigman status or his being considered simply an ordinary man. These "house pigs" also provide the security a man needs to make good to partners when others have not properly reciprocated to him and to give more than is required to heighten prestige. These pigs are also often used to increase partnerships. Women sometimes do withhold their pigs or give them informally outside a *tee* thereby depriving their husbands of publicly giving them. More often though, a woman threatens to do so if her wishes are not met.

However, husband and wife are partners in the *tee* enterprise, and the women's concern is equally clear and acknowledged. A man's political statement and the competitive side of his prestation is made by the size of his *tee*. It is, in a way, less important to him who are the recipients of it. He, of course, wants to keep his best and biggest contributing partners satisfied so they will make good returns in the next *tee*. The perspectives and interests of husband and wife in the *tee* are best understood as complementary: he is concerned with its size as a challenge to his agnatic competitors; she is more interested in directing pigs to linked partners and those persons important to her. Thus, their

**Table 7** Items from "House" Given in *Tee Saandi* 1968–1969

| Category of man | Number | Total pigs given in *tee* | Total pigs from house | Range in houses | Percentage from house | Other items given in *tee** | Total from house | Range in houses | Percentage from house |
|---|---|---|---|---|---|---|---|---|---|
| Bigman | 16 | 769 | 186 | 2–34 | 24% | 210 | 16 | 0–4 | 8% |
| Minor bigman | 4 | 150 | 40 | 2–22 | 27% | 57 | 1 | 0–1 | 0% |
| Ordinary man | 19 | 310 | 60 | 0–7 | 19% | 120 | 6 | 0–2 | 5% |
| Rubbish man | 3 | 37 | 14 | 2–8 | 38% | 11 | 0 | 0 | 0% |
| Total | 42 | 1266 | 300 | 0–34 | 24% | 398 | 23 | 0–4 | 6% |

* Includes pearl and other shells, cassowaries, salt, tree-oil, feathers and stone axes.

**Table 8**   Items from "House" Given in *Saandi Pingi* 1969–1975

| Type of *saandi* | Bigman [16] | Minor Bigman [4] | Ordinary man [19] | Rubbish man [3] | Total [42] |
|---|---|---|---|---|---|
| Total *mena sapya* given | 282 | 46 | 68 | 4 | 400 |
| *Mena sapya* from house | 86 | 10 | 11 | 1 | 108 |
| Range in houses | 0–20 | 2–3 | 0-3 | 0–1 | 0–20 |
| Percentage from house | 30% | 22% | 16% | 25% | 27% |
| Total *mena ita* given | 75 | 21 | 46 | 3 | 145 |
| *Mena ita* from house | 33 | 6 | 14 | 0 | 53 |
| Range in houses | 0–14 | 0–5 | 0–2 | 0 | 0–14 |
| Percentage from house | 44% | 29% | 30% | 0 | 37% |
| Total *mena saka* given | 244 | 84 | 122 | 6 | 456 |
| *Mena saka* from house | 134 | 32 | 60 | 2 | 228 |
| Range in houses | 0–38 | 1–27 | 0–11 | 0–2 | 0–38 |
| Percentage from house | 55% | 38% | 49% | 33% | 50% |
| Total other items given | 10 | 0 | 4 | 0 | 14 |
| Other items from house | 2 | 0 | 3 | 0 | 5 |
| Range in houses | 0–2 | 0 | 0–2 | 0 | 0–2 |
| Percentage from house | 20% | 0 | 75% | 0 | 36% |
| Total all *saandi* given | 611 | 151 | 240 | 13 | 1015 |
| Total *saandi* from house | 255 | 48 | 88 | 3 | 394 |
| Range in houses | 1–47 | 3–30 | 0–15 | 0–2 | 0–47 |
| Percentage from house | 42% | 32% | 37% | 23% | 39% |

**Table 9**   "House" Pigs* Contributed in *Tee Saandi* and *Saandi Pingi*

| Category of man | Total pigs given | Total pigs from house | Percentage from house |
|---|---|---|---|
| Bigman | 1370 | 439 | 32% |
| Minor bigman | 301 | 88 | 29% |
| Ordinary man | 546 | 145 | 27% |
| Rubbish man | 50 | 17 | 34% |
| Total | 2267 | 689 | 30% |
| All Items | 2679 | 717 | 27% |

* *Mena sapya* and *mena ita* are counted as one pig
Combining pigs given in *tee saandi* and those given in *saandi pingi*, the total pig contributions to the *tee* by this sample of houses are shown.

motives are not in conflict and there is no competition in a *tee* between wife and husband. A man who tries to coerce his wife's interests is likely to be the eventual loser; in fact such attempts are rare.

In sum, women do own and can direct the pigs they help

produce. An infrequently quoted, early source on the *tee* makes this same point. Wirz (1952a:44) writes of the ability of women to "own" pigs, "lend" them out, and "demand" reciprocation for them at the next *tee*. Some Tombema women are more active and assertive in the *tee* than others; they are the feminine equivalents of bigmen.

## Strong-Willed Women

Women who vigorously participate in the *tee* affairs of their husbands and kinsmen are called "strong-willed women" (*enda pupu lenge*).[13] There is no other Tombema term which means "bigwoman", and indeed "strong-willed" women are not simply female versions of bigmen. The rivalry and ranking of men is more clear-cut. Men gain renown through their transactional ability and oratory, through the wealth they publicly display, and by their influence over others. These channels for prestige distinguish and elevate the names of men, not women.

But there are other, feminine traits and abilities which set some women apart from others, and make men and other women speak admiringly of them. To a lesser extent than among men, such women can exert influence over other women. If a man calls a woman *enda pupu lenge,* most likely he is speaking of her ability to look after pigs and raise strong herds, and to work with industry in the gardens. But also included in that designation is an evaluation of her strength in *tee* dealings, of her penchant for making her feelings known forcefully, and of her capacity to secure wealth from her relatives through wise investment and integrity in reciprocation. These are male-perceived qualities of a strong-willed woman. This praise is, though, tinged with ambivalence. Men and their strong-willed wives can conflict over a *tee* payment and men know such women are tenacious in asserting their views. Men sometimes compare such women with hard-to-control pigs: they are unmanageable and have minds of their own. In this way too, these women are similar to bigmen; once they have made up their minds, Tombema say, others are powerless to do anything about it. Some men say that a strong-willed woman "gives pigs where she likes; her husband will not disagree".

When a woman calls another woman strong-willed, she is also speaking of the qualities that men value. But women emphasize more the obstinate side of such a woman: she can win a confrontation with her husband. Strong-willed women are often said to possess supernaturally given "good luck" in raising crops and producing pigs. Influential women can often "finance" pigs from other women and men for *tee*-related exchanges they are urging their husbands to make. There is also some evidence of a subtle hierarchy among women. One minor example was recorded from dialogue between two women, one an *enda pupu lenge*, the other not. In discussing their herds, the strong-willed woman used *kapa* to describe the "fat" of her pigs, the other woman continually used *katai*.[14] When I enquired as to the reason, informants told me that *kapa* is used only by important women, *katai* by others. *Kapa* is a boasting term as in "my pigs have more fat than yours" though less blatant and obvious than this. A status distinction was conveyed through language, it was a prestige marker for this woman. Women, too, gain renown from other women.

Information was collected on 12 recognized, strong-willed women, seven married to Mamagakini men, five married to non-agnatic co-resident men.[15] As in the achievement of the status of bigman, there appear to be no overriding structural determinants which apply to the women. The 12 women come from eight different clans, some located nearer to Mamagakini than others; seven women have fathers who are or were bigmen; six have husbands who are currently bigmen. Only four of the 12 have both. Every Mamagakini subclan is represented. In two cases of polygyny, one wife only is singled out for acclaim. Strong-willed women are those who are firmly settled as wives and have several children. As with bigmen, strong-willed women are in mid- to late-middle age and rely on personal characteristics as the predominant element of their higher status.

The pig herds that these women care for, and to some extent, direct, are large. In brief, Mamagakini residents had, at the time of the census, 2,023 pigs in their possession. Each separate household (of which there are 124)[16] contained, on average, nearly 14 pigs (range 0–47). The households of stong-willed women contained on average 29 pigs (range 17–47), about twice as many as others.[17] Not every pig was "owned" or "produced" by the couple, some were held for future transit.

Households with a strong-willed woman raised more pigs (*mena palo anda*) and invested them into the *tee* system than others, both in *tee saandi* and *saandi pingi* (see tables, 7, 8, 9). Detailed transactional information was collected from eight of the 12 households of these women. In *tee saandi,* their household contributions amounted to 29 per cent (140 of 480 pigs given) of their total prestation, nearly 6 per cent more than average (23.6 per cent, 300 of 1,266 pigs given). During *saandi pingi*, their house production accounted for about 5 per cent more (44.5 per cent, 180 of 404 pigs given) than the average (38.8 per cent, 389 of 1,001 pigs given). These households also took *saandi* for themselves (live pigs or consumed sides of pork) twice as much as other households, a further reflection of their productive ability. *Saandi pingi* was sought for house-raised pigs that would be passed on to the *saandi* contributor in the *tee* later. In sum, households of strong-willed women produce more pigs for the *tee* and consume more pork through *saandi* for pigs they have raised, than do others.

The rewards for this productive effort, it could be argued, accrue unequally. Men gain the public recognition and prestige, women do the hard work. This view, if adopted, must be tempered with the facts that *tee* negotiations are difficult and protracted, and require men to be away frequently and spend much time in other places. Men too must transport pigs from place-to-place and hunt for stray animals. The other salient fact is that through effort, women also gain a measure of prestige in their own right, apart from their husband. Women can be known as strong-willed while their husbands are only ordinary men. Again, the complementary, non-competitive side of husband-wife involvement in the *tee* is emphasized. There is prestige to be gained by both for a successful performance.

Pigs are the inalienable property of the woman whose labour produced them. This fundamental fact is embodied in the notion of "pigs of the house sleeping stall". The dichotomy of "house pigs" and "pigs of *tee* roads" further illustrates the combined production and exchange aspects of the *tee*. Obviously, all pigs start out as "house pigs" somewhere along the *tee* network; thus the very foundation of the *tee* system ultimately rests on women's production of pigs. The acknowledged and vital role of Enga women in the production process and in their potential

A Yalingani woman makes *tee* to reciprocate her deceased husband's debts.

control of the items of highest exchange value, extends much further what are only symptoms among the Melpa. It is clear in A.M. Strathern's (1972) account, that Melpa women exert some moral coercion over the disposal of pigs they have produced. But "production" as a category of activity is devalued in Mount Hagen; "transactional" activities are the more valuable. Melpa men appear to have propagated this fiction. With pearlshells, Mount Hagen men appear to have easily dismissed women altogether from the exchange process. They control both their production and exchange. Pearlshell exchange is a pure transactional activity, and to Hagen way of thinking, could only be the province of men. Tombema cannot so easily separate the production and exchange of pigs; Tombema men cannot therefore deny the crucial importance of women in producing pigs for exchange in the *tee*.


## Conclusion

In this and the previous chapter, I have attempted to place the Tombema *tee* and neighbouring Melpa *moka* into an historical and comparative perspective. These are the two great Highlands exchange systems; they link the widest number of communities and largest populations. Exchange is important throughout the New Guinea Highlands, but the systematic interconnection of communities within one single institution is nowhere as significant as it is in the Melpa *moka* and to an even greater extent, in the Enga *tee*. It could, in fact, be argued that they together form a single regional system, for at their interface, men apparently participate in both sets of activities, converting Enga pigs into Melpa pearlshells (A.J. Strathern, 1969a, Meggitt 1974). Furthermore, it has been argued by some that the *tee* grew out of, or expanded from *moka* activities, moving from east to west. Whether or not this is so, I have portrayed the *tee* as if it represents an historically prior form of exchange institution to the *moka*, historically prior in that pigs, not pearlshells, were the first items of value that were exchanged.

Melpa society is situated geographically nearer the source of entry of pearlshells into the Highlands. As they made their way, probably slowly and few in number at first, into the Mount Hagen area via interpersonal trade links from the Papuan coast, they became the most treasured items of value. South of Mount Hagen in the Mendi and Erave areas, Hides (1936:125) reported how an "old chief" showed him a beautiful pearlshell, how "he held it up with the utmost reverence . . . The expression on his face told us plainly that he was asking if we had such a beautiful thing in our possession". Meggitt (1956:103) describes how among the neighbouring Waka of the Southern Highlands, only "an important man owned a piece of pearlshell, which would then cost at least a big pig". Perhaps initially because of their scarcity, they became valuable. An ideology developed around them as increasingly they were concentrated in the hands of the powerful few. A.J. Strathern (1979:534) writes of this ideology. "Shells which did in effect come from the outside world were thought of as wild things (*mel romi*) which men in a sense hunted by their magic. . . . Shells could be seen as symbolic of the whole nexus of exchange relations." Because of the very nature of the items, pearlshells, and their foreign source, powerful Melpa men could, both ideologically and in fact, separate the equally crucial aspects of production and exchange which had enabled the prior pig *moka* to operate. When this separation was made and applied anew to the basis of valued items, it was an easy next step to confine Melpa women to the mundane and much less valued position of mere producers of pigs: a less important process and less important items of exchange. As A.J. Strathern writes, "Men saw themselves as obtaining the shells without any intervention from women's labour", and in exchange "men liked to see themselves as in control and independent of women" (1979:534). Men thus recombined the production and exchange of pearlshells under their total control.

In the previous chapter, it was argued that some men built a system of stratification by controlling these precious pearlshells. When inflation occurred after European contact, the "chiefs" monopoly of shells was broken and "since that time, they have struggled to reassert their advantages" (A.J. Strathern 1979:533). In the post-colonial era, the prevailing system of Melpa stratification collapsed and bigmen emerged as the legacy of pearlshell inflation. Anthropologists described them as models of pan-Melanesian political systems, men who could not quite ascend the evolutionary heights of Polynesian chiefs. The two areas have been distinguished on this basis ever since. The bigman model was taken as timeless rather than historically recent and specific, at least in some areas of Melanesia. Synchronic studies proliferated the cases of existent bigman systems.

As Melpa society changed from "chiefs" to "bigmen" in the post-contact period, the processes of political legitimization were transformed as was the exchange economy. Bigmen sought influence in oratory, renewed warfare, and increasingly, in the management of money from cash cropping, when they could no longer keep tight rein on pearlshells. "Chiefly lineages" were reduced to what Strathern has described as the ability of a bigman to bequeath wealth and knowledge to a son who could then become influential in his own right. Women regained some of their influence as "producers of money", influence they once had as producers of pigs. The pre-colonial basis of stratification in Melpa society, the control of pearlshells, had stripped women of their role in the *moka* system, by devaluing pigs, and hence downplaying the productive ability of women. No woman was allowed to participate in shell *moka*. Such devaluations made them nonessential political persons and placed them right outside the activities of exchange.

But it was not simply the presence of pearlshells which made stratification a reality among the Melpa while the Enga remained more or less egalitarian. Enga certainly did not have access to pearlshells to the same extent as did Melpa. Yet, a more widely encompassing answer must be sought as to why "chiefs" did not appear among the Enga. Women are the key to such an answer. The Enga structures of marriage, warfare, and exchange immediately point to women as more crucially significant to *tee* than Melpa women perhaps ever were to the *moka*. Women are essential to every *tee* activity, and with its links to warfare and marriage, men could never have excluded them from active involvement in it. Enga women produced not only the exchange items, but the very partnerships on which the *tee* is founded and on which it originated. Perhaps too, the processes of inflation had already begun to be recognized by the Enga when pearl-shells became more available to them. Overall, I have argued that Enga women and their part in the production and reproduction of the exchange system, exerted a constraining conservative force, which meant that pigs remained the most valued *tee* items and women themselves remained crucial to the *tee* system. In so doing, the *tee* retains its ties to the past. This is evident even to-day.

There are, no doubt, many problems in trying to view the *moka* as a transformation of an exchange system like the *tee*. Interpreting the present *tee* as a precursor to the pearlshell *moka* is perhaps unwarranted. But the Enga *tee* presents a situation in which the means of pig production were available to all, and in which the production and exchange of pigs allowed women a nearly equal say with men. The Melpa *moka* clearly did not. The contemporary differences in comparing the two exchange systems, can be explained by the historical processes and factors which have brought them about, and by the structural features in which they have operated.

In the following two chapters I will analyze the contemporary workings of the *tee*. Its egalitarian nature, stemming from open access to pig production is clearly evident in the system's processes and loci of competition. The importance of groups as exchange units in the *moka* which are coordinated by a bigman give way to individual transactions in the *tee*. The political significance of the *moka* and bigmen for intergroup relations which, I have argued, have historical roots, are lessened in the

Enga *tee*. Interpersonal transactions predominate and the political consequences of *tee*-making are evident within groups.

## Notes

1. See Chowning 1966. Based on my calculations, about 65 per cent of all current *tee* partnerships are linked by living women. In some cases, more than one woman links men (for example MZS). Such double links are counted as one to arrive at the above figure.
2. This is especially so if the children are much too young to manage *tee* affairs in any way.
3. I have shown (Feil 1981) that marriage payments and *tee* payments are much the same. It is very difficult to distinguish them and when a divorce is being settled only bridewealth payments should be returned. The *tee* debts between affines are not considered, even though bridewealth was the beginning of a chain of *tee* transactions.
4. However, a man may claim pigs as compensation for wayward acts by his wife; for example he may take pigs intended for his affines in the *tee*, and give them elsewhere.
5. He was believed to be a potential bigman prior to the divorce. After about two years, he married a widow, but by then, his rise was affected and he is not now regarded as a future bigman.
6. I have examples in which young girls contributed pigs under their care to death payments. In one, a girl gave pigs to her mother's brother as *laita pingi* after her mother's death, when her father staunchly refused to make the payment. He must certainly have given tacit approval to her, however, and her mother's brother later returned two pigs which she took "in her name" and looked after.
7. To avoid paying compensation, a man sometimes says that pigs of his own belong instead to his wife, daughter, or son, and that he cannot use them to satisfy the complainant. This rationalization is, however, taken seriously enough by the court, which further suggests that ownership of pigs by wives, sons, and daughters is taken seriously by the Tombema.
8. There is potential for conflict over some pigs, for example, those pigs "in transit" which bear litters. According to *tee* rule, all of the litter should be passed on, but in practice, some deal involving division is usually worked out, and the couple who are holding the pig when it has the litter usually take a larger share of it.
9. Actions of women thus have ramifications for *tee* relations between in-laws. A woman can be responsible for the loss of *tee* pigs to her own kinsmen. Men confront the woman, not each other if disputes arise over such incidents.
10. This is the same sample of men used in the following chapters.
11. This is probably a slight understatement. This information was usually elicited from men, whose knowledge, they admit, of *mena palo anda* is less precise than that of their wives. Men often told me that if I wanted a more precise count, I should speak to their wives. I did in a number of cases and recorded slightly higher numbers.
12. There is no Tombema gloss for "minor bigman". I discuss status of men in the next chapter. However, "minor bigmen" here means rising and aspiring

men (three men) and a former bigman still active in the *tee* but on the decline due to old age.

13. *Pupu lenge* carries the further meaning of being obstinate, strong, and disobedient.
14. Men used *katai* and *kapa* interchangeably, they are synonyms. Only women of different statuses use them to convey other meanings.
15. These women are the most often mentioned, most widely-recognized "strong-willed women" resident in Mamagakini. Only one strong-willed woman married to a nonagnate is a Mamagakini woman.
16. "Households" measured here are headed by a wife. In cases of polygyny, each wife's pig holdings are counted separately. Some current bachelors (of which there are 36) attach themselves to other men's houses, but this is rare and their pigs are not counted here. Most maintain separate residences. Bachelors have 268 pigs. Thus, 2,023 pigs minus 268 equals 1,755 pigs. This number divided by the number of households equals an average of 14 pigs per household. Strong-willed women had twice that number.
17. One man had 66 pigs and these were looked after by two wives, one of which was considered an "*endu pupu lenge*". She has 42 pigs in "her herd". The household of 47 pigs is headed by a woman who most people consider to be the hardest-working, *endu pupu lenge* in Mamagakini.

# FIVE

# The "Holders of the Way": Tombema *Tee* Partners

> We don't call a person *kaita miningi* without reason. A *kaita miningi* is a person who gives pigs and makes *tee*. He remains when other men have gone. *Kaita miningi* have the same heart.
>
> Kama, a Mamagakini bigman

This and the following chapter examine in detail the patterns and breadth of Tombema *tee* partnerships (*kaita miningi*), the individual ties of exchange upon which the *tee* institution is built. A man's *tee* contributors form no acknowledged entity, his recipients recognize no tie or bond except the dyadic one to him as giver. *Tee* partnerships are in no sense collectively held or sanctioned (for example by groups), nor determined by other than individual considerations. In Tombema, all transactions are between individuals: there are no situations when groups exchange valuables, or when precise accounting, placement, or direction of specific items of value might be confused, taken from individual hands, or might not matter. *Tee* accounts are strictly individual ones. One of the purposes of these two chapters is to demonstrate just how ideographic and non-overlapping *tee* networks are.

The present chapter deals mainly with *tee* partnerships of men from different clans. Intraclan partnerships have been briefly dealt with earlier. The major differences between them concern frequency and intensity of exchange. The majority of a man's *tee* partners, and in nearly every case, his most important ones, are members of clans other than his own. These partners fall mainly into matrilateral and affinal categories. Intraclan partners are made to resemble them (Feil 1978a).

Existing literature yields little for the analysis of *tee* partnerships. Elkin (1953), Kleinig (1955), Bulmer (1960a, b), A.J.
Strathern (1969a), and Meggitt (1974) give some details of who
*tee* partners are and what relationships they share and, in some
cases, the frequency of transactions between them. These
authors generally treat exchange partnerships as epiphenomenal
of cognatic kinship and affinity.[1] Tombema themselves are quite
clear and explicit in distinguishing *kaita miningi* as a separate
category of persons. All are related, mainly in matrilateral or
affinal ways, but in no sense are they the automatic outcome or
simple reflection of these ties, nor strictly determined by them.
In sum, *kaita miningi* is a category of persons best labelled
"friends" which has a kinship component. This chapter
endeavours to elaborate the significance of friendship and
behaviour of friends in Tombema society, friendships which
have as their basis and most fundamental feature, exchange
interest in the *tee*. *Kaita miningi* means "to hold the way".
Although *tee* concerns predominate among "holders of the way",
much more than just pigs and valuables pass along the *tee* "roads"
which connect them. Common *tee* interests and mutual
exchange support are a *sine qua non* for being called a *kaita miningi*, but a wide range of obligations and appropriate behaviours,
not strictly *tee*-related, are observed by persons who share that
status.

## The Ways of Friends

A person calls another *kaita miningi* only if he is a *tee* partner.
Tombema recognize the difference between being "friendly"
and being "friends" and they enjoy easy-going relationships with
a wide range of persons, not just *kaita miningi*. But, *kaita miningi*
are special, close, or true friends. As in our own society, friendship here connotes obligations of all types, but most importantly
in Tombema, these are associated with *tee*-making. Tombema
make further distinctions among their *kaita miningi*, mainly on
the basis of frequency, volume, and intensity of their *tee* transactions (see below). In sum the often quoted Mendi refrain (Ryan
1961:301) that "exchange means friendship. . . . Only friends can
exchange and all friends must exchange" is equally applicable to
Tombema *tee* partners.

In Tombema society, there are few, if any, intrinsic exchange obligations embedded in affinal or other kinship relationships (compare Glasse 1969:36–37). A person does not give pigs and other valuables to a person simply because he is related to him in a certain way. Moreover, the whole range of obligations, in addition to those of exchange that exist between certain categories of kin, are activated only among those who also share an exchange relationship; in Tombema society, the *tee*. In short, affines and other kinsmen are socially recognized as such only if *tee* commitments also exist between them. Affines for example who are not *kaita miningi* are not recognized as affines, and concomitant obligations and behaviours are not binding. Minor aspects of courtesy and protocol, like name taboos between certain affines, lose conviction and usage unless *tee* obligations persist. Axiomatically: affines and matrilateral kin exchange; those who do not exchange are not affines and matrilateral kin. *Kaita miningi* make good affines, and while the reverse might also be true, it need not necessarily be so.

*Kaita miningi* are called by other, descriptive terms which characterize the expected behaviour of *tee* allies (see Meggitt 1974:79). *Kaita miningi* are known as "*tee* men", "remaining men", those who stay and are dependable. Tombema also say that *kaita miningi* should not fight in any way, they should always share food, they should sleep with each other when visiting nearby to talk *tee* or for any other reason, and they should offer help in gardening, house-building and in other chores. *Kaita miningi* are believed to feel empathetic illness with the same symptoms when a partner is afflicted. *Kaita miningi* should not bring court cases against each other, and any differences between them should be handled privately with "gentle talk". Disputes between *tee* friends that become public are usually an indication that the relationship is coming to an end, and that one or other is seeking some advantage in the public eye. *Tee* partnerships are personal, private relationships, and decision-making and discussions about *tee* matters should be handled quietly. When scoring rhetorical points in public speech, a man never mentions individual *tee* partners by name or allusion; remarks are general in nature and seek to heighten fame by boasting of personal achievement, rather than by defaming the performance of others. *Kaita miningi* as a category of persons is often distinguished from ordinary men (*mee akali*) with whom no *tee* or other obligations are felt to be binding.

These considerable obligations, incumbent on friends, show one side of the nature of *tee* relationships. The other, more personal side, though perhaps less tangible, is equally important in informing our perspective on the spirit of *tee* alliance and the great trust shared by partners. More recent writers on the *tee* and systems of exchange in the Highlands generally have, in my view, neglected this aspect. An indication of the spirit of friendliness between *tee* partners is mentioned in a paper by Kleinig (1955:6) which I quote at length:

> Older natives have expressed the thought that the Te nowadays has lost much of its real spirit and significance and the reason for this seems to lie in the fact taht (sic) each and every transaction nowadays is not valued as highly as it was in the days gone by. One old man told me that when they made Te the procedure was as follows: A friend from a nearby tribe would come to his home in the evening and after a pleasant visit would go home again. During his stay his guest would unostentatiously place a small package behind his back, and after the friend had left he would open the package. Expertly bound in the choicest leave and bound-up in the tastiest spinach-like greens would be a small cooked pig, stuffed with the best seasoning and deliciously salted. So delighted and honored would he feel at this splendid gesture that the next morning he would take his best and biggest pig, and cut a slit in its ear, thus designating it as the reurn (sic) payment for his friend's gift to him. From this we can perhaps infer that the present generation has overlooked a feature of the Te which gave to it a distinctive quality, by placing too much importance on the material value and number of transactions. (See also Wirz 1952b:71, and Elkin 1953:197–98.)

It has been emphasized that *tee* payments (for example, those in *saandi pingi*) are not given without prior request, or at least some indication by the recipient that a pig is needed and will be returned in a forthcoming *tee*. Furthermore, no transaction in Tombema society is "free", that is, without some expectation of return or some strategy or option in mind by the giver.[2] Rather, *tee* transactions are inspired by a multitude of motives, both of self-interst and magnaminity. While the former is often more readily apparent, the latter cannot be ignored. Furthermore, the spirit of friendship in Tombema society should not be deprecated simply because self-interest is an element in exchange dealings between friends. The above instance cited by Kleinig is a good case in point. It can be anticipated that the giver of the cooked pig would expect the return payment set aside for him, but his unpretentious generosity, privately demonstrated, hints of a deeper involvement between the two men than mere self-seeking material reward. The personal content of friendship can never be overlooked: it is an important consideration in the initiation and continuation of partnerships, and it will become increasingly important to the argument when the nature and locus of exchange competition and rivalry is discussed.

Two aspects of the content of *tee* partnerships which are essential to an understanding of their breadth and importance need elaboration. The first involves residence and changes in residence, and the allocation of garden land. Chapter two has shown the high percentage of nonagnatic residents in the Mamagakini clan. A large proportion of these have established residence in Mamagakini territory through their mothers. Typically, following the divorce or death of a husband, a Mamagakini woman brings her children back to her natal clan and her children have subsequently become permanent members. Sister's children are welcomed, given garden land by a mother's brother, and their children, if they maintain Mamagakini residence, become "true" Mamagakini members (*tolae* Mamagakini). In a number of other instances, however, different circumstances have precipitated a change in residence. In these situations the prominence of existing *tee* exchange ties between men come into play. *Kaita miningi* status can be a determining one in the sponsorship of residential change. *Kaita miningi* "hold the way" for their partners to settle and garden with them on their land. Evidence that prior *tee* ties are significant ones can be seen in the following example.

> Iki, a bigman from the Malipio clan, is a sister's son (*mandipae*) of Mamagakini; his deceased mother was a member of the Kopane subclan. Several years ago, while resident in Malipio territory, he became embroiled in some bitter disputes with his fellow clansmen over charges that his pigs had destroyed their gardens. He was accused on two separate occasions and forfeited three pigs in the court settlements. Fearing more incidents, he decided to move, and approached Suluwaya, a Mamagakini bigman, whom Iki called *kaingi*, (maternal cross-cousin).[3] Iki's mother's brother and his mother's brother's son in the Kopane subclan had died and his *tee* connections to other living Kopane members were weak. However,

his ties to Suluwaya, a member of the Munimi subclan were very strong. The relationship had begun several years earlier when Suluwaya made a death payment of one pig to Iki as compensation for the death of Suluwaya's father's brother's son, himself a *mandipae* of Malipio. The relationship subsequently flourished when Iki reciprocated the pig with "interest". In time, Iki's relationship with Suluwaya far outweighed any *tee* dealings he had with Kopane men. He and Suluwaya became major *tee* partners. Following the trouble in Malipio, Suluwaya invited Iki to live with him, gave him land to plant, and he remains there now with wife and family. Both Iki and Suluwaya justified the move on the grounds of their status as *kaita miningi*, as *tee* partners and friends.

Of course, other considerations can also be important: for example, the availability of land, and in some cases the status of the sponsor, but existing *tee* ties are a powerful factor that may influence the choice of a residential change. Iki might have been expected to seek refuge with Kopane, but his exchange ties to Suluwaya took precedence over the closer genealogical, maternal ties to them. Iki is a bigman in his own right. The relationship between him and Suluwaya is not, therefore, simply one of a bigman attracting a man of lower status (and a non-agnate) to settle with him as follower and dependent helper. The two men were already strong *tee* partners before the move, and the most plausible interpretation is that Suluwaya was providing a haven for his exchange ally. There are many more such examples that can be mentioned. The status distinction between the sponsor and the person taking up residence is not often the crucial variable: in another case that occurred during my stay, an ordinary Mamagakini man took in his wife's brother, a bigman from the Kirapani clan who had left for similar reasons as Iki.

Intraclan *kaita miningi* may also sponsor the residential shifts of partners from other subclans. The reasons for changing residence in these instances are often the same as the above. Additionally, *tee* partner status appears to be a determining one in two other aspects of clan organization. Tombema grant gardening rights to *kaita miningi* as a feature of their friendship. As well as allotting garden land to others, Tombema divide gardens they have individually prepared and parcel these segments to others. In this allocation, *kaita miningi* status is again a determining one.

In sponsoring residential changes, in allotting garden sites and segments, relationships based in the *tee* provide for more than just the exchange of valuables. *Tee* status serves in many ways to define the pattern of interaction between men in a variety of social situations. *Tee* friendships cut across descent-unit boundaries and allow individuals choice in their relationships with others. *Tee* partnerships provide a wider set of possible relationships yet define a narrower set of persons, and of a quite different sort, than those based simply on descent or other kinship principles.

In Tombema, descent units are also the warring units. The brief discussion of warfare in chapter two has shown that it is thought to be a clan activity, and throughout Tombema country as elsewhere in Enga (Meggitt 1965a, 1977) a clan's most bitter enemies are contiguous neighbours. As mentioned, there is also the seeming paradox, in the pattern of Tombema social relations, that clans who are unequivocal enemies also provide marriage partners and, more importantly, a person's most valued *tee* partners. Herein lies a key feature of the nature of *kaita miningi*, and the role they play in Tombema society. *Kaita miningi* and the requirements incumbent on their relationship as *tee* partners, supersede the usual hostility expected of members of opposed clans. The entailments of a *tee* relationship in an environment of constant warfare are evident in a variety of situations explained by Tombema men.

One of the most obvious is that a man cannot actively participate in *tee* discussions, nor make public speeches about *tee* matters in clan areas, or when clans are present, in which he has no important *tee* partner. Tombema say simply that if any man, no matter how important or influential he may be, does not have a *tee* connection of substance in a certain clan, he is not allowed to talk *tee* there; he "does not have a way". Acknowledged bigmen become silent onlookers in such situations, while less important men, beneficiaries of a propitious friendship, take the lead in *tee* discussions. Tombema say that if men talk where they have no major *tee* allies, no one would listen. "Why should they? These men take no pigs from him and he none from them". An equally important concern is whether or not a man has a protector in that place. Tombema say that in times past, only the foolhardy would dare go and listen to *tee* discussions in places where they had no *tee* partner.

It has been remarked that *kaita miningi* should not fight in any way; but they have the additional, more active role, of defending their *tee* partners when they are visiting for *tee* discussions, to take pigs away, or, for any other reason, are present on a partner's clan territory. This responsibility is often in conflict with the wishes of fellow clansmen, who may want to treat another's *tee* partner in a less than friendly way. One incident will be sufficient to make the point.

> An old man named Lipu of the Mapete subclan, told of a time when a *kaita miningi* came to take a pig away. While leading the pig out of Mamagakini territory, another Mapete man followed, ambushed and killed him, and then stole the pig. When the cry went out and the body was found, Lipu traced the tracks of the pig to the culprit's house. He confronted him with the accusation of murder, drew his axe and struck, seriously wounding his friend's killer. The man did not die at this time, despite other attempts.[4] He later tried to take revenge on Lipu who then fatally wounded him with a spear, after incurring a large axe wound himself which is clearly visible today. Lipu was both angry and ashamed that he had permitted a valued friend to die at the hands of his 'brother' while under his protection in Mamagakini territory. He did not question the propriety of his own act of revenge, and there are many other cases in which clansmen have been pitted against each other over the defense of a *kaita miningi,* an act which amounts to a defense of the *tee* system itself.[5]

*Kaita miningi* should also warn each other of impending attack by their respective groups, thereby demonstrating their loyalty and friendship. This is especially true of major *tee* partners. Messages might be sent through women or delivered personally. The warnings were often phrased in highly metaphorical language to avoid detection, but the meaning would urge a friend to stay well clear or to avoid the area where the other would be fighting. There is no question as to what would happen should two partners meet on the battlefield: they would tell each other to get away, to move out of spear and arrow range, and to keep alert for the shots of others. One of the most sorrowful mourning laments was composed by a man whose arrow went astray and by accident, felled a *kaita miningi* who had ventured too close.

More often, however, the two enemy sides ended hostilities in order to await and participate fully in the *tee*, an event known as to "fasten together the weapons" (*yanda tambuingi*).[6] Individual *kaita miningi* were instrumental, through this transaction, in bringing the fighting to a halt, if only temporarily. The initiation of *yanda tambuingi* was an individual decision in the first instance. It is no surprise that bigmen often made the decision, but in a number of recorded examples, lesser men decided with their *kaita miningi* of the enemy clan to end the fighting. The act was simply to agree with a partner to meet at a given place and time, and exchange pigs of precisely equal quality and size. By announcing their intention to engage in this transaction, and by challenging their fellow clansmen to do the same, hostilities could be brought to an end. The risks to the individuals initially involved were great. To meet at a designated spot (usually near the battlefield) was dangerous and a man depended on the safety provided by his *tee* partner with whom he exchanged. The number of pigs exchanged was not great, nor important. The demonstration that an individual *tee* partnership was more significant and vital than the demands of group warfare was at issue. This act of friendship was also a direct challenge to fellow clansmen. If a single *tee* network was opened up while the others remained closed, the potential gains in prestige and wealth were enormous. Through *yanda tambuingi*, Tombema individuals re-affirmed the greater value of exchange over warfare. The *tee* became, once again, the ultimate value for society. It was in the interests of all men to participate in *yanda tambuingi* so that the *tee* could occur and all could take part in it. If hostilities did end at this time, outstanding homicide payments could be made at the closely following *tee*, and there was a chance for a more lasting truce.

*Tee* partnerships are relationships of a very special kind. *Kaita miningi* are relationships which partially overlap with others, but are unique in their requirements and obligations. They are similar to Tangu friendships (Burridge 1957) in that *kaita miningi* share duties and responsibilities that are not inherent in other relationships of descent and kinship.

## Becoming Partners

Once, Komba, a Mapete man, went to visit a *kaita miningi* in a distant clan. He was preparing for a forthcoming festival and had no drum. He took with him a metal shovel bought at Kompiama, in the hope of trading it for one. Upon arriving, he discovered that his friend was absent. Persisting, he showed the shovel around but could find no takers. A man named Tambili recognized Komba. Their wives were distant cross-cousins they discovered, but they themselves knew each other only slightly, and had certainly never made *tee*. Realizing that Komba had no place to stay, he invited him home. His wife gave him food and asked after Komba's wife. Tambili traded the shovel for a drum of his own, and in addition, gave Komba a tube of tree oil (*topa*) to take with him. Both drum-making materials and tree oil are plentiful in that area. Komba brought the tree oil back and gave it to Saka, an existing *tee* partner. In a subsequent *tee*, Saka returned a small pig for the oil, and when Komba in turn made his *tee*, he gave the pig plus an additional one from his own herd to Tambili. When a few years later, the *tee* reversed, Tambili gave Komba two pigs, two tubes of oil, and two pearlshells, and then later when another *tee* was made, he gave Komba another pig. Komba has since returned two pigs to Tambili in advance of the next *tee*.

This is a good example of the genesis of a *tee* partnership, the way in which a *tee* road "had been made" (*tee kaita pingi*) or "begun", (*tee kaita pyanjingi*). The verb *pyanjingi* more precisely means climbing from one tree to another without touching the ground; in *tee* terms, that two men who once stood on their own, have created a link or bridge between them so that *tee* transactions can now take place.

All *tee* partnerships are not, of course, left to such haphazard and fortuitous incidents for their inception. Some of a man's partnerships are inherited from his father or are taken up by a former partner's son. But nearly two-thirds of all recorded partnerships are made by a man himself, and here I examine the processes by which this occurs. Most of a person's intraclan partnerships come about from an initial marriage contribution. Fellow clansmen receive marriage payments and a *tee* partnership between clansmen as new "affines" is the result (see Feil 1981).

One of a person's more pragmatic concerns in the establishment of a *tee* friendship is to keep both sides of his network as close to evenly balanced as possible. A man's *tee* network is discretely divided between givers and takers in any *tee*. When a new partnership is established, it creates a potential imbalance in the total set. In this situation, the recipient of a pig from a new partner will in turn seek another new partner to give it to, rather than give it to an established one. In this way, partners become "matched" and *tee* accounts are more manageable. Subsequent requests for pigs by one, are relayed to the linked partner: he is given first opportunity to supply the needed payment, and later to receive its reciprocation. If he is unable to supply it, the request may then be made to another man. Stable, enduring *tee* chains are built by this process. A person has major partners who are linked with his other major partners in the opposite direction, men who can handle the volume of pig flow. A man stands in the "middle" of his total *tee* network, with evenly matched sets of partners alternating as contributors and recipients in a *tee* sequence. The existing partnerships of 45 Mamagakini men, a total of 2,176 partnerships, were recorded. Of these, the indivisible sets of contributors/recipients numbered 1,101 and 1,075. Thus, on average, half of a person's partners give pigs to him in any *tee*, while the other half receive them.

The majority of all *tee* partnerships begin simply within the context of *tee* giving. In table 10, *tee* is an all-inclusive category. Also included are the majority of relationships passed on from the father. The original type of payment made to begin the relationship has, in some instances, been forgotten. Typically, a man, recognizing the possibility of a *tee* relationship because of an appropriate female tie, asks another man with whom he has not previously transacted for a pig. This request may be made during the preliminary phase of giving, the night before the live pig distribution is to take place, or during the distribution of killed pigs.[7] A request granted begins a partnership. Tombema characterize this type of beginning as "simply in the *tee*" (*mee tee*). The other situations in which a *tee* partnership can begin are slightly different. Circumstances occur in which it is appropriate to make an unrequested payment to another man, with whom *tee* has not previously been made, but always in the hope that an initial gift will be returned and a partnership established. In these instances, too, female connections are essential. Consider this example.

> Lungu, a Mamagakini man, has several existing exchange ties with men of his mother's clan. His father, still alive, has strong *tee* partnerships there also. A younger brother of Lungu died and it became appropriate for he and his father to make a death compensation payment to members of his mother's clan, Yauwani. Lungu gave many pigs, some to existing *tee* partners, but used the opportunity and occasion to initiate partnerships with six other Yauwani men, more

distantly related, with whom he had not previously made *tee*. All of these men of course, fall into the mother's brother and cross-cousin kinship categories. In due course, these six men reciprocated the initial death payment pigs in their *tee*, and the partnerships continue now. Lungu proliferated his partnerships on an occasion when giving to many Yauwani men was appropriate. As noted earlier, death compensation payments are easily turned into fruitful *tee* contacts.

**Table 10** *Tee* Partnerships: Initial Type of Transaction

| Transaction | Number | % of Total |
|---|---|---|
| *Mee tee*, including *saandi, tee,* and *yae pingi* | 1,493 | 70 |
| Marriage payments (*enda yole pingi*)[8] | 491 | 23 |
| Death compensation (*laita pingi*) | 102 | 5 |
| Homicide Compensation (*bungi pingi, kepa singi*) | 35 | 2 |
| Other: | 12 | 0 |
| Child growth (*wane yangi*) | 4 | |
| War-ending payment (*yanda tambuingi*) | 4 | |
| Marriage related (*yokeya pingi*) | 1 | |
| Death related (*endakali pole kenge*) | | |
| (*kumanda pyalyo nyingi*) | 1 | |
| Injury related (*kondo pingi*) | 1 | |
| Totals | 2,133* | 100 |

* Sample of 44 men. Details of the 45th were not available.

Marriage payments are the most important non-*tee* transactions for beginning exchange partnerships. In marriage and in other types of payments, bigmen are the most active participants. They can muster the required wealth to be able to give to a wider set of persons, thereby proliferating their *tee* contacts. An ordinary man making a death payment would probably have fewer pigs to give and these would be sent to satisfy existing partners. A bigman, however, can find more pigs through financial channels and give them to persons with whom he has not previously made *tee*.

By comparison, however, strict *tee* transactions are used to begin partnerships much more often than all other types of payment combined. This fact seems to support my earlier point that exchange obligations do not result simply from kinship and affinal relationships. A man initiates a partnership in the *tee* and, after that beginning, death, homicide, and other payments to that partner become appropriate *because* he is a *tee* ally, not because he is a kinsman or affine. *Tee* status defines the pattern of exchange in any specific context (see also Feil 1979).

A majority of partnerships beginning by *tee* payment occur during the *yae pingi* phase. Ironically, as I pointed out earlier, it is also a time when many partnerships dissolve. During *yae pingi*, more pork circulates between partners than can ever be consumed. Thus, *yae pingi* is a time of high investment opportunity, but the returns are never as high. Some recipients of pork will return a pig in the next *tee*, and new partnerships will be established. All contexts of giving in Tombema become possible *tee* beginnings between two individuals. Men sharing a female link are always potential *tee* allies.

## Succession to Partnerships

The process by which a young girl acquires pigs of her own has been mentioned above; young boys are also given pigs by their fathers to look after and eventually, to make *tee*. In this way, a young boy is slowly but surely introduced to *tee* procedure and set up with a small *tee* network of his own. In early adolescence the boy takes fuller responsibility of his small herd, which in theory contains those animals previously alloted by his father, their offspring, and the returns gained from earlier *tee* investments. His mother's brother may approach him directly now and he is encouraged by his father to make investments on his own, and learn the rules of *tee*-making. When the time comes for his marriage, his own pigs (not his father's) are used as bridal payment, pigs that he had raised and received in exchange. He gives these pigs to his new affines who form his first set of supporters. If he is the only son, or otherwise the youngest, he and his father may line their *tee* sticks in a single row and, though their transactions and accounts are always kept separate, they make the *tee* together. Eventually, the father's role diminishes and a son's partners take the majority of the pigs tethered. The father has helped make his son's early *tee* roads, and now the boy "takes his place". If his father is a bigman and the son looks likely to step into that status, he is referred to as a man who "takes the ropemarkers", that is, *tee* partners of his father.

The partnerships a person inherits from his father, how many and which ones, depend on many factors. Sons whose fathers die while they are still young, are unlikely to inherit many. A mother on her own, who does not remarry and remains within her husband's clan, can sometimes, nominally, keep up the *tee* partnerships of her husband. She holds them until her son can take over for himself. Sometimes there is a break in *tee* relations lasting up to several years, until the boy is old enough to make *tee* on his own. Then, his father's former partner, or that man's son, may remind him how they once made *tee*. With a token gift, he invites him to begin transacting again. Sons of former bigmen and those aspiring to that status tend to inherit more partnerships from their fathers than do sons of ordinary men. Nearly half of their current partnerships have been taken from their fathers, or are with their father's partner's sons.[9] Nonagnatic residents inherit fewer *tee* partners than agnates, for if a woman leaves her husband and brings a son to live with her clansmen, his relations through his father do not develop and he will have few *tee* partnerships with his clansmen. Similarly too, if his father died and he took up residence with his mother's clan. However, if a man resides with his wife's clan, as nonagnatic brother-in-law, and does not die or divorce prematurely, many partners devolve to his son, regardless of his nonagnatic status.[10] While nonagnatic residents may inherit fewer partnerships from their fathers than agnates, this minor disadvantage is more than overcome by the fact that as a resident nonagnate, a man has vast potential support with co-resident mother's brothers and cross-cousins. Men linked by women, potential *tee* partners, are readily available to them, giving them advantages over agnates in respect to exchange. They are thus equally able to achieve the status of bigman if that is their ambition. This point is more fully elaborated below.

The partnerships that are handed down to the son are usually those which were begun while the father was still actively transacting. Other things being equal, a son continues to make *tee* with his own *apange* (father's brothers-in-law) and maternal and paternal cross-cousins. A man may also continue to transact with partners whom his father called cross-cousins and their sons, but these partnerships are rarely important to him. New marriages establish new links which may mean that old, discontinued partnerships are taken up afresh. Finally, same clan, and same subclan partnerships, are passed on more frequently than partnerships with men in other clans. Proximity is an important factor in inheritance of intraclan partnerships, but it will be shown that these partnerships are in general inconsequential. More precise information from which these general trends are abstracted is provided in the following table.

Succession to *tee* partnerships can involve other than father-to-son inheritance. Fathers whose sons contract propitious marriages, may use this link to begin *tee* relations with a son's affines, for example, his son's wife's father or son's wife's brother. This is extremely rare however. Fathers may use these ties to make *tee*, but other subclansmen of his son may not. A man whose father-in-law is old and about to die, and is without a son, may bring a linked partner with him to his wife's clan seeking a replacement for the old man. A member of his wife's subclan who is not already a *tee* partner, may agree to succeed his ageing subclansman. In other situations, a son-in-law may directly inherit an important partnership from his father-in-law, if the latter is without sons. But some female link is always necessary between two such men.

**Table 11**  Succession to *Tee* Partnerships: Inherited from Father, or Men whose Fathers were Partners

|  | Partnerships in other clans | Different subclan partnerships | Same subclan partnerships | Total |
|---|---|---|---|---|
| Inherited partnerships | 521 | 189 | 79 | 789 |
| New partnerships | 1088 | 197 | 59 | 1344 |
| Total | 1609 | 386 | 138 | 2133 |
| % Inherited | 32% | 49% | 57% | 37% |
| % of New Partnerships | 68% | 51% | 43% | 63% |
| Number of men: 44 | | | | |

Partnerships begun by a father may cease on his death. But later, a new link creates a new *tee* partnership which is not strictly inherited. In a number of cases the following occurred:

A made *tee* with B, his mother's brother's son, and C, his mother's brother's son's son. A died when D was very young and *tee* relations with B and C ceased. However, C later married E, a member of the same subclan as D, and, as "brother's-in-law", D and C began *tee* relations again. They even occasionally address each other as "cross-cousins" acknowledging the relationship of their fathers.

Usually, two men in a *tee* network know they are linked by a third man. If that middleman dies, the network of payments will also come to an end. Should this happen, partners have no recourse. In some cases however, the network can be "patched up", but only if a suitable tie exists between the two men, who have never directly transacted before. Consider this example:

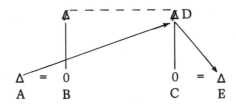

In this *tee* chain, A gave pigs to D (his wife's father) and D gave the pigs of A to E (his daughter's husband). A and E were not directly involved in the *tee*. When D died, rather than abandoning what had been a fruitful relationship, A and E approached each other and decided to begin their own *tee* partnership, with B and C, subclan sisters, as their links. They call each other "brother", and succeeded to the partnership of their father-in-law. Such succession is not always possible. Female links of the type that B and C provide must already be present for this result to occur.

In theory, Tombema maintain that all *tee* partnerships are self-perpetuating. In practice they realize they must decide which of their father's partners are most valuable to them as *tee* allies and friends, men whom they will continue to count on and to whom they will continue to give support.

## Frequencies of Friendship

Tombema expect certain people to be *kaita miningi*. They realize that things do not always turn out as they should, but, in theory, certain categories of kinsmen and affines are counted on to provide exchange support. A payment of some kind, usually in the *tee*, initiates the partnership. After that, existing partners may use any occasion to make *tee* payments.

Unrelated persons, not linked by a woman, cannot be *tee* partners. All *tee* partners can be called by a kinship term (some by more than one, for example, intraclan partners) but often, *tee* partners address or refer to each other simply as *kaita miningi*. Meggitt (1974:188) found that 16 per cent of *tee* partners in his sample (of 14 men) were unrelated. I found no such occurrence. Elkin (1953:192) and Bulmer (1960a:373) likewise found that unrelated persons made *tee*. Tombema continually emphasized to me that relatedness was necessary. As shown earlier, the situation could not be more different than the *moka*, in which large percentages of partnerships and transactions are between unrelated men.

Table 13 shows the kinship categories into which fall the current *tee* partners of 45 adult Mamagakini men, and men co-resident with Mamagakini. For comparison, the same sample of men is used throughout this and other chapters. The men are further distinguished below by status and whether or not they are Mamagakini agnates. Their intraclan partnerships are given in Appendix 3. Their total number of partnerships is 2,176. Table 13 enumerates the kinship categories of partners in other clans only. The connecting female tie is further distinguished: one of different subclan, one of the same subclan, or an "actual" (*angi*) relationship.[11] For example, the relationship MMZSDH – different subclan intragenerational link – should be read: "own mother's mother's different subclan sister's own son's daughter's husband". The first intragenerational tie is denoted in the table. All other ties are actual genealogical relationships, as are the ones in the column showing actual kinship and affinal connections. Relationships of two links only, for example ZH or WB – same subclan intragenerational link – mean a man's same subclan sister's own husband – and a man's own wife's same subclan brother. The "strength" of different subclan and same subclan intragenerational connecting ties is assessed.

**Table 12**  Interclan *Tee* Partnerships

| Category | Kinship Relationship | Different subclan intra-generational link | Same subclan intra-generational link | Actual link | Total |
|---|---|---|---|---|---|
| | ZH | 42 | 126 | 21 | 189 |
| | WB | 35 | 179 | 41 | 255 |
| | MBDH | 11 | 16 | 1 | 28 |
| | WMZS | 5 | 7 | 0 | 12 |
| | WFZS | 9 | 20 | 0 | 29 |
| | WMBS | 9 | 21 | 0 | 30 |
| | FZDH | 3 | 10 | 0 | 13 |
| | WBDH | 1 | 0 | 0 | 1 |
| *palingi* | MMZSDH | 2 | 0 | 0 | 2 |
| | MMZDH | 1 | 0 | 0 | 1 |
| | FMBSDH | 1 | 0 | 0 | 1 |
| | WBS[a] | 0 | 4 | 0 | 4 |
| | MZDH | 0 | 3 | 0 | 3 |
| | WFFZ | 0 | 1 | 0 | 1 |
| | WFS | 0 | 0 | 1 | 1 |
| | WMZDH | 0 .. 119 | 0 .. 387 | 1 ..65 | 1 .. 571 |
| | MB | 47 | 53 | 14 | 114 |
| | ZS | 47 | 71 | 15 | 133 |
| *apange* | MMZS | 4 | 1 | 0 | 5 |
| | MBDS[b] | 2 | 0 | 0 | 2 |
| | MFZS | 0 | 3 | 0 | 3 |
| | MZDS | 0 .. 100 | 1 .. 129 | 0 .. 29 | 1 .. 258 |
| | MZS | 31 | 33 | 2 | 66 |
| | WZH | 15 | 31 | 5 | 51 |
| | WMZH | 6 | 0 | 0 | 6 |
| | FMBSS | 4 | 9 | 0 | 13 |
| | FFZSS | 3 | 2 | 0 | 5 |
| *yangonge* | MMZDS | 2 | 0 | 0 | 2 |
| | FMZDS | 2 | 0 | 0 | 2 |
| | FMBSS | 1 | 0 | 0 | 1 |
| | FMBDS | 1 | 0 | 0 | 1 |
| | WFZDH | 1 | 2 | 0 | 3 |
| | SWF | 0 | 1 | 3 | 4 |
| | DHF | 0 .. 66 | 0 .. 78 | 1 .. 11 | 1 .. 155 |
| | WZS | 6 | 20 | 4 | 30 |
| | FZSS | 6 | 5 | 1 | 12 |
| | MBSS | 5 | 5 | 2 | 12 |
| | MZSS | 5 | 2 | 0 | 7 |
| *ikiningi* | WBS | 1 | 0 | 2 | 3 |
| | WMZSS | 1 | 0 | 0 | 1 |
| | FZDS[c] | 0 | 2 | 0 | 2 |
| | MMZDS | 0 | 1 | 0 | 1 |
| | WMBSS | 0 .. 24 | 1 .. 36 | 0 .. 9 | 1 .. 69 |

**Table 12** (cont'd) Interclan *Tee* Partnerships

| Category | Kinship Relationship | Different subclan intra-generational link | Same subclan intra-generational link | Actual link | Total |
|---|---|---|---|---|---|
| | DH | 0 | 0 | 14 | 14 |
| | BDH | 11 | 57 | 0 | 68 |
| | WF | 0 | 0 | 17 | 17 |
| | WFB | 7 | 51 | 0 | 58 |
| | ZDH | 2 | 7 | 1 | 10 |
| | WMZH | 1 | 5 | 0 | 6 |
| | MBDDH | 1 | 0 | 0 | 1 |
| | WFMBS | 1 | 2 | 0 | 3 |
| | WMB | 0 | 16 | 3 | 19 |
| *imangi* | WDH | 0 | 5 | 1 | 6 |
| | WZDH | 0 | 3 | 0 | 3 |
| | WBDH[d] | 0 | 2 | 0 | 2 |
| | WFZH | 0 | 2 | 0 | 2 |
| | ZHF | 0 | 1 | 0 | 1 |
| | FZSDH | 0 | 1 | 1 | 2 |
| | MZSDH | 0 | 1 | 0 | 1 |
| | FMDH | 0 | 0 | 1 | 1 |
| | DHFZS | 0 .. 23 | 0 .. 153 | 1 .. 39 | 1 .. 215 |
| | FMZS | 4 | 2 | 0 | 6 |
| | FMBS | 4 | 4 | 0 | 8 |
| | FFZS | 3 | 0 | 0 | 3 |
| | MZH | 3 | 9 | 0 | 12 |
| *takange* | MFZS | 2 | 0 | 0 | 2 |
| | MMBS | 1 | 0 | 0 | 1 |
| | FMBDH | 1 | 0 | 0 | 1 |
| | FFZH | 0 .. 18 | 10 .. 25 | 0 .. 0 | 10 .. 43 |
| | MBS | 82 | 68 | 14 | 164 |
| *kaingi* | FZS | 56 | 76 | 9 | 141 |
| | MMZSS | 2 .. 140 | 0 .. 144 | 0 .. 23 | 2 .. 307 |
| | ZSS | 1 | 0 | 0 | 1 |
| | BDS | 1 | 1 | 0 | 2 |
| *kauwange* | FZH | 0 | 3 | 2 | 5 |
| | MFB | 0 | 2 | 0 | 2 |
| | FFZH | 0 .. 2 | 2 .. 8 | 0 .. 2 | 2 .. 12 |

Grand Total  1,631

[a] may also be called *kauwange*  or  *ikiningi*
[b] may also be called *ikiningi*
[c] may also be called *apange*
[d] may also be called *palingi*

Summary of 2,176 Partnerships

| | | |
|---|---:|---|
| Interclan partnerships | 1,631 | (76% of total) |
|    Different subclan intragenerational link | 491 | (30%) |
|    Same subclan intragenerational link | 962 | (59%) |
|    Actual link | 178 | (11%) |
| *Different subclan partnerships | 396 | (18% of total) |
| *Same subclan partnerships | 143 | (6% of total) |
| *Different subclan partnerships, no known female link | 6 | (Less than 1% of total) |

(* see Appendix 3)

Partnerships traced through a wife or sister are the most numerous, accounting for over half of the total. Together with partnerships traced through the mother and father's sister, these four linking women account for over 90 per cent of the total.[12] Tombema unambiguously assert as dogma that women alone make *tee* partnerships possible. Living women who provide the links of most current partnerships can always be named, for they themselves are prominent in their working. Partners whose linking woman is dead can usually explain the connection, but may not be able to remember the woman's name.[13] But the question arises whether or not Tombema themselves conceptualize *tee* partner relationships as these tables portray. Does a partnership labelled, for example, *ikiningi* – MFZDSS – represent the cognitive knowledge of the person describing the relationship?[14] If so, it seems that Tombema do not share the lack of interest most Highlanders show in genealogical reckoning. Consider the following hypothetical example:

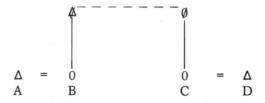

Tombema would say that A and D are probably *tee* partners. The decision of course depends on other factors, their personal preferences, financial ability, and so on.

If they are partners, it is explicitly so by virtue of the fact that B and C are cross-cousins, the link in this case being the common clanship of the two women's linking step. The women themselves (B and C) have probably initiated the relationship by giving a pig to each other, or suggesting that their husbands become partners. Assume then that A and D are *tee* partners.

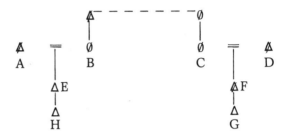

A and D continue as *tee* partners; their sons, E and F inherit the partnership, F then dies and G inherits the relationship from him and continues to make *tee* with E. If G and perhaps even E are asked the nature of their *tee* relationship, they may not know precisely. They may simply say that they took over the partnership of their fathers. They can probably name C and B, E surely can. The women are now dead, but their importance, as symbols of a *tee* road, remains. The *tee* relationship originally involving A and D, in which connections were well-known and the basis for the partnership clearly understood, has devolved to E and G whose knowledge is imprecise and their reasons for transacting do not parallel those of men who instigated the partnership. Portraying the relationship of E and G as one of FMMBDS is slightly stilted and conveys little of the process whereby the relationship of E and G has come about. The original *tee*-makers must be kept in mind to understand "multi-termed" partnerships.[15] Only a small percentage of all partnerships involve a two-generational link, however. Of course, there are individuals who know (or believe they do) that grandparental or great-grandparental links exist and use the knowledge to begin a *tee* partnership even though their fathers or father's father did not choose to use the connection themselves.

Kinship ties with linking women are essential to *tee* partners. Furthermore, it is arguable that Tombema place a greater value on genealogical knowledge for exchange purposes than they do on knowledge for reckoning membership in descent groups. Chapter two gave the correct impression that Tombema are unconcerned with ancestors and the placing of individuals in groups determined by them. But for activating ties of exchange based on female links, Tombema become almost expert practitioners of heraldry. *Tee* relationships do different things and are determined differently than those of descent.

Persons calling themselves *palingi* form the most numerous category of *tee* partners, just under one third of the total. Adding to it the *imangi* category, they represent 43 per cent of all partnerships. These two affinal categories provide the core of a man's *tee* network. Partners in the *apange* category and more than half of those in the *kaingi* category are maternally linked. Affines and maternal kinsmen are not only the most numerous *tee* partners, they are also a man's most important ones.

**Table 13**  *Tee* Partners: Kinship Category and Connecting Link.

| Kinship Category (all uses) | Different subclan link | | Same subclan link | | Actual link | | Total | |
|---|---|---|---|---|---|---|---|---|
| *palingi*   | 202 | (29%) | 418  | (61%) | 67 | (10%) | 687  | (32%) |
| *apange*    | 107 | (39%) | 136  | (50%) | 29 | (11%) | 272  | (13%) |
| *yangonge*  | 254 | (61%) | 146  | (35%) | 14 | ( 4%) | 414  | (19%) |
| *ikiningi*  | 58  | (48%) | 55   | (45%) | 9  | (7%)  | 122  | ( 5%) |
| *imangi*    | 30  | (13%) | 158  | (68%) | 44 | (19%) | 232  | (11%) |
| *takange*   | 78  | (61%) | 50   | (39%) | 0  | 0     | 128  | ( 6%) |
| *kaingi*    | 140 | (45%) | 146  | (47%) | 23 | ( 8%) | 309  | (14%) |
| *kauwange*  | 2   | (17%) | 8    | (66%) | 2  | (17%) | 12   | ( 1%) |
| Totals      | 871 | (40%) | 1117 | (51%) | 188 | (9%) | 2176 | (100%) |

Partners of different clans use subclan women as connecting ties and actual links more than 70 per cent of the time (table 12) to form partnerships. Immediate kin relationships carry the most conviction: ties between a woman and her fellow subclansmen are close, both genealogically and emotionally. Her subclan brothers and fathers have aided and protected her through youth; they receive the greatest share of her bridewealth in repayment. They benefit further for she makes fruitful *tee* partnerships possible, and directs her productive effort (pigs) to them. A woman's subclan sisters and, to a lesser extent father's sisters, are her closest female friends and it is this friendship that makes partnerships between their husbands important and frequent. When two women from the same subclan or clan marry into the same group, they are constant companions and allies, and *tee* relations grow from their association to their husbands who are clansmen. But the ties between subclan sisters often lead to *tee* partnerships between their husbands no matter what distance is involved or what their clan affiliation is. Intraclan *tee* partnerships are based on different subclan female links more often than interclan partnerships. The use of different subclan female ties between intraclan partners equals the percentage (70 per cent) of same subclan and actual female links used by partners in different clans. Overall, about 40 per cent of all partners use connecting ties of women from different subclans as the foundations of *tee* partnerships.

## *Tee* Partners and Status

Tombema distinguish men by status. There is reasonably high concensus for men in each status category, and within each, men are considered equals.[16] Most Mamagakini subclans have several bigmen, but there is no man who is "biggest". Further-

A bigman addresses the crowd before giving his pigs.

more, in the *tee*, bigmen do not form "power bases" from the membership of the clan segment they belong to (see following chapter). The *tee* is not concerned with groups and bigmen leading them. Bigmen have virtually no say over the *tee* affairs of other men of whatever status. The hierarchy too, at least at the top, is relatively stable (compare Meggitt 1967, 1971, 1972). Bigmen do not lose their position except when they grow old, and although a poor *tee* performance diminishes their prestige, it is not permanent, and they are still widely regarded as bigmen. Men of lower status may move up, but they need not displace a current bigman to attain that status.

Bigmen are most often referred to as *kamongo*. Metaphorically, they are like "*talyili*", a lizard which climbs tall trees, or "*laima*", cassowaries. Bigmen are men "with names", men who "hold the talk", "fixing men", and "large men". A man is a bigman only if he is influential in the *tee*, can make a large display of pigs, and is a skilled orator on *tee* occasions. No other activity (for example in war or ritual) makes a person a bigman. Bigmen have more pigs than others, but more importantly, they have more *tee* partners and transact more frequently in the *tee* than other men. Details are given below and in the following chapter of 16 Mamagakini bigmen.

Men referred to in table 14 as minor bigmen form a nebulous category (compare Bulmer 1960a:323; A.J. Strathern 1971:187). They are called in Tombema "small bigmen", or less frequently "just bigmen". This category includes both emergent bigmen, and men who, due to old age, are declining in *tee* importance. The four examples include three young, rising men, and one man who was once a bigman but is no longer.

Tombema refer to men of middle status as "just men" or "small men". I term them ordinary men. They are married, often keep many pigs, but are unlikely ever to be regarded as bigmen. Ordinary men, however, are often key links in networks of bigmen spanning many clans. In such cases (and there are several), Tombema suggest that bigman status hinges less on pigs than on a powerful personality, *tee* sense, range of contacts, and oratorical ability.

Men of lowest status have been referred to in Papua New Guinea as "rubbish men"; Tombema term them "poor men". They are always bachelors, may behave eccentrically, and are sometimes called "mad". They are further described as men who "eat and run" and "those who do not laugh or speak". But, rubbish men do keep pigs, have *tee* partners, and make *tee* as individuals.

**Table 14**  Number of *Tee* Partners per Person by Status and Agnation and Nonagnation

| Category of men | Number | Number of Partnerships | Average | Range |
|---|---|---|---|---|
| Bigman | | | | |
| Agnate | 11 | 729 | 66 | 34 − 151 |
| Nonagnate | 5 | 390 | 78 | 31 − 132 |
| Sub-Total | 16 | 1,119 | 70 | 31 − 151 |
| Minor Bigman | | | | |
| Agnate | 3 | 156 | 52 | 32 − 84 |
| Nonagnate | 1 | 32 | 32 | − |
| Sub-Total | 4 | 188 | 47 | 32 − 84 |
| Ordinary Men | | | | |
| Agnate | 16 | 578 | 36 | 19 − 77 |
| Nonagnate | 6 | 245 | 41 | 26 − 75 |
| Sub-Total | 22 | 823 | 37 | 19 − 77 |
| Rubbish Man | | | | |
| Agnate | 2 | 33 | 17 | 12 − 21 |
| Nonagnate | 1 | 13 | 13 | − |
| Sub-Total | 3 | 46 | 15 | 12 − 21 |
| Totals | 45 | 2,176 | 48 | 12 − 151 |
| Agnates | 32 | 1,496 | 47 | 12 − 151 |
| Nonagnates | 13 | 680 | 52 | 13 − 132 |

Table 14 confirms numerically what might reasonably be expected. Acknowledged bigmen have more partnerships on average than men of other statuses. The ranges however, show a great deal of overlap: for example, a bigman named Pyawa (non-agnate of the Tareyane subclan) has just 31 partnerships while a minor bigman and several ordinary men have almost three times as many. Pyawa exemplifies one strategy, albeit less often used, in the formation of a *tee* network. In his discussions with me, he made it clear that he preferred fewer, stronger partners with whom he could exchange larger numbers of pigs. He is a partner of some of the biggest men in surrounding clans and also in other Mamagakini subclans. His *tee* partners are able men of high reputation and status on whom he can safely rely. Additionally, he told of only one incident in his active *tee* life when a partner defaulted to him and he had to be dropped from his network.

Thus Pyawa's pool of *kaita miningi* is relatively small, but highly stable and composed of important men from whom he can take sufficient pigs and valuables to be acclaimed a *kamongo*.[17]

Nonagnatic residents have more *tee* partners on average than agnates. Nonagnatic residents transact less frequently with their own agnates resident elsewhere, but make *tee* more often with co-resident men than do agnates. Co-resident nonagnatic men have the essential *tee* connection to resident agnates: a linking woman who, in most instances is alive or still remembered. While clansmen must "straighten the way" (Feil 1978a), non-agnates have a straight path to potential *tee* allies. Nonagnates also make use more often than agnates of other subclan female links to form partnerships. Other writers (Meggitt 1965a:34–45; A.J. Strathern 1972) have argued that, in some Highlands societies, nonagnates suffer greater or lesser disadvantages because of their status in such activities as bride acquisition, gathering bridewealth, access to land and in wealth generally. The reverse could well be argued for Tombema, at least as reflected in the number of *tee* allies a nonagnate can muster.

A co-resident nonagnate, Tuingi, a bigman whose mother is Mamagakini, has over 40 partnerships (of his total of 121) with Mamagakini men, from every other subclan, not just that of his mother. He has used his nonagnatic and bigman status to establish *tee* relations with a wide range of cross-cousins and mother's brothers with whom he lives. Men living with their wife's group have similar opportunities to transact with her kinsmen, his brother's-in-law and father's-in-law.

Furthermore, resident nonagnates frequently use the marriage of a female cross-cousin or a wife's sister to begin *tee* relations with their husbands. The advantages of a nonagnate to prolifer-ate near *tee* partnerships are great.

Bigmen, as might be expected, have a higher percentage of partners in other clans than do lesser men. The prestige and resources of bigmen allow them to contract *tee* relations with a wider range of individuals than ordinary men, who are con-strained by limits of wealth and deal more often only with the subclansmen of their mother or wife for example. In addition to expanding numbers, bigmen tend to take pigs from individuals in more clans than do ordinary men. By so doing, they gain a foothold into the *tee* activities of many different clans at different locations. With partners widely spread, they can make *tee* speeches and participate forcefully at many *tee* grounds. The next chapter will explore this theme more fully. The figures do not support the notion that bigmen have, more frequently than others, *tee* partners who are members of their own clan and subclan. This assumption has led to the view that, by monopolizing exchange contacts in their own groups, bigmen "act as channels through which wealth flows into and out of their clans" (Meggitt 1974:81). My data suggests the opposite.[18] An alternative hypothesis is that bigmen have the influence and resources to transact more often with persons in other clans, not direct competitors, who offer the possibility of more stable partnerships. Other men of lower status are bound to contacts closer to home. The Tombema ideal is to draw support from outside, to receive pigs from as many men as possible in other clans. Bigmen are more successful in this pursuit than other men. A man may use investments taken from clansmen, channel them to outside partners, and when the return comes, default to them. Partnerships with men of different clans always have the potential to grow into significant ones; intraclan and especially subclan partnerships never do. The discussion turns to consider who a person's major partners are, their placement and stability.

## Big *Tee* Roads and Partnership Stability

The previous section showed that, on average and depending on status, a person has between 12 and 150 exchange partners in the *tee*. A large proportion of these will contribute or receive valuables in every *tee*; some will not, but will remain in good standing for future transactions. A fraction of a man's partners are designated as "big or major *tee* roads". These are his most important *tee* allies, they participate more actively in his planning and give and receive the biggest, single shares of his pigs and pearlshells when he makes his *tee*. Tombema say these *tee* roads are "heavy", "full", and "abundant" ones, and that the number of pigs travelling along them is enough to "bury" a man. What one man considers a big road, another man may not. A man of low *tee* status who receives a few pigs only, would consider a contribution of two a "big" road. An important man on the other hand thinks of 15 to 20 as a major contribution. In discussion, a man will characteristically signal a big road by clapping together several times his closed fists, to represent ten pigs taken or given for every clap. The essence of a "big road" however, is that a person so called can always be counted on to provide valuables. The ideal is summed up by a current Mamagakini bigman, Ango, as a lesson gained from his dead father Angu, himself once a powerful man in the *tee*:

> Angu told me how to make *saandi pingi* (initiatory payments): send lots of pigs to one man to pull all of his pigs when the *tee* comes. But I should also befriend several men in case some don't return straight. I should have "best friends" though who will always give pigs to me, who will not tire of my face, and whom I can trust. I have followed his advice and I have taken his place in the *tee*.

A person's major partners are usually linked by him: he takes pigs from one and gives them to the other. This means, of course, that each partner must be able to operate at that transactional level. If, for example, a man takes ten pigs from one major partner and gives them to another, that man must be able to return a similar quantity to be passed back subsequently. In some cases, a man may take ten pigs from a major partner and give them to ten different persons. But this practice is usually avoided as too risky, and every attempt is made to find a partner "big" enough to handle the flow of pigs. The linking of major partners leads naturally to the creation of chains of important partnerships built on interpersonal ties. These become well-established, enduring, and as will be pointed out in the next chapter, it is these partnerships that are the major competing units in the *tee*. Major partners are never members of the same subclan and rarely are they fellow clansmen.

A large proportion of important partners of Mamagakini men in the sample, are members of clans only a few removed from Mamagakini in the *tee*-making sequence (see chapter three). This again reflects the restricted social universe of which men are a part. A person's marriage is contracted nearby and his *tee* partners, including his most important ones, come from neighbouring clans. To the south, the clans Wakenekoni, Kirapani/Malipio and Sauli which all share common boundaries with Mamagakini, and precede, in that order, Mamagakini in the *tee* sequence, account for 39 per cent (86 of 222) of partnerships described as major. The clans which immediately follow Mama-gakini in the *tee*, Yauwani/Angaleyani, Poreyalani, and Malipani, again all contiguous clans, contain a further 32 per cent (70 of 222) of major partnerships. Major intraclan partner-ships account for a further 8 per cent (18 of 222). Thus nearly 80 per cent of all major *tee* partners are members of clans within three steps of Mamagakini in *tee*-making order. The kinship categories into which major partners fall, parallel in many ways the overall pattern of *kaita miningi* (see table 13).

Slightly more than one-third of important partnerships have been inherited from the father or taken up with a partner's son, these being predominantly in the *apange* and *kaingi* categories.[19] But the majority of major partners are those a man makes for himself, his *palingi* and *imangi* (in-laws). The emphasis is on relationships a man's wife, sisters, and daughters make possible, relationships an individual has shaped and sustained by his own acumen in *tee* affairs, and those with whom he has chosen, for personal and other reasons, to transact.[20]

Important partners of bigmen are, in nearly every case, other bigmen. Furthermore, a greater portion of their total *tee* network (33 per cent) is made up of bigmen. Ordinary men associate with bigmen as major partners about half of the time, while of their total number of *tee* partnerships, bigmen make up less than one-quarter. *Tee* disputes which lead to the dissolution of partner-ships are most numerous between bigmen and ordinary men. It is more often the latter who are dissatisfied with the *tee* performance of bigmen. Bigmen prefer other bigmen as partners, major ones or not, and some *tee* transactions between them may involve up to 50 pigs and other valuables. However it is slightly misleading to equate bigman status solely with the ability to attract and provide large numbers of pigs. There are several Mamagakini men who are major partners of bigmen, supply and receive from them large numbers of pigs, yet still are not acknowledged bigmen themselves. Bigmen, remember, are not merely those who "hold the pigs", but they also are those who "hold the talk". Thus some unassuming men, not known for their rhetorical or organizational skills, are key links in the *tee* net-works of bigmen.

All *tee* partnerships but especially important ones, are remark-ably enduring and free from conflict and tension. There are numerous examples, of unbroken *tee* relations between men lasting for many decades. The longest in the sample I collected involved Lipu the oldest Mamagakini man.

Born in 1905 approximately, he made his first *tee* called *kupi ee* (see Appendix 2) in about 1925. He was not yet married, but had established, by then, an important relationship with a sister's husband named Ale (Yauwani clan). As Lipu grew older, the relationship continued to flourish, and both he and Ale became bigmen together. Ale died and his son Mapusa took up the partnership, which also became an important one for him. By the time of *alekiki tee* (about 1940), the two were major partners and Mapusa would soon become a bigman, helped along by Lipu. In 1976, when I questioned both Lipu and Mapusa separately about their major partnerships, they acknowledged each other. Counting Ale's and Mapusa's subsequent inheritance of the partnership, Lipu has enjoyed over 50 years of uninterrupted *tee* relations with them. Regretably, neither Lipu nor Mapusa have sons to take their places, and for Lipu, his old age now prevents him from fulfilling the obligations of a major partner to a current bigman. Such duration in *tee* relationships is not unusual.

To gauge in an approximate way the stability of major partnerships, each man in the sample was asked in which *tee* he began to participate, and then at which *tee* each of his major partnerships began. The men are grouped in the following categories: "young men", those who made their first *tee* between 1960 and 1965; "middle-aged men", those who made their first *tee* between 1950 and 1955; and "older men", those who made their first *tee* in the early 1940s or before. These time periods were then measured against the years of *tee* activity with major partners. Table 15 gives the results.

**Table 15**  Average Years of *Tee*-Making with Current Major Partners to 1976

|  | Number of men | Years of *tee*-making | Average years of *tee*-making with major current partners |
|---|---|---|---|
| Young men | 8 | 11 − 16 | 12 |
| Middle-aged men | 26 | 21 − 26 | 23 |
| Old men | 8 | 31 − 36 | 31 |

The younger men have, in all cases, retained all of their major partners from their first *tee*. Middle-aged men have retained most, and older men, also, have many long-standing partnerships, though many of their partners have died. Some older men do, however, have major partnerships which began only eight or nine years ago. These are major partnerships brought about by their daughters' marriages. It is clear that these major roads of men, the relationships through which most pigs and valuables pass, are highly durable arrangements.

## Equality and Inequality

The *tee* is essentially an interclan institution and, as such, *tee* partners are always linked by women, following the rule of clan exogamy. Intraclan partnerships also have a mediating female link, and are modelled on interclan partnerships. Thus, *ipso facto*, relationships with exchange potential fall into nonagnatic categories, while simple agnatic connections hold no promise of exchange. Furthermore, a linking woman is essential for the daily workings of a partnership. In this view, the categories agnatic and nonagnatic assume secondary importance. The main point for Tombema is that with a pivotal female link between men, a *tee* relationship is possible. The present chapter has confirmed that nearly every *tee* partnership is mediated by a woman, the majority of them by living women.

What makes a relationship through a woman different, special and not of the same order as relationships of men linked only through other men? Conversely what makes agnatic ties similar, mundane, and equivalent? In Tombema society, at one level, an ethic of egalitarianism among men exists. In Tombema there are no status differences of any kind which are ascribed by agnation; there are no avoidance or other taboos which suggest inequality or bring embarrassment to agnates. There may be temporary inequalities between men, but they are not believed to be permanent or socially prescribed. Tombema say as much themselves when discussing the vicissitudes of life. They firmly believe, with justification, that a man can become as important or remain as ordinary as he chooses to be. As well, the open access to pig production ensures at least the potential of *tee* equality.

A man's relationships through other men are, of course, confined to his fellow clansmen. In material dealings with them, equality means strict accounting in giving. Debts, whether in goods or labour, are expected to be reciprocated *quid pro quo*, and the sooner the better. A clansman who is lackadaisical in meeting this return is publicly criticized at the earliest opportunity. Furthermore, there are tensions of co-residence which surface during local court proceedings, usually involving pigs, gardens, and the insults and slights inevitable with frequent interaction. In these cases too, men strive to maintain balance and equality. The man guilty of slanderous one-upmanship is put back in his place and a fine paid to the offended party. Frequent pig disputes between clansmen are adjudicated in much the same way, without regard to the status of the concerned parties. Instructively, when, as often happens, guilt cannot be assessed or both persons are deemed culpable, they are urged to exchange precisely identical things at the same time, thus reinforcing the notion of their status equality. For men whose tie to each other is through other men, the maintenance of equality requires constant vigilance.

The equality of individual men has, as its analogue, the equality of groups: clans, indistinguishable from each other except by name. Here too, continual watch is needed to achieve equality. Clans are the war-making units, and threats and attacks are countered by similar units. Battles in the past were not often decisive, and in the long run, advantages gained in warfare were seen only as temporary. Just as individual agnates assert their equality in dealings with other agnates, agnatic clans defend theirs. Relationships between men and androcentric groups are "symmetrical" in Bateson's sense (1936[1958]:311): "a relationship between two individuals (or two groups) is said to be symmetrical if each responds to the other with the same kind of behaviour, e.g., if each meets the other with assertiveness". The example of assertiveness is a particularly apt one for the study of Tombema agnates and agnatic clans, the implications of which will be explored in the next chapter.

The equality of relations between men linked by other men stand in marked contrast to those between men sharing a female tie. The reasons and manifestations are several. The most obvious is that relations between the sexes are complementary, inter-dependent, and not of the same order. Bateson (1936[1958]:308), describes a relationship as complementary if "most of the behaviour of the one individual is culturally regarded as of one sort (e.g., assertive) while most of the behaviour of the other, when he replies, is culturally regarded as a sort complementary to this (e.g., submissive)." In Tombema society, the tasks of men and women, their parts in pig production and exchange, and more importantly, their roles and perceptions of the *tee* are complementary (Feil 1978b, c). It might be expected that relations of men through women would reflect and assume a character different from that of men related through other men. In fact, it is so. Interpersonal relations between men related through women reflect inequality: name taboos between persons of the *imangi* category, slight embarrassment and stiffness in the presence of a brother-in-law, exaggerated generosity and punctilio when an *apange* or *kaingi* is visiting. These persons are clearly dignitaries, people different from oneself with whom formalities and protocol are essential. Differences are further expressed in the simple fact that female-linked men belong to different clans and usually live in different places. Relations between men with a female point of reference come about only through marriage, the beginning of inequality in exchange (see Feil 1981).

Forge has made the point clearly:

> From the point of view of the equal men, women are a source of inequality, in fact they are in some senses the only source of inequality, an inequality not between men and women where the equal/unequal distinction has no meaning but the source of inequality between men. Basically men related to each other through women cannot be equal to each other and they cannot therefore carry on equal exchange. (1972:536)

In Tombema society, the paramount expression of inequality is unequal exchange between *tee* partners, distinct as a category of persons, for they alone are linked by women. Women are the source of inequality between men. Inequality in giving does not here refer to the kinds of goods involved, but rather to the nature of *tee* transactions. The *tee* flows first in one direction and then years (often many years) later, in the opposite direction; this prohibits any immediate equality in a *tee* partnership. One partner or the other is always in debt. *Tee* relations are by definition unequal, but it is a shifting, alternating inequality. When a dispute between partners leads to the dissolution of a *tee* partnership, the debtor gives what is owed, the men become publicly equal, and the *tee* partnership which is unequal by definition

comes to an end. Equal men cannot make *tee*. For *tee* partnerships to be possible, women must provide roads between men,
equality must give way to inequality. The symmetrical relations
between men linked by other men have as their counterpart,
complementary relations of men linked by women. Symmetry
means equality in behaviour and transactions. Complementary
relations are behaviourally unequal and allow for altering
inequality in *tee* process.

Some relationships of men linked by women are further
"different" from those of men linked by men, by the very
substance connecting them. Tombema, like other Highlands
peoples (for example, the Mae [Meggitt 1964a, 1965a]; the Daribi
[Wagner 1967]; and Melpa [A.J. Strathern 1972]) believe that
blood (*taeyoko*) is passed by a woman to her children, and it is
this transmission (both symbolically and literally) which binds a
child through his mother to its maternal kinsfolk, both male and
female. The nature of the internal substance, blood, shared
between a man and his maternal kin is of a significantly different
and complementary sort to the external characteristics a person
"receives" from his father. A person's face, hair, skin, and bones
are made possible by his father's semen. Semen (*pongo ipange*) is
here symbolic of agnatic connections in general, a "patrilineage"
is referred to as the "mark/boundary of a man's penis" (*pongo lili*).

The tie of blood is a fundamental one between a person and his
maternal kin. Maternal kin are known as the "owners of the
child" (*wane tange*). In this capacity, any injury, blood spilled, or
death of a sister's child must be compensated; payment must be
given to the maternal kin of the child. Thus, one set of female-
linked relations are further differentiated from male-linked ties
by transmitted substance. Men in the categories of kin bound by
blood are major *tee* allies as has been shown. But brothers-in-law
are also linked by women, yet share no blood, and form the
largest category of *tee* partners. What about the nature of their
relationship? In exchange terms, Tombema conceptualize the
relationship between a man and his sister's husband as if the
sister's husband is holding the rights of exchange for his son,
until such time as the child can assume the partnership for himself or, in the hope that a child will be born to his sister and that
an exchange relationship will then be possible. *Tee* payments
"begin" between *apange* while the child is still nursing, and "child

growth payments" (*wane yangi*) are often made in the child's name by the father. Relations between brothers-in-law are also unequal and the blood idiom remains an important one to those partnerships. Tombema have created an exchange system in which the interaction of men is patterned in one of two ways: equality-seeking behaviour among men related by other men, and behaviour stressing and recognizing inequality among men linked by women.

The result of these patterns reflects the processes of competition within the *tee*. To maintain equality is extremely burdensome and men linked by other men, that is, fellow clansmen, seek always to ensure that equality. Fellow subclansmen, the most equal of all, are the fiercest *tee* competitors. Men linked by women are, however, unequal, hence by definition not viable competitors. In an ever-changing political world in which nothing is fixed, *tee* relations of men linked through women provide certainty and stability. Competition for status and advantage does not enter into the workings of their *tee* exchange arrangements. *Tee* partners are not competitors at all. They offer a "haven of rest from strife" (Forge 1972:537) and from the constant vigilance that equality-seeking among clansmen demands. Friendship and competition are incompatible in Tombema ethos, and *tee* relations do not allow their mixture. Men whose ties are through women are the surest, most trustworthy allies and supporters in exchange. A man's *tee* support comes from them and his performance in the *tee* is a direct challenge to those with whom he competes, his fellow subclansmen and clansmen, to prove they are his equal. The processes of competition will be examined in the context of *tee* transactions. It will be shown how sets of men compete with each other for the prestige and renown that *tee* performance can bring.

## Notes

1. Bulmer (1960b:10) however, notes that "*moka* partnerships to a very large extent follow these lines of individual affinity and cognatic kinship". He adds (1960b:11) that the *moka* "adds extra weight and content to the web of affinal and kinship ties . . .".
2. There is no Tombema term which I know of that means "free gift". Tombema do say that *saandi* and other payments, large or of the smallest bit of pork, make a partner feel happy and honoured, but reciprocation for any

gift is always expected. Even when Tombema use the phrase "*mee maingi*" (give for no reason) some return by the recipient is expected. Every gift is interpreted in this way and men went to some length to explain the meaning of any gift they received. Thus, when a man received some pig intestines from a woman at a bridewealth transaction, it was in repayment for a similar bit of pork he gave to her years earlier. I am sure that this too was in the woman's mind. Children are brought up to realize that any gift must be reciprocated and that, in *tee*, one must be wise and prudent and not eat a pig for which it might be difficult to find a replacement later.

3. Suluwaya and Iki more often call each other *kaita miningi*. Here I am stressing the point that Iki's mother is not from Suluwaya's subclan. It might be suggested that the fact that Iki was forced to move is demonstration that he is not a bigman. He is considered so in Malipio on the basis of his *tee* performances. He did not become a bigman only after his move. In the "classic" bigman mould, it would appear as if Iki was moving from his "power base". But his clansmen are far from his *tee* supporters and he was seeking relief with his *tee* ally, Suluwaya.

4. Lipu admits that he tried to sorcerize him. Mai speakers on the opposite side of the Sau River are thought to be sorcerers. Lipu asked a Mai *tee* partner to provide the service against his "brother". It apparently failed. But also in this context, I was told that when sorcery was suspected as a cause of death, men would go to their *tee* partners in enemy clans and try to find out who it was that was performing sorcery. They apparently believed that *tee* partners would inform on their own brothers if they knew.

5. Meggitt (1977) shows that one-quarter of recorded homicides involved clansmen. Perhaps some of these result from clansmen avenging the deaths of *tee* partners.

6. During my stay in Kompiama, as the *tee* moved in the Tsaka Valley, a fight occurred between the Yambatani and Kepa clans in which five deaths occurred. Yambatani give pigs to Kepa in *tee*, and immediately precede it in *tee*-making order. Despite the deaths, when the *tee* arrived two weeks later, Yambatani men made it and their Kepa partners took pigs away. I was told that Keke, a Yambatani bigman, made the point in his *tee* speech that fighting could wait; war involved only two clans, the *tee* involves everyone. He also said that the *tee* is more important than continuing war. Thus, warfare ceased temporarily at least, as Yambatani made the *tee* onward.

7. Requests to new partners are most often made during *saandi pingi*. But "house pigs" are often given in the *tee* to initiate new partnerships with men who have not given *saandi pingi* for them.

8. This figure shows only those partnerships established by payments made at the time of bridewealth. It disguises the extent to which *tee* partnerships with distant affines follow upon the marriage payments to more immediate ones. The others are given under *mee tee*.

9. Eleven men in the sample are sons of acknowledged former bigmen. Of their current *tee* networks, a total of 760 partnerships, they have inherited 373, or just under 50 per cent of them. Eight of the 11 are themselves current bigmen. There are eight other bigmen in the sample, but they inherited only 20 per cent of their father's partnerships. In all, bigmen (16) inherited about 37 per cent of partnerships begun by their fathers. Although half of them inherited substantially from their fathers, the other half managed through their own ability to build up large *tee* networks and achieve renown in the *tee*. One bigman inherited no partners from his father and is a resident nonagnate, but is acclaimed one of the most influential of all men in *tee* activities.

10. The 31 Mamagakini agnates in the sample inherited 40 per cent of their current partnerships (595 of 1478), the 13 nonagnates inherited 30 per cent of their current partnerships. In the group of nonagnates, men who then took up residence in their mother's group at an early age, after the divorce of their parents, inherited few partnerships. (For example, none of 30 inherited, four of 26, and three of 26.) Other men, whose fathers lived in their mother's clan, inherited many partnerships from their nonagnatic fathers (for example 78 of 130, 24 of 59). These are examples of bigmen. Similar circumstances of death and divorce effect the succession to partnerships by agnates. For example, one man inherited only six of 62 partnerships from his father who died when he was young, but two men inherited 24 of 48 and 66 of 128 from their fathers who lived and made *tee* until old age.

11. Again I emphasize that all partnerships are different, separate ones with men in other clans and their reciprocals are not given. Each partnership is listed according to the kinship relationship provided by the man in the sample.

12. Partnerships traced through sisters number 334, through wives, 540, through mothers, 424, through father's sisters, 175. The total through these female links is 1473, or 90 per cent. Partnerships traced through mother's mother, (14) and father's mother, (34) equal 48, through father's father's sisters, 20 and through son's wives (4), or daughters (86), 90. A wife or sister who links partners is almost always alive. Daughter's or son's wives are also always living links. While a mother or father's sister may be dead, partnerships traced through these women are thought to be permanent because of the transmitted blood linking such partners (see below).

13. Some partners whose links are many generational are, of course, linked by more than one woman. The tables show the initial, intragenerational link to which the relationship is traced. For example, a partnership listed as MMZSDH contains four linking women. Three of these linking women are probably dead and have no part in the current partnership. However, the daughter of a man's MMZS is still alive and is the important link between her husband and her FMZDS. She is the woman of significance to the relationship, but her tie to the linked partner originates in the grandparental generation.

14. I have listed all genealogical steps, but realize that Tombema use kinship terminology to "leapfrog" through their genealogies: MFZDSS is mother's father's cross-cousin's son's son, and so on. A kinship category and the identification of a clan may be all that is needed to demonstrate precise genealogical connection.

15. By "multi-termed" I mean many intergenerational steps.

16. Each Mamagakini man was asked, during census taking and afterwards, to rank other men of his own and other subclans. I asked which men were considered bigmen, which were considered minor bigmen, ordinary men, and rubbish men. Then, when the sample of men was selected, the responses were tabulated. There was virtual unanimity about bigmen and about rising minor bigmen. Rubbish men were also easy to distinguish. There was some ambiguity about some "ordinary men" who are rising, and some men who are too old to be considered bigmen. However, I emphasize that within categories, informants stressed rough equality. They could not distinguish within the clan or any subclan, a bigman "bigger" than another, or "biggest" of all.

17. In chapter six I state that the number of pigs a man can take and give away defines his status, not the number of partnerships he has. In the last *tee,*

Pyawa gave away more pigs than some men with twice the number of partners. Pyawa is not rationalizing; the absolute number of pigs and valuables count, not just the number of partners.

18. Nearly 80 per cent of the partnerships of Mamagakini bigmen are with men of other clans, compared to 70 per cent for ordinary men. Rubbish men also have a higher percentage of partnerships (74 per cent) with men in other clans than do ordinary men, though the reasons why this is so are unclear.

19. Most fathers of men in the sample were dead and I could not always discover if important partnerships had been inherited by their fathers from their fathers. I expect that such inheritances are rare.

20. A wife may demand that many pigs go to her brother and father; over 50 per cent of important partnerships are with these men.

# SIX

# The "Holders of the Way": Transactions and Competition

I've been to see my friends in the Sauli and Kirapani clans and have taken all of their pigs. Is there any man here who can do as I've done? Some men say they will make a big garden, but they never do. Some men say they will be big in the *tee* but where are they now? Look at all of these pigs. Do you see them? My name clings to this *tee*, yours has been lost.

Kepa, a Mamagakini bigman,
addressing fellow clansmen
during his *tee*.

The bases of *tee* partnerships and the behaviour and obligations incumbent on them were examined in the previous chapter. Here I describe the transactional side of *tee* partnerships. The contexts of competition, both individual and collective, are also discussed. In connection with the processes of *tee* competition, I also briefly analyze a *tee* which occurred in Kompiama during my stay there, and present an extended example of one man's *tee*, that of a Mamagakini bigman, Kepa. Many of the processes described so far in this book will thereby be highlighted. Some details of an actual *tee*, who the contributors and recipients were, and so on, have been given by other writers (for example Elkin [1953]; Kleinig [1955] and Meggitt [1974]). My aim is to understand, as far as is possible, the motivation and planning of a man and his wife when they make a major *tee*.

## Individual Transactions

The historical workings and transactions of major *tee* partners reveal the numerous and varied contexts in which they have exchanged pigs and, in the wider perspective of time, the basic equality in number of valuables given and received. Every context of giving is a suitable one for *tee* transactions. The temporary, shifting inequality which results from the alternative direction of *tee* sequences, belies the overall equality of giving when the partnerships are viewed through time (compare A.J. Strathern 1971:223). Major partnerships often begin with the initiatory gift of a single side of pork or a small pig, then blossom into a relationship in which tens of pigs change hands in a *tee*. The overall equality is also a good indication of the integrity which partners show in returning at least what they have received. One example will suffice.

> The bigman Ango began a *tee* relationship with Takyo (Tinlapini clan) in the early 1950s. Takyo is a "brother" (MZS) of Ango's wife, the two men call each other *"palingi"*, brother-in-law. Before the partnership began however, during a fight with the Wakenekoni clan, Ango injured Takyo. Takyo was present to fight as an ally of a Wakenekoni *tee* partner. Soon after this altercation, peace came to the Kompiama area. Ango, recognizing the chance to convert an enemy, offered a large side of pork to Takyo as injury compensation. Then, they further acknowledged their status as "in-laws". Takyo returned an axe, and Ango subsequently gave a pig to Takyo saying that "he had earlier married his sister and this payment was bridewealth that Takyo had never received". The marriage had taken place ten years earlier. *Tee* relations were on. Through three death payments, another injury compensation, a homicide payment, a child-growth payment, and several *tees*, Ango and Takyo gave pigs to each other. Their relationship flourished and remains a very strong one today. Their tally sheet is impressive: before the last *tee* in 1969, Ango had given Takyo at various times, and on various occasions, 86 live pigs, two cassowaries, 14 pearlshells, two pork sides, a total of 104 items. Takyo has given Ango 79 pigs, four cassowaries, 18 pearlshells, one axe, a total of 102 items. In the 1969 *tee*, and since as *saandi pingi*, Ango has given a further 13 live pigs, two pearlshells, and four pork sides; Takyo has sent one live pig in advance of his *tee*. In this awaited *tee*, Takyo will send Ango a large payment to reciprocate these outstanding debts and establish new credits with him. Invariably, partnerships of this duration exhibit similar equality.

Throughout 1974 to 1976, I recorded the transactions of 42 men, the same men used in the samples in chapter five. Initiatory payments given and received as well as live pigs given and received in advance of the *tee* were noted. To these exchanges, however, must be added the transactions of the previous *tee* of 1968-69, known as *tee saandi*. In the early 1960s a *tee* (called *tee mamaku*) was sent towards Wapenamanda and Wabaga, and the return *tee* to be known as *tee lyunguna* was expected later in that decade. When it failed to come (see below) men from "down below" in the Kompiama and Wapi clans sent a smaller, second *tee* (*tee saandi*) to encourage partners "on top" to make *tee lyunguna*. *Tee saandi* was sent in the same direction as *tee mamaku*, but the number of pigs given, and partners given to, was probably smaller than usual in major *tees*. Information on "house items" given in *tee saandi* and *saandi pingi* was presented in chapter four; tables 16-19 show all valuables given during these times.

The men in this sample strongly emphasized that this *tee* was small by "normal" *tee* standards and really was only an added inducement to "pull" down a *tee* which was their due anyway. *Tee mamaku* plus *tee saandi* would, they argued, bring a large return *tee*. The outcome is described in a later section.

**Table 16**   Valuables Given in *Tee Saandi* 1968-69*

| Category of man | No. | Pigs Given | Range | Average | Other items given in Tee** | Range | Average |
|---|---|---|---|---|---|---|---|
| Bigman | 16 | 769 | 17-101 | 48 | 210 | 0-31 | 13 |
| Minor bigman | 4 | 150 | 21- 68 | 38 | 57 | 4-23 | 14 |
| Ordinary man | 19 | 310 | 7- 34 | 16 | 120 | 0-19 | 6 |
| Rubbish man | 3 | 37 | 8- 17 | 12 | 11 | 1- 8 | 4 |
| Totals | 42 | 1266 | 7-101 | 30 | 398 | 0-31 | 9 |

\* See table 7, chapter four
\*\* Includes pearl and other shells, cassowaries, salt, tree-oil, feathers, and stone axes.

Table 16 shows, predictably, that bigmen were much more active transactors than others. The overlapping ranges are significant, however, and signal possible movements between categories of men on their way up, and those men now older who are becoming less active in the *tee*. The difference between bigmen and minor bigmen and ordinary men in number of pigs given is perhaps surprisingly large. In *tee saandi*, financial support was hard to muster, which affected ordinary men more than bigmen. Greater numbers of "house raised" pigs were also needed and used in *tee saandi*, a fact which would also favour bigmen. While the bigmen of the sample (38 per cent of the total) control a disproportionate share of the valuables given (58 per cent), the figures further reveal that the bulk of the wealth was not financed from fellow clansmen. Bigmen did not take the pigs and shells from members of their communities and invest them elsewhere in their own or their clan's or subclan's name. Of the 979 valuables given by bigmen, only 39 (5 per cent) of them were donated by fellow clansmen. Adding minor bigmen, only 59 of 1,186 valuables (5 per cent) given in the *tee* were contributed by other clansmen. Further details and the implications of this data are presented below. In all, only 6 per cent of valuables given in *tee saandi* by the sample of men were contributed by fellow clansmen.

In the years since *tee saandi*, additional *saandi* in all forms have been sent to partners as credits for the expected *tee* which is approaching slowly. These credits and accompanying debts are now enormous, and whereas two *tees* were earlier sent in the same direction, it is now generally felt that at least two *tees* in reciprocation will be needed to settle all outstanding debts.

I have recorded the complete *saandi* details of the sample of men. In most cases, it was difficult if not impossible to trace both the complete, precise "path" the payment had travelled, (that is, the number of partners whose hands it had passed through) and also, the precise purpose (if any) for which the payment had been sought and given. In most cases, men know three or four steps along which the *saandi* payment had moved, but beyond this narrow range, they shrugged their shoulders when asked and said, "How can I know?" I did, however, record instances of *saandi* made to fulfil all of the obligations and types of transactions mentioned in earlier chapters. The longest chain which I recorded from "supplier" of a pig to "user", comprised 17 men. I lost track of it when it passed beyond Wapenamanda. The chains are often much shorter. In cases where pork sides are needed immediately there may not be enough time for long chains to develop. Every *tee* man thrives on such situations for investment. There may be no clear-cut reason for a *saandi* payment or request immediately apparent to any dyad of men along the chain. A request filters down from partner to partner until one can satisfy it by providing the necessary, requested

**Table 17** Valuables given in *Saandi Pingi*: 1969–75*

| Category of man | Number | mena sapya | Range | Average | mena ita | Range | Average | mena saka | Range | Average | Other items given in Tee** | Range | Average | Totals | Range | Average |
|---|---|---|---|---|---|---|---|---|---|---|---|---|---|---|---|---|
| Bigman | 16 | 282 | 6–45 | 18 | 75 | 0–20 | 5 | 244 | 0–63 | 15 | 10 | 0–8 | <1 | 611 | 9–99 | 38 |
| Minor bigman | 4 | 46 | 6–21 | 12 | 21 | 2–10 | 5 | 84 | 1–63 | 21 | 0 | 0 | 0 | 151 | 10–94 | 38 |
| Ordinary man | 19 | 68 | 0–17 | 4 | 46 | 0–9 | 2 | 122 | 0–21 | 6 | 4 | 1–3 | <1 | 240 | 1–47 | 13 |
| Rubbish man | 3 | 4 | 0–3 | 1 | 3 | 0–3 | 1 | 6 | 0–4 | 2 | 0 | 0 | 0 | 13 | 1–10 | 4 |
| Totals | 42 | 400 | 0–45 | 10 | 145 | 0–20 | 3 | 456 | 0–63 | 11 | 14 | 0–8 | <1 | 1,015 | 1–99 | 24 |

* See table 8, chapter four
** Other items are not often given in *saandi pingi*.

valuable. Table 17 gives the rates of *saandi pingi* for the period of transaction after *tee saandi*, that is from 1969 to 1975.

Adding valuables given in *tee saandi* and *saandi pingi*, the sample of men engaged in at least 2,679 separate transactions over a six-year period. The tables also show that pork sides and live pigs are the most common *saandi* items. As noted earlier, pork sides are the best investment, for a live pig for each is the usual return.

Table 18 combines all valuables given in *tee saandi* and *saandi pingi*. These figures again show the transactional edge of bigmen and minor bigmen over others. The ranges however, show significant overlap:

**Table 18** Valuables Given in *Tee Saandi* and *Saandi Pingi* 1969–75*

| Category of man | Tee Saandi | Saandi Pingi | Total | Range | Average |
|---|---|---|---|---|---|
| Bigman | 979 | 611 | 1,590 | 29–216 | 99 |
| Minor bigman | 207 | 151 | 358 | 36–185 | 90 |
| Ordinary man | 430 | 240 | 670 | 11– 67 | 35 |
| Rubbish man | 48 | 13 | 61 | 14– 29 | 20 |
| Totals | 1,664 | 1,015 | 2,679 | 11–216 | 64 |

\* See table 9, chapter four

Chapter four showed that about one-third of all pig contributions for the sample of men originated from their own stocks, two-thirds were financed from other partners. Bigmen and their wives inject more of their own "capital" into the *tee* than do other men, evidence both of the ability to produce more and a greater willingness to invest it.[1]

The sample of houses contributed over 700 valuables (table 9, chapter four) as *saandi* to *tee* partners as credits for the forthcoming *tee*. The returns from these may be taken from the *tee* to replenish depleted stocks, or to reinvest. However, these men have also incurred debts of their own by seeking *saandi* for various reasons. They have consumed the pork of others, used the pigs to meet obligations, or are holding the pigs with some other end in mind. These debts will have to be reciprocated, perhaps from the gains made by their house investments, or from existing stocks, nearer to *tee* time. I recorded the *saandi* taken by the sample of men, and table 19 sets out the details. This table, then, measures the indebtedness of the sample of men.

**Table 19**  *Saandi* Held, Used or Consumed after 1969

| Category of man | No. | mena sapya | mena ita | mena saka | Other Items | Range | Average | Total |
|---|---|---|---|---|---|---|---|---|
| Bigman | 16 | 53 | 4 | 24 | 0 | 0 – 20 | 5 | 81 |
| Minor bigman | 4 | 11 | 3 | 3 | 0 | 0 – 8 | 4 | 17 |
| Ordinary bigman | 19 | 25 | 3 | 12 | 0 | 0 – 6 | 2 | 40 |
| Rubbish man | 3 | 0 | 0 | 0 | 0 | 0 | 0 | 0 |
| Totals | 42 | 89 | 10 | 39 | 0 | 0 – 20 | 3 | 138 |

A person takes *saandi* for himself much less often than he does provide *saandi* for other men from his own holdings. For example, an average bigman took *saandi* for himself only five times, but gave *saandi* 38 times of which 16 were from his own stocks. A person is more willing to chance investing pigs of his own than to consume pigs of others and become indebted to them. However, earlier chapters have described how a person asks *saandi* for a pig he and his wife have raised and thereby gains a gift for a pig they might have given "for nothing" anyway. But usually, a man tries to minimize his own *saandi* requirements or supply them from his own stocks and to act as agent for other men as often as possible. The figures bear out the Tombema maxim that "only old and foolish people eat pigs" or, more correctly, the pigs of others. A person must think before he eats a pig given to him as *saandi*, for if he does, he must provide one of his own herd to replace it in the *tee*. The "proper" use of pigs is to give them to partners as investments which will eventually increase the size of a man's own *tee* and hence his prestige.

### Recipients and Contributors

It has been noted that the range of interaction of individuals and groups is highly circumscribed (Feil 1980, 1981). Marriages are concentrated, enemies are proximate, and the chain-like nature of the *tee* system places heavy emphasis on nearby partners who are members of clans which immediately precede or follow one's own in the *tee*-making sequence. The firmly established order in *tee*-making among clans has, as its analogue, the step-like character in the movement of pigs between individual partners which make up *tee* networks.

A man tries to control his pigs prior to presenting them in *tee pingi*.

For the men in Mamagakini clan, the majority of their *tee* partners and hence the range of their immediate *tee* influence, does not extend beyond three or four clans which precede or follow it in *tee*-making. About 60 per cent (1,293 of 2,176) of all *tee* partners of men in the sample come from the Wakenekoni (89 partners), Kirapani/Malipio (273), Sauli (285), Yauwani/Angaleyani (278), Poreyalani (190) and Malipani (178) clans. Nearly two-thirds of all recorded marriages were contracted in these same six clans. Counting intraclan partners, the sample of men have over 80 per cent of all partners in just seven clans. The remaining partnerships of these men are spread among 23 additional clans. Most major partnerships are with men of the same six clans (see previous chapter) though few are within Mamagakini. Thus, in any *tee*, the biggest share of pigs come from men in three of the clans, and Mamagakini men pass them on to partners in the other three clans.

But while the majority of transactions take place within this narrow sphere, some men, mainly bigmen, move beyond this constraining universe and utilize their contacts to establish partnerships further away. The reasons are not surprising: there is prestige to be won by merely having contacts in clans other than the usual, near ones. Personal fame is spread to varied locales. Not to be overlooked, however, is the desire to find pigs where other men cannot. Vying for pigs close to home means direct confrontation with clansmen who may share the same contributor. More distant partners may belong uniquely to one man in a clan; his resources are untouchable to fellow clan and subclan competitors. Thus, the bigman, Ango, has 12 partners in the Yalingani clan whom he shares with no other Mamagakini man; Suluwaya, another bigman has nine partners in the Tinlapini clan, near Wabaga, distant cross-cousins of his father, who alone give pigs to him. Important men in the *tee* must go beyond the near sources to tap new ones.

When the number of clans in which a man has partners is examined, significant differences by status emerge. Bigmen have *tee* partners in 12 different clans on average (range 8–19), minor bigmen in ten (range 9–12), ordinary men in nine clans (range 5–13) and rubbish men in five on average (range 3–7). Being a bigman means having a say in the transactions of men in many different places: if a man has partners there "he has the way to speak there". As well, individual pigs that come from afar are objects of prestige and boasting: "this pig came from beyond Wapenamanda, I went that far to get it". The implication is that lesser men find their pigs nearby, in clans where everyone has a friend. In the competitive world of the *tee*, men of high status use such seemingly innocuous differences when the number of pigs they give fails convincingly to distinguish them from other men.

The *tee* community of seven clans which provides most Mamagakini partners, has a total adult, male population of about 1,000 men.[2] But while *tee* relationships, based on marriage, are largely restricted to individuals in relatively few clans, there are rules, stated and unstated, which produce individual *tee* networks which are essentially unique. Thus, on the one hand, the *tee* community is narrowly circumscribed; on the other, within it, there are processes which prevent overlap in the partnerships of men. Competition lies at the root of these processes.

Amongst the most important is the lack of subclan-based marriage prohibitions (Feil 1981). Men of a subclan often marry women from the same subclan, even the same lineage. Individuals, not subclans, are the exchange units, and personal genealogies alone determine whom a person can or cannot marry. By duplicating a marriage in a certain subclan, a man secures exchange partners of his own there, he establishes a major partnership or two in opposition to those of fellow subclansmen. On both ends, these unique ties become competing ones: the subclansman who takes the most pigs from another subclan's members gains the most prestige. Subclan members furthermore hold no right to use specific exchange links which result from the marriage of one of its members (compare Meggitt 1965a:93). This is an explicit rule. The circle of men who receive a man's bridewealth are for his *tee* "use" alone. Other subclansmen cannot "step-over" him to deal directly with his affines in the *tee*.

There are no major *tee* contributors or recipients shared by two men who make *tee* at the same ceremonial ground. While a small number of major partners are fellow clansmen, none of these are co-subclansmen. In other words, there are no major partners who openly compete for prestige by making *tee* on the same occasion. *Kaita miningi* are never brought into open competition. As had been shown in the last chapter, only 6 per cent of all *tee* partnerships are intrasubclan ones. Thus, all major contributors and recipients are outside the local "political" community, the subclan, in *tee* matters. The picture that emerges from these details and previous discussion is of independent men with essentially independent and idiographic *tee* networks. Due to the narrowness of the wider *tee* community, networks can never be absolutely unique, but important partners are never shared by other clansmen or subclansmen.

To demonstrate these points, I compare the *tee* networks of three sets of men of the Mapete subclan. Each of these sets contains three men of roughly equal status. Within the set, each man has some similar connections through marriage in neighbouring clans. Mapete is a subclan of 21 adult men: there are three acknowledged bigmen, 15 men whom I call "ordinary men" and three "rubbish men". These are the categories represented in the example. The first set are bigmen: Ango, Kama, and Pimbiki. Respectively, they have the following number of *tee* partnerships: Ango (151), Kama (58),[3] and Pimbiki (130).

Ango's mother is a Kirapani woman, Pimbiki married a Kirapani woman, and Kama was once married to a Kirapani woman who is now dead, but his current wife's mother is from Kirapani. Additionally, Ango has a Yalingani wife. Kama's mother is from Yalingani. Thus, these three status equals of the same subclan have potentially overlapping ties to the same clans, and men.[4]

The ordinary men are represented by Lakai (40 partnerships), Meyu (45) and Mungi (39).

Lakai's sister married a Wakenekoni man, Meyu has a Wakenekoni wife; Meyu's sister married a Poreyalani man, Lakai has a Poreyalani wife, and Mungi's wife's mother is Poreyalani. Mungi's sister also married a Poreyalani man. Mungi has a Yauwani wife, while Meyu's wife's mother is a Yauwani woman.

The rubbish men include Takeyoko (12), Kilipalene (13), and Imbu (21 partnerships each).

Both Takeyoko and Kilipalene have Wakenekoni mothers; Kilipalene and Imbu have sisters who married Yauwani men, and both Takeyoko and Imbu have Yalingani connections.

Thus, in all cases, these men have ties which should lead, *ceteris paribus,* to overlapping *tee* networks.

Comparing the lists of partnerships for men of each status, table 20 shows the duplications which occur. None of the shared partners are considered major or important ones. When the partners who have actually received or contributed valuables from (and including) *tee saandi* to the present are compared,[5] overlapping partnerships are further reduced.[6]

**Table 20**  Mapete *Tee* Partnerships: a Comparison of Men

| Men | Combined Partnerships | Partnerships in common | % of Partnerships in common |
|---|---|---|---|
| Ango and Pimbiki | 281 | 45 | 16% |
| Ango and Kama | 209 | 21 | 10% |
| Pimbiki and Kama | 188 | 26 | 13% |
| Ango, Pimbiki and Kama | 339 | 17 | 5% |
| Lakai and Meyu | 85 | 6 | 7% |
| Lakai and Mungi | 79 | 3 | 4% |
| Meyu and Mungi | 84 | 1 | 1% |
| Lakai, Meyu and Mungi | 124 | 1 | <1% |
| Takeyoko and Kilipalene | 25 | 1 | 4% |
| Takeyoko and Imbu | 33 | 1 | 3% |
| Kilipalene and Imbu | 34 | 1 | 3% |
| Takeyoko, Kilipalene and Imbu | 46 | 0 | 0 |

**Table 21**  *Tee* Recipients and Contributors to Mapete Men: A Comparison

| Men | Combined Recipients | Recipients in common | % in common | Combined Contributors | Contributors in common | % in common | Recipients & Contributors Combined | Recipients & Contributors in common | % in common |
|---|---|---|---|---|---|---|---|---|---|
| Ango and Pimbiki | 85 | 5 | 6 | 83 | 4 | 5 | 168 | 9 | 5 |
| Ango and Kama | 67 | 3 | 4 | 56 | 3 | 5 | 123 | 6 | 5 |
| Pimbiki and Kama | 58 | 3 | 5 | 63 | 2 | 3 | 121 | 5 | 4 |
| Ango, Pimbiki and Kama | 105 | 1 | 1 | 101 | 2 | 2 | 206 | 3 | 2 |
| Lakai and Meyu | 32 | 1 | 3 | 42 | 2 | 5 | 74 | 3 | 4 |
| Lakai and Mungi | 29 | 2 | 7 | 28 | 1 | 4 | 57 | 3 | 5 |
| Meyu and Mungi | 29 | 1 | 3 | 44 | 0 | 0 | 73 | 1 | 1 |
| Lakai, Meyu and Mungi | 45 | 0 | 0 | 57 | 0 | 0 | 102 | 0 | 0 |
| Takeyoko and Kilipalene | 13 | 1 | 8 | 10 | 0 | 0 | 23 | 1 | 4 |
| Takeyoko and Imbu | 14 | 1 | 7 | 12 | 0 | 0 | 26 | 1 | 4 |
| Kilipalene and Imbu | 15 | 0 | 0 | 14 | 0 | 0 | 29 | 0 | 0 |
| Takeyoko, Kilipalene and Imbu | 21 | 0 | 0 | 18 | 0 | 0 | 39 | 0 | 0 |

These figures confirm that stated partners of men of the same status, those men who are major competitors, overlap very little. The overlaps are highest where it might be expected, among men with most partnerships, bigmen. But with bigmen especially, the busiest transactors, men whom they have given to and taken from in the *tee* period, overlap significantly less than they do in theory. This suggests that during a *tee* sequence (as exemplified by this period of time), competing bigmen muster support from different men and invest with partners who do not have ties with a rival in the same subclan. When ties of marriage make *tee* relations with all rivals possible, contributors choose with whom to align. These discrete networks are the major competitive units in the *tee*. The individual representatives in each subclan compete, using this support, with status rivals who are drawing valuables from different channels.

But it is not simply bigmen who are rivals and competitively vie for the most prestigious positions. Other, lesser men, including those referred to as "rubbish men" are also involved.

Obviously, there is no danger of them challenging bigmen, and their *tee* performance cannot be so regarded or measured. Yet these men, who can give only a few pigs, refuse anonymity and by their *tees*, make statements about their financial viability and their standing "as men" in the community. Ordinary men do as much themselves, but the younger of these are a threat to the hegemony of established bigmen. Their *tee* performance is a direct and constant reminder to bigmen that they, too, can give many pigs and that, in time, their *tee* may equal those of bigmen. Thus, at all levels within the subclan, albeit for different reasons, competition is taking place. It is the individual with his network of loyal supporters outside the local group, who is opposing men within his own subclan.

Furthermore, very few fellow clansmen transact in any *tee*, and their lack of importance is further reflected in the number of valuables clansmen received and contributed to other clansmen during *tee saandi*, and the intervening period of *saandi pingi*. If all transactions are combined, the 42 men engaged in a total of 4,641, counting valuables given and received, in *tee saandi* and *saandi pingi*. Of these valuables exchanged, only 261 (6 per cent) involve different subclansmen, and only 124 (2 per cent) fellow subclan partners.

The overwhelming impression given by these figures is that the *tee* is an "outward looking" institution; it places little value in transacting with clansmen or subclansmen. It is also an institution which forms fairly discrete units of men for the exchange of valuables. The discussion now moves to examine the intricacies and performance of some specific *tee* chains and their competitive aspects.

## *Tee* Chains

A man's most important *tee* partners are called "big roads" and their characteristics and stability have been described previously. The discrete, non-overlapping ties between individual men of a subclan and their major partners outside, means that distinct chains made up of interpersonal links are created. Subclans, as well as clans, have a set order of *tee*-making, once the *tee* has reached the clan.

**Table 22** Different Subclan and Same Subclan Recipients and Contributors, *Tee Saandi* and *Saandi Pingi*

| Category of Man | Valuables given in Subclansmen | Number of Valuables given to Different Subclansmen | Number of Valuables given to Subclansmen | Totals | | Valuables Received in Subclansmen | Number of Valuables Rec'd from Different Subclansmen | Number of Valuables Rec'd from Subclansmen | Totals | |
|---|---|---|---|---|---|---|---|---|---|---|
| | *Tee Saandi* | | | | | *Tee Saandi* * | | | | |
| Bigman (16) | 979 | 35 | 18 | 53 | 5% | 777 | 24 | 15 | 39 | 5% |
| Minor bigman ( 4) | 207 | 16 | 16 | 32 | 15% | 166 | 18 | 2 | 20 | 12% |
| Ordinary man (19) | 430 | 52 | 12 | 64 | 15% | 364 | 14 | 8 | 22 | 6% |
| Rubbish man ( 3) | 48 | 6 | 3 | 9 | 19% | 34 | 0 | 1 | 1 | 3% |
| Totals (42) | 1,664 | 109 7% | 49 3% | 158 | 9% | 1,341 | 56 4% | 26 2% | 82 | 6% |
| | *Saandi Pingi* | | | | | *Saandi Pingi* | | | | |
| Bigman | 611 | 38 | 20 | 58 | 9% | 356 | 12 | 8 | 20 | 6% |
| Minor bigman | 151 | 3 | 7 | 10 | 7% | 103 | 6 | 5 | 11 | 11% |
| Ordinary man | 240 | 19 | 8 | 27 | 11% | 152 | 17 | 1 | 18 | 12% |
| Rubbish man | 13 | 1 | 0 | 1 | 8% | 10 | 0 | 0 | 0 | 0% |
| Totals | 1,015 | 61 **6%** | 35 3% | 96 | 9% | 621 | 35 6% | 14 2% | 49 | 8% |

* **Valuables given in the *Tee* and *Saandi Pingi* equal valuables received plus house items. See tables 16, 17, and 18, and tables 7, 8, and 9 in chapter four.**

**Figure 4** Clan and Subclan *Tee*-making order

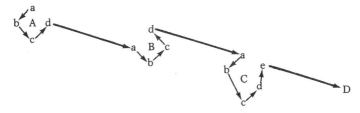

The component subclans a, b, c, d, (of clan A) make their *tees* before subclan a of clan B and so on. A major chain of partners might be composed of a man in Ab who gives pigs to a man in Bc who is a partner to a man in Ca and so forth. Men Ab, Bc and Ca form no recognized social entity, but it is this collectivity based in the *tee* that is the focus of a man's primary allegiance in exchange. The *tee* involves "vertical units" of men in many clans in opposition to similar units, rather than competing "horizontal" groups, for example, the clans A, B, and C. A man and his recipients and contributors in various clans form a sort of network in competition with men of his subclan and their network of backers. Major *tee* chains thus cut right across clan and subclan boundaries. A man's main loyalty in exchange matters lies with his important partners and the *tee* chains they comprise. He is the chain's representative when his subclan makes its *tee*.

The lines of competition are drawn in a number of ways. With the wider *tee* community so circumscribed, it is almost inevitable that subclansmen will have *tee* ties with different men in another clan's subclan. For example:

> Each of the three bigmen of the Tayowe subclan has an important link to the same Sauli subclan. Two bigmen have Sauli wives, the third a Sauli mother. As a result, each has a major partner in the Wayuwa subclan, and each of these supporters is himself a bigman. In *tee saandi*, the three Tayowe men, Leyambo, Kambi, and Ngoo gave the following to their major Wayuwa partners:

| Leyambo | | Kambi | | Ngoo | |
|---|---|---|---|---|---|
| ↓ | 10 valuables | ↓ | 8 valuables | ↓ | 8 valuables |
| ↓ | | ↓ | | ↓ | |
| ↓ | Sauli/Wayuwa | ↓ | Sauli/Wayuwa | ↓ | Sauli/Wayuwa |
| Ango | (*palingi*-WB) | Pyakiya | (*apange*-MB) | Pyalamuna | (*palingi*-WB) |
| ↓ | | ↓ | | ↓ | |
| ↓ | | ↓ | | ↓ | |
| ↓ | Kirapani | ↓ | Kirapani | ↓ | Kirapani |
| Watao | (*palingi*-ZH) | Amaiyu | (*palingi*-ZH) | Wapulao | (*kaingi*-FZS) |

While Leyambo and Ngoo **gave** three valuables to other "ordinary" men in Wayuwa subclan, Kambi gave only to Pyakiya. These three Tayowe men did not give to the major partners of each other or to any other "bigmen" in that Sauli subclan. When the Sauli men made their *tees*, they each gave pigs and pearlshells to their respective partners in the Kirapani clan, again three bigmen, and the *tee* chains were extended.

It is not known precisely how many of the Tayowe men's valuables were actually passed on to Kirapani via Wayuwa, or how many additional items the Wayuwa men added, but the Tayowe men believe their valuables went along these roads, and they expect their return along them. After this step-by-step progression through three clans, the pattern was disrupted. Watao and Wapulao next gave to Yalingani men, but Amaiyu sent his pigs from Kambi via Pyakiya to a Tinlapini man. This is usual. Important *tee* chains do not always have representatives in every clan or follow, step-by-step, the *tee*-making order through more than a few clans. The Tayowe bigmen are rivals for the top position in that subclan. These men have allied their interests in the Wayuwa subclan with men who are also rivals, and the Wayuwa men in turn with Kirapani. To a large extent, the Tayowe men's claim to bigman status depends on the returns they will gain from their Wayuwa partners and other major ones. These returns will be used to validate their status in opposition to other claims at their *tee* ground.

Potential partners that all men of a subclan may equally share (for example, a sister's husband or mother's brother) are allotted.[7] These men align their interests with a specific supporter, which *ipso facto* excludes others. The Mapete subclan provides numerous examples.

Two full sisters have married bigmen in the Sauli and Sokone clans. The bigmen Kama and Ango have each become identified with one: Kama has invested 20 pigs in this *tee* series with one brother-in-law, Kaketao (Sauli), but does not even count as a partner (that is, has never transacted with) Langa (Sokone), the other brother-in-law. Langa has given seven pigs to Ango. Ango and Kaketao have not transacted since before *tee saandi*. The exchange ties made by two sisters have been split among two competing bigmen of the same subclan.[8]

It does not often happen, but some major allignments change, just as major partners occasionally dissolve over a *tee* dispute.

Ango and Kaketao have never been major partners, but did transact continually until a dispute over repayment lessened their commitment to each other. Kama was then a man on the way up, and quickly became an important partner of Kaketao as Ango's influence with him waned.

Major partners like those above, bring secret messages to their partners about *tee* movements; they discuss strategy in private and make general comparisons about the support others are likely to attract. They also, on occasion, spread false reports to confuse others or blatantly lie to hide their own intentions.[9] The *tee* is a personal undertaking and relationships with major partners have a guarded air to them. I have been present when the competition was made explicit. Thus, when Langa's son died and Kama received no payment, he complained bitterly in public that Langa was more interested in making *tee* payments to Ango than in compensating the boy's death. No doubt, Langa was. Langa and Kama are not *tee* partners.[10] Ango, of course, did not say a word.

It is not simply bigmen who are rivals or have a stake in important *tee* chains. A Mapete rubbish man through a propitious marriage, has important connections with a bigman's *tee* chain, which reaches Wapenamanda. The uniqueness of this tie lifts his standing in the subclan; he has a connection that even bigmen do not possess. The bigman outside may not consider him to be an important contributor, but the man of low status gains from being recognized as a member of a bigman's *tee* circle. A man and his supporters, whether major or minor, share a loyalty and unity of interest based on *tee* dealings. The success of one often means success to the others.

There are numerous, important *tee* chains running through Mamagakini. Two will be mentioned to illustrate their extent. They demonstrate the known links of interlocking pairs of individuals. They are also the major competitive networks. Many investments of *saandi* are made along these paths of men and the return *tees* are large. Each chain is composed exclusively of bigmen. My personal knowledge of these chains is of a few steps only; each partner also knew of only some of the men involved. At both ends it continues to places and persons unknown to me.

These chains are the longest elicited from participants. The longer of the two, from Kapumanda (Yuwai) to Walya (Yopondo) is well over fifty miles in direct distance. The Mamagakini men in these chains have not been to either end, nor have they met most of the men who make them up. Ango has given Lemaita 18

**Figure 5** "Big Road" *Tee* Chains

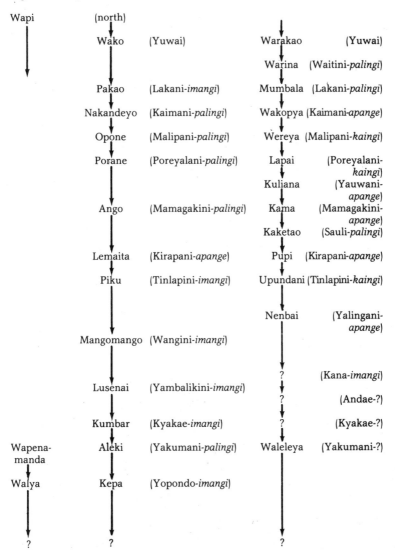

| Wapi | (north) | | | |
|---|---|---|---|---|
| | Wako | (Yuwai) | Warakao | (Yuwai) |
| | | | Warina | (Waitini-*palingi*) |
| | Pakao | (Lakani-*imangi*) | Mumbala | (Lakani-*palingi*) |
| | Nakandeyo | (Kaimani-*palingi*) | Wakopya | (Kaimani-*apange*) |
| | Opone | (Malipani-*palingi*) | Wereya | (Malipani-*kaingi*) |
| | Porane | (Poreyalani-*palingi*) | Lapai | (Poreyalani-*kaingi*) |
| | | | Kuliana | (Yauwani-*apange*) |
| | Ango | (Mamagakini-*palingi*) | Kama | (Mamagakini-*apange*) |
| | | | Kaketao | (Sauli-*palingi*) |
| | Lemaita | (Kirapani-*apange*) | Pupi | (Kirapani-*apange*) |
| | Piku | (Tinlapini-*imangi*) | Upundani | (Tinlapini-*kaingi*) |
| | | | Nenbai | (Yalingani-*apange*) |
| | Mangomango | (Wangini-*imangi*) | | |
| | | | ? | (Kana-*imangi*) |
| | Lusenai | (Yambalikini-*imangi*) | ? | (Andae-?) |
| | Kumbar | (Kyakae-*imangi*) | ? | (Kyakae-?) |
| Wapena-manda | Aleki | (Yakumani-*palingi*) | Waleleya | (Yakumani-?) |
| Walya | Kepa | (Yopondo-*imangi*) | | |
| ? | ? | | ? | |

live pigs and six sides of pork as *saandi*, of which 14 live pigs and four sides of pork have come from Porane. Kama has invested 11 live pigs and nine sides of pork with Kaketao of which eight live pigs and four sides of pork have come from Kuliana.

The *tee* fosters unity and co-operation with men outside the immediate social group, and at its expense. In any *tee*, chains of men, individuals in a network of allies, compete to make the biggest *tee*. Competition between men in different groups has little significance or objective. Men of the same political unit, the subclan and clan, are rivals for the positions of leadership and the prestige and renown that go with it.

## A Brief History of *Tee* Activity in Kompiama: 1960 to the Present

To demonstrate the rivalry and competitiveness of *tee*-making, a brief history of *tee* activity in Kompiama follows. I emphasize the positions taken by opposing Mamagakini bigmen in their quest to gain prestige at the expense of fellow bigmen. A chronology of *tees* that have occurred in Kompiama since the early part of the century appears in Appendix 2 and provides a framework for the events described here.

The last major *tee* (or "big" *tee* as Tombema refer to it) was *tee mamaku*, which occurred in the early 1960s. All men and clans participated. It was sent towards Wapenamanda and originated in the Wapi. Tombema regarded it as reciprocation for a previous *tee mamaku* which had "come down" from Wapenamanda in the early 1950s. About 1955, *tee lyunguna* was sent towards Wapenamanda. From 1955 to the early 1960s (the time of the second *tee mamaku*), a number of minor, local *tees* occurred but did not move beyond Kompiama. After they sent *tee mamaku* in the 1960s, Kompiama men expected to receive two *tees* in return: *lyunguna* (for the similarly named *tee* of 1955) and *mamaku* (for the one they had just made). After this *tee mamaku*, they also expected Wapenamanda men to take a *yae pingi* to them. It never happened. The reasons why are unclear. In Kompiama, during my stay, the failed promise was mentioned endlessly. Pigs were killed, however, but under different guises than *yae pingi*, and were area specific. Still, Kompiama men waited for the promised *tee*, *lyunguna* and *mamaku*.

In the late 1960s two chains of men with Mamagakini representatives attempted to "pull" the *tees* down. The first attempt which came to be known as the "*tee* of adopted pigs" (*tee mena mondo*) began with men in the Poreyalani clan. Pigs were passed between partners until they arrived in Mamagakini. Two bigmen, Ngoo (Tayowe subclan) and Lyupa (Tareyane subclan), decided to make this *tee* upwards. They received pigs from partners linked to Poreyalani, they added pigs from their own stock and through other finance, and made the "*tee* of adopted pigs". Ngoo and Lyupa competed to make the biggest *tee* and also hoped that their efforts would be enough to stimulate *tee* activity in the direction of Wapenamanda. If *tee lyunguna* began, they could claim that it was due to their efforts. Other Mamagakini men staunchly refused to participate saying too many pigs had already been sent that way and they would wait. Even Mamagakini men who received pigs as part of this small *tee* refused to send them on. In discussions with Ngoo, he remarked to me that his independent action was an attempt to cop the prestige of being the instigator of *tee lyunguna,* should he be successful. His name would adhere to that *tee* if he could make it "come down" with his contributions now. The "heightening of one's name" is a common theme when men talk of "bringing the *tee*". Only Ngoo and Lyupa made this *tee*; their performances were compared. But this *tee* fizzled, it did not proceed beyond the Kirapani clan and had no effect in stirring the *tee* in Wapenamanda. It was a defeat for Ngoo and Lyupa. In a public *tee* discussion in 1974, when the subject came up, Leyambo, Ngoo's rival in the Tayowe subclan, made the point that "I was strong in refusing *tee mena mondo*; your (Ngoo's) name went loose in that *tee*. I threw your name away then." Ngoo had gambled and lost in his effort to pull the *tee*. Leyambo had "won" by refusing to participate.

Another two years passed without indication that *tee lyunguna* was progressing in the area beyond Wapenamanda. Again the idea of making a *tee* upwards, thereby repeating the earlier ones, was broached in the Kompiama area. Who originated the idea is unknown, but inside Mamagakini a number of bigmen, including Ngoo, were in favour of it. Clearly, they reasoned, the *tees* in Wapenamanda needed further inducement. But the strategies for making a *tee* were a point of contention within

Mamagakini and outside. Ngoo, Kamambu (Munimi bigman), Pimbiki (Mapete) and others decided the best course was first to send a small *tee* towards the Wapi, and pull a bigger return which could then be sent towards Wapenamanda to bring *tee lyunguna*. This would be a preliminary payment and an inducement for a *tee* from the Wapi. These three men argued that the earlier attempt failed because of the small number of pigs sent upwards, not due to organizational problems. Leyambo, Suluwaya (Munimi), and Ango (Mapete), all bigmen, were against the idea. They reasoned that if a payment was made towards the Wapi, the return *tee* (to be passed towards Wapenamanda) would be too large, and represent yet another *tee* which might be difficult to retrieve as *lyunguna* and *mamaku* were now. In these slight differences of view, the competitive element among status equals of the same subclan is obvious. It appears as if men purposely take opposing positions. Furthermore, this account closely parallels the way men talk about the *tee* and its processes. Mamagakini men feel they have a great impact on *tee* happenings as far away as the Wapi and Wapenamanda. The range of their immediate relationships is narrow, but by compounding the steps, they believe they have some policy-making power at the starting points of the *tee*. Their repeated failures to bring about the hoped-for *tee* have not yet diminished their feeling that they have some influence and control over distant *tee* forces.

Ngoo, Kamambu and Pimbiki, and other Mamagakini men of all statuses made a downward *tee* in the expectation of compelling a large return to send towards Wapenamanda. To counter this move, Leyambo, Suluwaya, and Ango at first did nothing. They then went to their *tee* partners in the direction of the Wapi and asked them to make a *tee* to them without any preliminary payment. They asked their immediate partners to pass the word on and begin an upward-moving *tee*. Their *tee* would move in an opposite direction to the other one. The alliances, if they be so-called, of Ngoo and that group, and Leyambo and that group, were only temporary ones. In due course, the men would be competitors themselves to make the most of what they had collectively sought. They simply endorsed the same general position. The *tee* begun by Ngoo and the rest proceeded slowly, but the counter proposal gained momentum rapidly. Men in the Wapi started to make the *tee* suggested by the Leyambo group, spurning the offer of pigs (from the Ngoo-led faction) which they knew would have to be more profitably returned. The *tee*, initiated by the efforts of the Leyambo group, soon "collided" with the other *tee* moving downward. When this happened, the latter *tee* (Ngoo group) was abandoned and all turned to make the upward *tee* instead. It became *tee saandi* (1968–69) referred to above. The ill-fated *tee* became known as the "*tee* of the red pig". The name itself is of interest. Ngoo had given a "red pig" to a *tee* partner on the other side of the Sau River. When the pig was carried across a cane bridge, the holding ropes broke, and the pig fell to its death in the river. This prophetic occurrence was taken to be a bad sign at the time, and indeed, just as the pig died, the *tee* also failed. The Ngoo group were the losers, Ngoo himself for the second time. These events again provided rhetorical ammunition for his rivals. Ango boasted to a gathering of men that his "*tee* had covered theirs up"; they had tried to block his *tee saandi*, but instead he had "met their pigs on the path, and had made a frightening noise and had scattered them". Their pigs were lost while his had succeeded in finding their way. All men and clans made *tee saandi* in 1968–69, a victory in itself for those who had wanted it so. It was "better" than previous *tees* in which only a few men had participated. When men made this *tee*, the competitive arena shifted to the narrower, intraclan, and subclan one. Men competed to make the biggest *tee*, the biggest contribution upwards, which would "pull" *tee lyunguna* and put their name on it.

*Tee saandi*, however, was not successful. The *tee* reached Wapenamanda and beyond, but it failed in its larger objective to bring *tee lyunguna*. When I arrived in the Kompiama area early in 1974, men were shaking their heads, wondering what had happened to their *tee*. Later, while in the Wapenamanda area, I was told that *tee saandi* had "met" *tee lyunguna* moving slowly towards Kompiama in the Tsaka valley. Two *tees* were again moving in opposite directions and *tee lyunguna* was abandoned. Men in the Tsaka "turned and made their *tee* go the other way". Laiapo men criticized their Kompiama counterparts for hasty action and impatience. They admitted that so many new debts had been incurred that several *tees* would now have to be made towards Kompiama to settle the accounts. It was in this context too that they enviously talked of Kompiama as the richest, most productive Enga area for pigs. But they also mentioned that Kompiama men had to send pigs towards Laiapo, the "crossroads" of the *tee* system.

In Kompiama, the recalcitrance of the *tee* led to more localized developments. In 1971, a young Tayowe man, Tima, died and members of the clan of his mother (Yauwani), urged a large and prompt death payment for him. Yauwani is located in a receiving position from Mamagakini. If *tee lyunguna* had come, Mamagakini men would have given pigs to their Yauwani partners. Several Yauwani men made an initiatory payment (*wara kingi*) to Tayowe partners. Tayowe men then made a *tee*-like payment, under the guise of a death payment. Many men sent pigs downward to their partners, not just to Yauwani, but to men in the Poreyalani, Malipani, Kaimani, Tsinani, Lakani, and Yapetalini clans. Men in the Kirapani, Sauli, Yalingani, Wakenekoni, and Yanjini clans contributed pigs to Mamagakini partners for the payment. In sum, this death payment became the occasion for a small, localized *tee* in the absence of a major one.

There was also an agreement, loosely resolved, that when *tee lyunguna* did come, a *yae pingi* would be made towards Wapenamanda as return and further inducement for *tee mamaku*. Two successive *tees* were expected from Wapenamanda; a *yae pingi* after *tee lyunguna* would ensure it. After the death payment for Tima, men who received the live pigs "held" them and suggested to their partners in the Wapi that if they killed a few pigs, these live ones would be given to them. The pigs given for the death payment would be passed on, just like the *tee*. Men in the Wapi responded, they killed pigs, and these, in exchange for the live ones, were given upwards and passed through Mamagakini and beyond. This payment was a *yae pingi* of sorts, and was called the "*tee* of cat's legs" (*yae kiti moko*), since the sides of pork were small, like kittens. But all Mamagakini men did not participate in this transaction. *Kiti moko* represented further investments towards Wapenamanda, and some men refused to send more *saandi* in that direction. Advocates of the large death payment and return *yae pingi* hoped yet again that this action would stir men in Wapenamanda to send *tee lyunguna*. Pimbiki and Ango of Mapete were arch-rivals during this period. Ango participated little, Pimbiki sent 25 live pigs downward. In the return *kiti moko*, he received over 40 pork sides which he invested with partners towards Wapenamanda, men whom he hoped would pull the *tee*.

In late 1974, *tee lyunguna* still had not arrived, and optimism waned, but *tee* discussions went on in the hope of bringing it off. Word came that the *tee* had gained little momentum and had been abandoned. Rumour was that a few men had made *tee lyunguna* and their pigs were on their way via selected partners. The bigman, Lumaita, of the Yambalikini clan, had made *tee lyunguna* as had others in Wapenamanda and Tsaka. No doubt this piecemeal effort had the same competitive component as similar *tees* in Kompiama: with only some men making the *tee* towards Kompiama in opposition to others who wanted to make a bigger *tee* later. Slowly, a few men in the Ninimbi River area made *tee lyunguna*; then a few men in the Wangini clan; two men in the Yalingani clan. Their partners in Yanjini, Kirapani/Malipio and Sauli followed, and finally *tee lyunguna* arrived in Mamagakini. Only a few men in these other clans made this *tee*. Fourteen Mamagakini men chose to make it, four bigmen and ten others. The idea developed among them that they would make this *tee* to the Wapi, seek another (if small) *yae pingi* and send these pork sides upwards to try yet again for *tee mamaku*. Indeed, all men agreed that *tee lyunguna* as a major *tee* was lost.

Abruptly, all talk of *tee lyunguna* was superseded with talk of "pulling" *tee mamaku* instead. Men in Mamagakini who made *tee lyunguna* boasted that they alone had not reneged on their partners down below, and they too would make *tee mamaku* later. "A few of us will make *lyunguna* now, we pulled it down when no one else could; we worked hard for *lyunguna*", and so on. Other men in Mamagakini tried desperately to stop it from proceeding. They wanted no *yae pingi* to begin in the Wapi nor to lose face over their failure to make this small *tee*. They reasoned that if men in the Wapi killed pigs in *yae pingi*, only those who had made *tee lyunguna* would receive sides of pork to reinvest. They also feared that their pigs (sent earlier as *mena yukupae*) would be killed too, and not be available to use when *tee mamaku* arrived later. Those in Mamagakini opposed to *tee lyunguna* tried to stall those planning to make it. They offered to join them if they would wait just a while longer; they called out the police from Kompiama when *tee lyunguna* participants discussed it on days devoted to road maintenance work. Some of the major participants were jailed and then bailed out by their supporters. The missionaries were alerted that Sundays were being used to "talk *tee*".[11] Sauli men who made *tee lyunguna* organized a *sandalu* for their bachelors to bring attention to their *tee* plans and to gather together men from many clans to discuss them.[12] Opponents also tried to block the financial sources of those men wishing to make *lyunguna*. Mamagakini was split into factions over this issue. False messages were circulated that *tee mamaku* was close and would overtake *lyunguna* before it reached the Wapi. In the end, these fourteen men made *tee lyunguna* while the others watched. One *tee*, that of Kepa, is analyzed in the next section.

This *tee*, though a small effort, was a triumph nonetheless. Ngoo was one of the *tee*-makers, and after repeated failures, he regained some prestige. So had Lyupa. When Ngoo made his *tee*, he publicly minimized it saying "this is a small *tee* from my house only; I've pulled no *tee* down". His self-effacement caused no commotion in the audience. He was boosting his weakened stature and belittling those men who had decided not to make this *tee*, or could not stop him from doing so. With a few men in each clan participating, *tee lyunguna* passed into the Wapi. It was renamed "copy stick" (*kopi yati*). A past officer-in-charge at Kompiama had invented a method for summoning persons wanted by his office. He sent out a "stick" which, when it reached the intended person, meant that he was to bring it immediately to the office. A similar, matching stick (copy) was held there. The sticks generally meant trouble and people throughout Kompiama were terribly afraid of them; even to touch or see them was a bad omen. Men who made *tee lyunguna* (or *tee kopi yati*) were "sending a summons" to men in the Wapi to kill pigs, to make a good *yae pingi* to be sent yet again toward Wapenamanda to bring *tee mamaku*. The men who made *tee lyunguna* and received *yae pingi* sides of pork would hope yet again to put their names on *tee mamaku*. Others inside Mamagakini and elsewhere stepped up their efforts to bring *mamaku* quickly lest they lose even more prestige.

The *yae pingi* return for "copy stick" in 1976 was not as great as expected. Men in the Wale-Tarua area, who also have *tee* contacts in the Wapi, had sent more pigs in the *tee* than Tombema men and received more sides of pork in return. Some Mamagakini men who had made this small *tee* also killed pigs in *yae* and sent them onward. As they did so, *tee mamaku* did finally start to move, and in 1978 was still moving in the Wapenamanda and Wabaga areas. When it arrived in Kompiama is unknown. After the *yae pingi* passed, men who had participated in it and in *tee lyunguna* spread the rumour that they would send a *tee* upwards in an attempt to foil *tee mamaku* moving downwards. They planted *tee* sticks signalling their aim. But when I left the area, they had made no further moves to implement that scheme. Perhaps they realized that such action would in the end be self-defeating since they too would benefit from a major *tee* reaching them from Wapenamanda.

In Wapenamanda it was said that men making *tee mamaku* had rubbed mud over their bodies to symbolize their sympathy with Tombema men. Tombema men had continually sent big pigs upwards to them and only now had they managed to send a *tee* to them. If a man sends lots of pigs to another, and he dies before being able to reciprocate them, the giver will go to the mourning house covered with mud to demonstrate this fact. Men in Wapenamanda had taken many pigs originating in Kompiama and had not returned them, at least until now. These men also made it clear that they would send another *tee* down immediately, it would be called "the pig's backbone *tee*" (*tee alekiki*) after a *tee* of the same name that had been made upwards decades earlier.

Details of this short history could be expanded. My basic aim has been to show the competitive positions of men in the *tee* in addition to those of man against man. The "alliances" of men in favour of one position or another are more apparent than real. Adherents to one viewpoint are still decisive rivals. Those who made the small *tee* for instance, fiercely contested it, to make a bigger one than other men who also chose to make it. Men who opposed it competed amongst themselves to invest as much wealth as possible to gain the biggest returns in *tee mamaku* when it eventually comes. Whose name will eventually adhere to *tee mamaku* is not clear, and probably never will be. A man

Kepa ties some pigs to stakes prior to his *tee* in November 1975.

does not win or lose absolutely; if that were so, a bigman such as Ngoo would by now be only lightly regarded. Men of the same status vie for the top position within it. They move up or down, but little can happen that would cause an absolute downfall. The Mamagakini man who gave the most pigs in *tee lyunguna* is Kepa of the Mupani subclan. An analysis of his *tee* sums up many aspects of this book, elements of competition and co-operation, the reciprocation of non-*tee* debts in the *tee*, and the place of women and their control over "house raised" pigs.

## The *Tee* of Kepa

Kepa, despite Mamagakini opposition, made *tee lyunguna* on 15 November 1975. His "small" *tee* amounted to 66 pigs, two cassowaries, and 16 pearlshells. He complained that he did not really want to make the *tee* but had been forced into it by his *tee* partners in Malipani, Kaimani, Angaleyani, and Yauwani clans. His *tee* partners asked him to make the *tee* and "if a friend tells you to do so, you must; you can't think that your pigs are still too small". Kepa was perhaps slightly more ambivalent about this *tee* than others making it. He had come to accept the position only after much prompting from *kaita miningi* on the Mai side of the Sau River. However, he felt that his *tee*, the biggest in Mamaga-kini, would result in a large *yae pingi* repayment which could be used to pull *tee mamaku*. Other men would then say that Kepa's *tee* and *yae pingi* made *mamaku* happen. A favourite Tombema ploy in rhetoric is to demean one's own *tee* performance when, by any standards, it is a very big and good show. Kepa claimed that his *tee* was small, that few men had helped him by sending pigs and these were all he could gather. In fact, at one point in the ceremony he said that this was not really a *tee* at all, but a death payment for a former wife. It mattered not that she was from a clan whose members would have given the *tee* to Kepa, not received it. Under the circumstances, his *tee* was very large and everyone knew it. Later when he addressed his fellow clans-men (see epigraph of this chapter), his speech became more pointed. Some information on contributors and recipients is given in table 24.

Kepa made each payment with specific intentions in mind or obligations to fulfil. Two brief, more specific examples will illustrate:

> Kepa gave ten pigs and one pearlshell to Yaka (Angaleyani clan). Yaka and Kepa became partners in *tee saandi*. Later, in 1971, Yaka's son married a woman, Kepa's "daughter", of the Mupani subclan. Kepa was given three pigs and one pearlshell of the bridewealth. Bridewealth became an occasion for a *tee* transaction between existing partners. In 1973 Kepa made a death payment for a deceased wife to partners in the Tinlapini clan. Yaka helped him make it.

|  |  | *tee saandi* |  |  |
|---|---|---|---|---|
| Yaka | 1 pig, 1 pearlshell | → → → → → | Kepa | |
|  |  | *saandi pingi* |  |  |
| Yaka | 5 sides of pork | → → → → → → → | Kepa | |
|  |  | bridewealth |  |  |
| Yaka | 3 pigs, 1 pearlshell | → → → → → | Kepa | |
|  |  | disposition of Yaka's payments |  |  |
| Kepa | 1 pig, 1 pearlshell, 2 pork sides | → | Ango | (Sauli) |
| Kepa | 1 pork side | → → → → → → → → | Kipu | (Tinlapini) |
| Kepa | 1 pork side | → → → → → → → → | Pakao | (Tinlapini) |
| Kepa | 1 pork side | → → → → → → → → | Ambo | (Tinlapini) |
| Kepa | 3 pigs, 1 pearlshell | → → → → → → | Self | (the bridewealth pigs were cut and distributed by Kepa; pearlshell was held). |

Kepa incurred debts to Yaka, but except for the four items he himself used, created credits of his own by reinvesting Yaka's valuables. Kepa's *tee* payment to Yaka was made up as follows:

Kepa's *tee* to Yaka

| Ango | 1 pig → → → → → → → → → | Kepa → → → → → → → → → | Yaka |
|---|---|---|---|
| Kipu | 1 pig → → → → → → → → → | Kepa → → → → → → → → → | Yaka |
| Pakao | 1 pig → → → → → → → → → | Kepa → → → → → → → → → | Yaka |
| Ambo | 1 pig → → → → → → → → → | Kepa → → → → → → → → → | Yaka |
| Puli (Sauli) | 3 pigs → → → → → → → → | Kepa → → → → → → → → | Yaka |

House contribution –

3 pigs, 1 pearlshell → → → → → → | Kepa → → → → → → | Yaka

Men who received *saandi* from Yaka via Kepa returned pigs which were passed back to Yaka by Kepa. Two sides of pork and one pearlshell (of Ango) given by Yaka remain unreciprocated. Kepa used the pigs given by Puli in their place, to preserve his important relationship with Yaka. Pigs from the bridewealth that Kepa distributed were reciprocated from his own house, and the pearlshell he gained was exchanged for another he received when his sister's daughter married. Kepa received 11 items from Yaka during *saandi* and returned the same number at his *tee*. He had to "juggle" the books for Puli had taken nothing from Yaka during *saandi*. The overall significance of Kepa's payment to Yaka was to reaffirm their friendship by making an adequate return and to show Yaka that he was considered an important *tee* partner.

The second example is more brief:

Kepa gave one pig to Amborali (Kaimani Clan). They had never before made *tee*; Amborali gave nothing to Kepa during *saandi pingi*. The pig given to Amborali was supplied by Kuriwana, a Mapete girl. Kuriwana and Kepa's daughter are close friends. The pig destroyed a garden of a Mapete man and fearing a dispute, Kuriwana gave the pig to Kepa. A *tee*-type relationship was established; Kuriwana's father and Kepa are not *tee* partners. A pig taken from a new partner created a new partnership with Amborali. But Kepa is also seeking a death payment from Amborali and other Kaimani men for the death of a "sister's son", a Kaimani man. Kepa let Amborali know that this pig "straightened the hand" for a return death payment.

The details presented in the above cases, compounded by the number of contributors and recipients, are necessary to understand the *tee* of any man. Listing only participants belies the complexity of *tee* transactions. With some contributions, Kepa was simply reciprocating what he had taken during *saandi pingi*, or exchanging pigs he had taken out of *tee saandi* and held. Kepa reciprocated non-*tee* debts thereby demonstrating a willingness to **begin** new partnerships. In many transactions, Kepa sent pigs to **induce** other payments later, for death compensation. To **some** recipients, he made only a token payment to preserve the partnership when there were not enough pigs to go around. Kepa created new partnerships with gifts he received from new sources. In most instances, Kepa was able to keep his accounts straight. Those men who received *saandi* from him returned pigs, and these were, in turn, sent to the original *saandi* makers. But not all contributing partners made *tee lyunguna* and Kepa was faced with the problem of spreading available resources and keeping as many partners as possible satisfied. His large house contribution indicates this point. *Tee lyunguna* was perhaps unusual, but during the preceding period of *saandi pingi* Kepa invested nearly 150 valuables. The return was less than one-third. However, the remaining credits will be reciprocated in *tee mamaku*.

**Table 23** Contributors and Recipients to Kepa's *Tee*

|  | Category | Number | Relationship | | Valuables Given/Received |
|---|---|---|---|---|---|
| **Contributors** | *yangonge* | 2 | WZH | (2) | 6 |
| | *palingi* | 9 | WB | (5) | 6 |
| | | | ZH | (1) | 2 |
| | | | WMZS | (2) | 15 |
| | | | WFZS | (1) | 2 |
| | *imangi* | 3 | DH | (1) | 4 |
| | | | ZDH | (1) | 1 |
| | | | MBSDH | (1) | 1 |
| | *apange* | 2 | ZS | (2) | 2 |
| | *kaingi* | 1 | FFZSS | (1) | 1 |
| | *wanenge* | 1 | BD | (1) | 1 |
| | Total | 18 | | | 41 |
| **Recipients** | *yangonge* | 8 | WZH | (7) | 27 |
| | | | MZS | (1) | 3 |
| | *palingi* | 8 | WB | (1) | 1 |
| | | | ZH | (5) | 8 |
| | | | WFZS | (2) | 13 |
| | *imangi* | 4 | WZDH | (2) | 7 |
| | | | DH | (1) | 6 |
| | | | WFZSDH | (1) | 1 |
| | *apange* | 4 | ZS | (4) | 5 |
| | *kaingi* | 5 | MBS | (2) | 7 |
| | | | FZS | (2) | 4 |
| | | | MMBSS | (1) | 2 |
| | Total | 29 | | | 84 |

Fellow clansmen and subclansmen received no valuables in Kepa's *tee*. Three clansmen, but no subclansmen, contributed four valuables. Kepa has a total of 89 *tee* partners, only 47 of whom contributed or received valuables in his *tee*. He did, however, transact in all fourteen clans in which he has partners.

Kepa gave 66 pigs of which 32 were "house raised". This number is higher than usual (see chapter four) because most of Kepa's partners did not make *tee lyunguna*. It has been argued that a woman controls the pigs she has raised and cared for. Endanganga, Kepa's wife, is considered by others to be a forceful, strong-willed, woman in *tee* concerns. When we consider the recipients of "house pigs" a clear pattern emerges:

**Table 24**    Recipients of Kepa's "House-Raised" Pigs

| Relationship to Wife | Number of Recipients | House-Raised Pigs Received |
|---|---|---|
| ZH | 4 | 7 |
| DH | 1 | 3 |
| ZDH | 1 | 3 |
| FZS | 1 | 3 |
| B | 2 | 2 |
| Total | 9 | 18 |

In addition to these 18 pigs, Endanganga gave two house pigs to a man "attached" to Kepa as helper, that is, a man who has also helped her in garden chores; she exchanged two pigs she took in *tee saandi*, and five pigs were given in return for a compensation payment which she received. In all, 27 of 32 house pigs (84 per cent) were either given by Endanganga to relatives linked to Kepa by her, or to persons in return for services or past payments to her. She gave the five remaining pigs to partners who had given *saandi* which Kepa sent to her relatives, but who had not returned them for this *tee*. In other words, her house pigs repaid those her kinsmen did not return. When her relations reciprocate in *tee mamaku*, Endanganga may take these pigs to replenish her depleted herd. In a *tee* like Kepa's, his wife held the key to its success, and had major control over who the recipients of her pigs were.

With the help of some partners, Kepa successfully made *tee lyunguna* when other clansmen could not. Or, so he could claim. In his *tee* speech, Kepa directed remarks to his intraclan opponents. "If they had any pigs", he said, "they were obviously too wild to tie to sticks". Kepa alone was making the *tee,* only he had tamed the pigs of others. Kepa made each payment with a specific, personal objective in mind. He represented only himself, and the "political" impact of his *tee* increased his prestige within his clan and elevated his name above his rivals. A *tee* is a man's individual statement about his financial ability and the value he places on his *tee* partners.

In the concluding section of this chapter I discuss aspects of competition: for what, by whom and their significance for Tombema society.

## Contexts of Competition

In the previous chapter I emphasized the generosity and loyalty which exists between *tee* partners. I suggested that *kaita miningi* are in no sense competitors, but non-competitive allies in the *tee* exchange system. The present chapter has looked at the transactions of *tee* partners and competition which arises from the *tee*. The competitive units, and the arenas of *tee* competition centre on personal networks of partners spanning many clans. When a man makes his *tee*, he is a "representative" of *tee* chains of which he is a member. It is these chains, rather than any named social entity, which share common exchange interests and a measure of satisfaction in the performance of immediate member partners. Members of *tee* chains feel rivalry with similar chains. A man who has just given many pigs in his *tee* to an important partner will be present when that man in turn makes his *tee*, he may help him allot his pearlshells or publicly count his line of pigs to verify their numbers. There is satisfaction in seeing an exchange ally (big or small) make a good show, especially in the knowledge that one helped bring it off. This is loyalty between individual men which finds no repetition in other spheres of activity. This sentiment is not diminished by the reminder that the helper of a partner's *tee* is also present to learn for future reference where and to whom his pigs have gone. The exchange efforts of a network, represented by a single individual making the *tee*, are pitted against fellow subclansmen and clansmen of other chains, to give the biggest and best performance, and gain the most prestige. But the rewards of a successful *tee* accrue only to the individual making it, he is measured against men of similar status, he gains at their expense, or his name diminishes as theirs rise.

This view of the locus of competition in exchange is not the prevailing one in other writings of the *tee*. Meggitt (1971, 1972, 1974, 1977) underplays the potential of the *tee* for creating competitive contexts within the clan.[13] Meggitt first shifts the locus of competition beyond the clan, and then lessens the overall significance of the *tee* for Mae society. In three of the above cited works, the same paragraph appears:

> Nevertheless, I think it would be a mistake to be led by the highly vocal concern of the Mae with the *Te* (especially during the phase of the pig distribution) into assuming that success in the *Te* is the ultimate value in their culture. As I have mentioned elsewhere (1971), the Mae do not compete for prestige just for its own sake. Prestige achieved through prestations helps a clan maintain its territorial boundaries by attracting both present military allies and women who produce future warriors. The basic preoccupation of the Mae is, it seems to me, with the possession and defence of clan land. Participation in the *Te*, as in other prestations, is but a means to this end.[14] (Meggitt 1972:116; 1974:170–71; 1977:9)

The competitive focus of the *tee* is, for Meggitt, purely between clan groups, the major territorial units. Throughout his writings, clans appear as solidary entities in exchange. Bigmen mediate *tee* proceedings by representing their groups, but the possibility that there might be competing bigmen in the same group is never mentioned. And, while individual transactions are admitted, they are given no significance. Clans act as a "corporate entity, confronting other corporate groups" (Meggitt 1971:196); "it publicly distributes pork to *its* pig creditors" (Meggitt 1972:111 [my emphasis]). "The clan (and hence its members)" (Meggitt 1972:115) is a telling phrase, implying that the two are inseparable. I maintain that Meggitt's approach to the *tee* and the level of abstraction used to analyze it has missed its significance. It is no mere epistemological quibble, for it turns on what the *tee* is and does in Enga society, and where the crucial competitive processes occur. Meggitt's approach masks the real arenas of competition in *tee*-making. Additionally, by any criteria, a person would be hard pressed to prove satisfactorily, that the *tee* is not an ultimate cultural value (whatever that may mean) for the Enga.

Moreover, Meggitt's sole emphasis on the epideictic (that is, adapted for display) element of the *tee* process has further flaws. In this role, the *"tee* provides regular opportunities for expanding clans to discover which of their neighbors are likely to be too weak to defend their territories" and it also "enables observers to gauge the number of allies it can effectively muster. In this way, other clans in the vicinity can readily assess the potential military capacity of that group and use the information when planning campaigns."[15] (Meggitt 1974:179, n. 27). The geographical narrowness of Tombema society has been noted throughout. For Mamagakini, a large majority of *tee* partners and valuables in the *tee* come from neighbouring groups. It is also these same groups who are Mamagakini's fiercest enemies. Meggitt's account of Mae society makes this statement equally true there. If Meggitt's proposition holds true, these enemies of Mamagakini would not be donors and recipients in the *tee*, rather they would attempt to gauge Mamagakini's strength by the valuables they receive. But the fact is, these clans, or rather, members of these enemy clans, give vast amounts of wealth *to* Mamagakini men. They cannot possibly have a stake or interest in Mamagakini's downfall. Without contributions from men in enemy groups, a man's *tee* would be miniscule. The *tee* cannot serve an epideictic role in the way Meggitt suggests, to alert enemies of weakness, for enemies provide exchange strength. Affines, maternal kin, enemies, and *tee* partners are all members of the same groups. While Meggitt may talk of the "mere lip service paid to these particular norms of kinship and affinity which emphasize pacific relations" (Meggitt 1974:179, n. 27) *tee* partners are not the automatic outcome of kinship and affinity, and the examples in chapter five show that *kaita miningi* place a high degree of trust and loyalty, not lip-service, in their *tee* friendships (see Wirz 1952b).

This book has argued that the *tee* is not "about" interclan competition at all. Rather, the major competitive locus of the *tee* is intraclan, that is, between close, agnatic relations. As Forge (1972:534) noted similarly for the *kula*, exchange partners are outside the immediate "political community" and are not competitors at all. *Tee* partners, like *kula* partners, are not rivals at all and their exchanges are not an expression of rivalry, but friendship and alliance. Most *tee* partners, and all major ones, are outside the immediate political community where prestige seeking is not at issue. Subclans and clans are the political units, subclans the *tee* units, and it is within these that competitive struggles take place.

A man makes his *tee* with close, fellow, subclan agnates. His performance, based on the length of his row of pigs, is compared with other subclansmen. Prestige is won at their expense. External judges decide, for, to have a "name" beyond the immediate group is part of the object of *tee*-making. Fame is gained at home but spreads abroad. Kama of the Mapete subclan, put the view forcefully:

> I am the "head" of *tee mamaku*. I've given lots of *saandi* to pull it down and when it comes, I'll take lots of pigs from it. I've held out for this big *tee* and expect to find lots of pigs. Some others have made the small *tee* but I've been strong. But the *tee* on top is mine, it belongs to me. It will bear my name. In future when people like you write about it they will say I "pulled" *tee mamaku*. When Sauli and Kirapani

A man calls the name of his partners to come and take their *tee* pigs. His partner is ready with a cordyline bush which he will plant to show the length of his row of pigs (*akaipu wai pingi*).

make the *tee* they too will say it is mine. They have followed my talk and have pulled the *tee* down.

When members of a subclan make their *tee*, the biggest men may, with great bravado, forcefully plant a cordyline bush to mark the length of their row of pig stakes. Later, they may refer to the growing bush to point out the extent of their past performance in order to diminish the prestige of others who did less well. Only within the immediate community do such markers have meaning. Other bigmen may burn down a small house at the *tee* ground, to show others they have conquered their intraclan rivals. A public count must be made to verify the number of pigs each man gives. The comparison with other subclansmen is thus blatant. All of these acts have only local significance. They distinguish men of high status from others within the group.

Among bigmen of the same subclan, status equals, like Kama, Ango, and Pimbiki of Mapete, the competition is for prestige within the group, renown outside it and maintaining a "name".

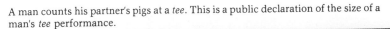

A man counts his partner's pigs at a *tee*. This is a public declaration of the size of a man's *tee* performance.

They vie to be the biggest bigman, and take opposing positions on *tee* policy as a challenge to the others to prove who can win. While temporary results may occur, there is no final outcome, but rather a juggling of positions within that status. Privately and individually these men would say, "If he (another bigman) is a true man he will win this bout; if I am, I will".[16] Publicly the verbal boasting makes the same point:

> If I don't succeed with this *tee*, I'll go hide in the bush. If I do, you'll make a platform at the *tee* ground and I'll speak from it, while you'll speak from the ground. If the big *tee* comes and you haven't killed pigs you'll become a crazy man.

Answer:

> I'm already crazy but if you come to my house and eat *tambu* (fern cooked with pigs), I'll call you crazy.

Bigmen compete to be able to claim that their efforts have brought the *tee*, that their name adheres to it, and that they have had an impact away from home in securing it. Some gain fame, and others are shamed, especially in situations when two forceful positions are put forward and one side wins, as in the case of the small versus large *tee* described above. Tombema realize that men and pigs are not easily parted and that "to pull" a *tee* requires strength of character and perseverence, as well as endless time spent discussing and persuading, away from home.[17] A bigman of Sauli, Kaketao (a partner of Kama's) put it like this:

> The *tee* is not like a house that I build and in which I have pigs, and tell Mamagakini to come and take them. Pigs come from other houses not just from mine alone. The *tee* must be pulled forcefully from others, it follows friendships and comes from a long way off. It is influence, and strength that brings it down. In each *tee*, we see who the real men are.

Aside from the prestige gained as a bigman and the acknowledgment of being a powerful, *tee* policy maker, the secondary rewards from *tee*-making are few. Bigmen may eat more pork than others, but accumulating live pigs for their own sake has no social value. Only in giving them away does a man gain. Hoarding would have the opposite effect.[18] Bigmen on average have more wives than ordinary men, but ordinary men with personal traits alone can attract several women. The direct power bigmen have over others is minimal and they in no way form a powerful interest group to subjugate others. It must be concluded that prestige has its own rewards. Public acclaim and "having a name" is satisfaction enough.

Once acknowledged as a bigman, a person does not lose that status until he becomes too old to move about and talk *tee*. There is remarkable stability in the hierarchy. Men known as *kamongo* jostle for position, but never fall out of the category. With ordinary men and minor bigmen with ambition, there is much to gain. To achieve bigman status does not require an existing bigman's retirement. Thus, ordinary men constantly compete with similar rising men to advance and move into the top rank. But ordinary men are also challenging current bigmen. If they gain that status, these men will be their competitors. While bigmen seek to maintain their standing, ordinary men compete with each other to achieve the top spot and eventually move up.

For ordinary men with ambitions, the way is open to become influential and to challenge the leaders. So-called rubbish men present no challenge. But, as often happens, a man of low status plants pig sticks for a forthcoming *tee*, perhaps only three or four, when in the next row, a bigman has over a hundred. The comparison is blatantly invidious and publicly so, and I wondered why the rubbish men bothered at all. Yet, by so doing, he maintained his autonomy, implicitly rejecting any notion that perhaps he should join his sticks to that of another, and mask his impotence as a *tee* man. They can, however, be known as able, self-sufficient men. Rubbish men, by making a *tee*, however small, are competing too, competing with popular opinion which says they cannot meet their own personal requirements and must depend on others. By making *tee*, giving pigs they have raised or financed, they are making a statement about their financial viability and personal autonomy. Their *tee* participation is the crucial means to that end. Tombema say that a man with in-laws can always find pigs, but have doubts whether an unmarried rubbish man can do so. Rubbish men, unmarried and frowned on, have a stake in *tee* proceedings – to prove to all that they are independent and, that they are equally men. That is their competition. These competitive situations are constantly occurring; I need only add the divergence of views over *tee* policy which mark *tee* history and the potential arenas for competition multiply. But there are some more general processes going on within and without the group.

In the last chapter, I referred to men related through other men, that is, agnates, as having a symmetrical relationship in Bateson's (1936 [1958]) sense, while men related through women shared a complementary one. The quality of interaction between individuals in these two types of relationship is quite different, but both, according to Bateson, exhibit potential schismogenesis: "a process of differentiation in the norms of individual behaviour resulting from cumulative interaction between individuals" (Bateson 1936 [1958]:175). Thus, men or groups sharing a symmetrical relationship respond to each other with the same kind of behaviour, thus heightening the symptoms and leading to a progressive change in the norms of their relationship, which Bateson calls "symmetrical schismogenesis". The same applies to men in a complementary relationship. Left unchecked and unmodified, "schismogenic strain" appears which threatens the "limits of cultural tolerance", leading to, among other things, instability in the relationships. These ideas have relevance in the context of the present analysis. Agnates of all statuses, sharing symmetrical relationships, directly confront each other in *tee*-making. They challenge each other to prove their equality. A competitive situation develops which has no final outcome. Men of roughly equivalent status are the major rivals, but even the lowest rubbish man, by making *tee*, is saying to the more powerful, "I am as good as you, I too can make *tee*". Agnates reply to other agnates with the same kind of behaviour, for why should they not, they are equals. But clearly such head-on confrontation can lead to schismogenic strain between clansmen and cause group and societal instability. The schismogenic trend is checked, I believe, in two ways, one of which Bateson himself mentions. Firstly, symmetrical schismogenesis is abated by uniting agnatic *tee* competitors in opposition to other agnatic groups, most notably in warfare (see Bateson 1936 [1958]:194).[19] Secondly, agnates can be converted to "nonagnates", thus potentially alleviating the strain. Symmetrical relationships come to be like complementary ones (Feil 1978a). Competition among some clan and subclan members at least, is reduced as behaviour is altered by their "new" relationships in exchange.[20] Clan and subclan partners have often transacted in the *tee* only once. But, appeal can be made to the time when, if only briefly, their *tee* interests appeared in common. Also, interclan and subclan factions may superficially unite men around one position, giving the illusion of agreement. But within these factions, competition is still rife.

Complementary relationships, those of *tee* partners, while lacking competition, are nonetheless potentially schismogenic. Complementary schismogenesis (a process in which the behaviour of one individual is continually met with behaviour of a complementary sort) is checked by the alternating sequence of *tee*-making. Here I agree with A.J. Strathern (1971:222–23). Donors in one series of exchanges are recipients in the next. Difficulties which might surface if payments were made in only one direction do not arise. However, some signs of strain are beginning to appear in the Kompiama area, as too many *tee* payments have been given in one direction without due reciprocation. Smaller, local *tees* however have reduced the tension. The idea of symmetrical relationships characterizes well those of agnates; complementary relationships those of nonagnates from which categories alone *tee* partners are drawn. Competition in the *tee* involves men sharing symmetrical relationships. Those in complementary ones are supporters, non-competitors, giving aid to their *kaita miningi* to make the best *tee* performance possible in opposition to other, similar networks of men.

## Notes

1. Eight of eighteen Mamagakini bigmen are polygynists; four who are not are married to "strong-willed" women; one has an attached bachelor (*kendamane pingi akali*) living with him. Bigmen thus appear to have more labour potential. However they also take more chances in investment, giving more house-raised pigs than others.
2. This figure is based on the 1971 census: Wakenekoni (42 adult men), Kirapani/Malipio (181), Sauli (151), Mamagakini (136), Yauwani/Angaleyani (106), Poreyalani (186), Malipani (160), a total of 962 adult men. These figures were taken from the Kompiama tax records, and are approximate only.
3. Kama has fewer partners than his rivals, but he is the most powerful orator and his *tee* connections are with two of the most important bigmen in neighbouring clans. His rhetoric and style are so forceful that he was recruited by the Australian Baptist Mission to be a travelling pastor; he refused when they forbade his polygyny. He has channelled his talents into *tee*-making. Additionally, his rise to fame has been meteoric and late in

life; there had been few signs when he was young that he would be a bigman.

4. All Kirapani connections are in the same subclan, Kama's and Ango's Yalingani connections are in the same subclan. It should also be pointed out that similar connections to other clans should, all things being equal, promote more and similar intraclan and intrasubclan partnerships. In fact, the reverse is the case.

5. These figures include all valuables given in *saandi pingi* up to 1975.

6. But these men are still considered partners in "good standing" and are likely to be called on at any time for *tee* assistance, and for reasons other than strictly *tee* ones (see chapter seven).

7. "Equally share" if the sister has no "actual" brothers or a mother has no sons, in which case subclansmen may compete for their subclan father's wife's brothers, their "mother's brothers".

8. There is also obvious competition between the two sisters to give the most to their respective brothers. At a *tee* of Mapete, both will be present to witness their brothers' performance, and Ango and Kama may make reference to them and their significant contributions to their *tees*. The women do not live together, but the competitive nexus between them and, through them, their brothers, is an important aspect of woman–woman *tee* involvement.

9. For example, Kama displayed his *tee* sticks to deceive his rivals into thinking he would make *tee lyunguna*. He never did. He hoped to forestall their intention to make it which might then diminish his prestige. Kaketao often spread false rumours about the *tee*'s movement in Wapenamanda, saying it was on the way and all should wait for it.

10. Kama is not a *tee* partner of Langa and did not expect to receive anything; yet it was an attempt to shame Ango and Langa, and to some extent, his sister as well.

11. The missions are generally opposed to the *tee* as too time-consuming and too dominating a force in their lives. But some churchgoers who are in opposing factions, have used the mission against their rivals and have prayed for their rivals' downfall.

12. The connection of *tee* and *sandalu* has been mentioned elsewhere in this book. The mission is also opposed to it and immediately after the Sauli *sandalu* withdrew its local pastor. Members of opposing Sauli *tee* factions wanted to stop *sandalu* for it brought attention to the *tee* plans of their rivals. They thus used mission influence to try to stop it. I was participating in the *sandalu* at the time and the native pastors came to the seclusion hut to try to disband it. After they left, the bachelors and I decided to stay, and we had to wash our eyes again (see Meggitt 1964b) for we had seen contaminated members of the community.

13. His paradigm and analyses are, of course, based on the co-operation and solidarity of descent groups in endeavours such as *tee*-making.

14. But Meggitt (1971:205, note 5) himself points out that active warriors are rarely true bigmen. Tombema reiterate that true bigmen are so as a result of *tee* and related activities only. Anybody can kill an enemy, but few can make a massive prestation.

15. Meggitt (1974:199, note 54) mentions that making a big *tee* prestation may have some negative repercussions for a clan; for example, a big *tee* means more pork sides in *mena yae pingi* are likely to be returned and more *enteritis necroticans* contracted. Members of clans who make big distributions are apparently more likely to die. Here too it seems that Meggitt does not recog-

nize that *yae pingi* pork must return to its sources, for a man's (or group's) *tee* has not been made only from his own pigs.

16. Tombema terms and phrases for competition include: "each man trying to put the other down"; "to compete"; "to win or conquer a man"; and "to look down on a prone man".

17. In the twelve months beginning May 1974, Ango was away from home for more than 200 days directly related to *tee* business. I lived next door and closely monitored his movements and often accompanied him.

18. In truth, the man who is most in debt and who finds the pigs to repay is the biggest man. Indebtedness and ability to repay have the greatest social value in the *tee*. A man who is not in debt is a man of no account; he is not asked for pigs and cannot acquire debts. He is in a state of financial balance which has no prestige value.

19. But this too is just an illusion, for clans are said to make war on other clans, but the effective fighting force is greatly reduced by ties of exchange to men in enemy clans.

20. If by chance, two agnates who share a complementary relationship must make *tee* at the same ground, one demurs and waits for the other to finish. I once witnessed this occurrence. But a comparison between such men is never made; onlookers remark that they are *tee* partners and could not possibly be competitors. I have also heard of such men making *tee* privately at their houses so as to honour obligations yet not confront partners using the same *tee* ground. But transactions between same subclansmen are not important nor frequent.

# SEVEN

# "Bending and Breaking the End": Decline and Dissolution of *Tee* Partnerships

During childbirth, the great pains cause a wife to say to herself "I will never again have intercourse with my husband, I will leave him". But later, she forgets, she stays with him and carries many more children. This too is the way of *tee* partners: one may consider leaving, but he remains and is a friend, and continues to give pigs in the *tee*.

Ango, a Mamagakini bigman

It has been shown that, in general, *tee* partnerships are quite stable relationships and that partners often develop into close friends and loyal allies. But there are situations which cause these partnerships to end abruptly. Some of the situations which lead to dissolution are clearly intentional: a person knowingly fails to give a pig rightly due to another, thereby causing a dispute. Other circumstances, such as the death or divorce of a woman linking two men in a partnership, may precipitate the end, but these are less calculable. These have been dealt with in chapter four. While the end result might be the same, the latter causes are reluctantly accepted, the former only so after bitter quarrels, perhaps even fights. The intent of this chapter is to elucidate the processes and infractions which cause *tee* partnerships to end.

The great majority of disputes between *kaita miningi* arise simply through the failure of one partner to give "correctly" to the other. "He doesn't give straight" is the most common complaint. A pig that should be given to one partner because an appropriate *saandi* payment has earlier been made for it, instead is given elsewhere, an infraction of *tee* rule called "bending or breaking the end" or "breaking the way".[1] A person fails to reciprocate properly and it is made the basis for dissolving the partnership. Accusations of this kind made by one party are extremely difficult for an observer to sort out with certainty, a problem which has led government officials in the area to refuse even to hear such charges in their courts. They are, however, voiced in informal discussions and courts nearer to home. As often happens, it is difficult from the testimony to distinguish the accuser from the accused. But failure to give or reciprocate properly are only two of the issues involved. *Tee* friends, as stated previously, should behave towards each other in special ways and fulfil certain non-*tee* obligations. To fail to observe these standards might also lead to a break-up. By examining these instances, some further idea is gained of the breadth and depth of the expectations of *tee* allies.

In addition to outright dissolution, the content — that is, the value — of a *tee* relationship between individuals can also diminish and become diluted over time. These occurrences are normally related to phases in an individual's life cycle. Tombema refer to dissolved *tee* partnerships as "*tee* friends who scatter" or "*tee* partners who abandon you". The contrast is that with that of a true, continuing *tee* ally, a "man who remains".

## Decline of Partnerships

A lessening in the number of pigs and valuables that two persons exchange in the *tee* may result from specific incidents such as default, but more often this leads to an absolute collapse. Rather, events in an individual's life cycle influence the content of *tee* transactions between partners.[2]

A person just beginning active *tee* involvement will usually have strong obligations to and credits with his mother's kin, particularly a mother's brother.[3] What began as a *tee* relationship between his father and his mother's brother (that is, between brothers-in-law) will later become a mother's brother-sister's son partnership, and much of the flow of valuables will, as the sister's son grows older, be directed to him at his father's expense. Initially then, a young man's biggest *tee* roads are with his maternal kin. These *tee* ties will normally remain strong, and will in time devolve to the maternal uncle's offspring, his cross-cousins. While cross-cousins are often strong exchange partners, there is a tenuousness in their relationship, for the children of cross-cousins are rarely major exchange allies. By that time, a man's primary obligations will be focussed elsewhere. There is a gradual weakening in *tee* relations from mother's brother to mother's brother's son to the children of cross-cousins, by which time the flow of valuables has either diminished or has discontinued altogether.[4] The process can be diagrammed as follows:

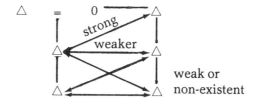

Coinciding with the strength of relations to his mother's kinsman, when a man marries, he begins to incur heavy *tee* obligations with his new affines, especially his wife's fathers and brothers. If *tee* partners on his mother's side have died, the focus of a man's strongest exchange ties is likely to shift from matrilateral partners to those among his affines. The wife's fathers/daughter's husband relationship normally remains strong until the wife's father becomes too old to hold up his side of the transactions: until he becomes a widower or drops out of the *tee*. The importance of that relationship gradually passes to the wife's brothers who take the exchange place of their father. In the process of transactional decline between partners, until a man reaches middle age when he is at the height of his *tee* involvement, he has been able to rely upon and benefit from men more senior, experienced and powerful in exchange matters than he is, namely his mother's brother or wife's father. With the increasing age and immobility of these men, a man's most important exchange partners then become his own generation mates, most notably those in the category of wife's brothers, sister's husbands and cross-cousins. The reduction in the flow of valuables to his senior partners means both an increase to his younger ones as well as a proliferation in the number of his partnerships. At this stage in life a man's pool of exchange supporters is largest: his maternal side is represented, he has his own affines, and those gained through sisters; he has used female ties to transact with some fellow clansmen; and when his daughters marry, they will bring other potentially important partners into his exchange network.[5]

This stage, too, is the beginning of his own decline. As a man grows older his most important partnerships will shift again: he becomes the mother's brother and the wife's father. Where he once drew strength from more senior men to raise his own exchange standing and interests, he now provides it for others. His contemporaries gradually leave his exchange network through death and illness, but until he also becomes too feeble, his sister's son and daughter's husband take up some of the exchange slack.[6] Soon enough though, he gives way to his own son and the cycle is repeated again. During a *tee* distribution, the giver of a valuable often calls the name not of his exchange partner, but of his son to come and collect the pig, saying "the handle of a bamboo knife cannot cut/eat pig". The handle of a knife is too dull and cannot cut, this represents the aging old man; while the top has the keen edge, which cuts easily, this represents the son who will now take his father's place (see A.J. Strathern 1971:212). *Tee* partnerships consequently have a life span of their own: they grow and decline in importance as an individual's life cycle progresses and as other primary friendships supplant and replace those formerly paramount. The life span of interclan partnerships for carrying obligations seem to be just two generations. But it has been poined out that intraclan partnerships rely on genealogical reckoning requiring greater depth of knowledge.

The pattern or process is, of course, rarely so simple as I have outlined here. There are also contingencies of death, divorce, default, and a man's financial ability, present at every stage. A person might develop partners in one kinship category who outweigh any others in importance. The major point, however, is that a man gains, *ceteris paribus,* new partners at fairly well-marked stages throughout his life. These reciprocally influence the strength of his ties to other partners, causing some to lose significance while others will slip away altogether.

## Individual Disputes

Like *tee* transactions themselves, disputes are strictly individual affairs arising from specific incidents between *tee* partners. If for example, a person defaults to one of a set of "brothers", the other "brothers" do not band together to force the defaulter to make good (using as a sanction the continuance of their relationship with him) in support of the brother's grievance. I recorded no such occurrences, nor does dispute settlement involve other than the immediate partners. Although brothers and other sets of close kin may have some exchange partners in common, their transactions with them are absolutely separate, and prosper or falter on their own merits without reference to the performance of others. Indeed, as is frequently the case, sets of close kin compete with each other for the pigs of a partner whom they all share, and his default to one of them may mean a gain to another. It is not too far-fetched to suggest that defaults are sometimes negotiated by promises and other inducements by one of a number of potential recipients all of whom might be close kinsmen.

"Disputes" that can be characterized as intergroup matters surface only on public occasions. But stinging rhetoric is never employed to chastise or shame a man's own important exchange partners in other groups. A speechmaker may deride the performance of men in other *tee* networks and by implication, the representatives of those networks in his own clan. He may say that other men do not have the resolve to bring the *tee* through negotiation, or that they take pigs as initiatory gifts and eat them rather than reciprocate. But his partners are different, they have the strength and ability to pull the *tee*. Individual exchange relationships are never jeopardized by indiscrete reference. A speech-maker may severely criticize the *tee* performance of men in other groups but immediately afterwards be in the company of his own partners from those same groups where an overwhelming atmosphere of friendliness prevails (see A.J. Strathern 1971:169).[7] In other words, a man rhetorically degrades the performance and capabilities of non-partners only on public occasions. *Tee* partners interact informally and on a personal level, and their negotiations are not a part of, nor open to, public scrutiny.

Much of the potential for group-scale disputes and struggles present in the *moka* system discussed by A.J. Strathern (1971: 175–83) are absent in the *tee*. The fact of "donor groups" withholding support, the apparent high degree of solidarity and unity of purpose in descent groups, and the crucial importance of the timing of gifts are important aspects of a major *moka*, yet they are of less importance for an analysis of the *tee*. There is no such thing in Tombema *tee* arrangements as "donor groups"; reliance on bigmen as organizers is less pronounced than in Melpa society; as mentioned, a person's contributors have only dyadic ties to him and recognize no unity or structure as a distinct, donating entity; and since the *tee* has a lineal sequence involving the making of prestations in a set order, the strategy of timing present in the *moka* is likewise largely absent in the *tee*. The *tee* is less meaningfully characterized as a struggle between competing groups than as a struggle between competing men of all statuses. Thus it is in the nexus of individual partnerships that defaults affect the *tee* process, and where complaints and strategies are most apparent.

The details, reasons, and circumstances of the disputes between partners which lead to their dissolution are as varied as they are in number. I present three examples of recorded disputes and offer them as "types" of complaints under which most fall. The first case is a clearly deliberate attempt at "breaking the end", the category in which most *tee* disputes are described by Tombema.

In the late 1960s, a pig which Lypita (of Malipani clan) received in *tee saandi* was sent on to his wife's sister's daughter's husband, Yokone (Kirapani clan), who in turn sent it on to Kokene, his brother-in-law (Yalingani clan), who also sent it onward a number of steps further to a place and person none of the principals know. Late in 1974, as *tee* activity increased in the direction that the pig was sent, its reciprocation came back along the same series of steps to Kokene's house. The pig given in the late 1960s was reciprocated by a single pig. The pig had not been given in any formal *tee* proceedings, but rather had come in advance of the *tee*. The pig should have been passed downward to Yokone, then to Lypita and on to its place of origin, but it was Kokene who held it. Yokone was apparently unaware of its arrival, where it had come from or, in fact, that it had come "along his road" and that he was entitled to it, if only in turn to pass it on to Lypita.

Kokene was preparing for a *tee* of his own (which he eventually made in June 1975) and was trying to increase his credits by making a number of quick investments. His own resources were dwindling and he was seeking gifts from others to invest for later return. He went to Yokone and asked him for a killed pig as a *saandi* payment, telling him for inducement, that he "had a pig in his house now" that he would pass on immediately. Yokone, young, but already a man of renown, sought to gain a greater share of Kokene's pigs when he made this *tee*, and asked Bokane (his brother-in-law in the Kirapani clan)[8] to supply the killed pig which would go to Kokene. Yokone made the same promise of an immediate return pig. Bokane had no pig to kill, but then asked Ango his "sister's son" (Mamagakini clan) to supply it, again making it clear that a pig would come immediately as reciprocation. Ango killed the pig, sent it to Bokane as *saandi*, then on to Yokone, then to Kokene, who disposed of it to another man as an investment to be returned, perhaps with increment, when he was to make the *tee* soon thereafter.

With the initiatory payment disposed of, Kokene sent the pig he had earlier received to Yokone, implying this was the one that the most recent gift of pork (that from Ango) had secured. But while the pig was with Yokone just prior to giving it to Bokane, Kokene's wife, a Kirapani woman, went and told Yokone that this pig was, in fact, the one he was entitled to from the earlier (1960s) payment. Her husband had wrongfully taken a second initiatory payment for the pig that should have been passed on without another payment being necessary. Yokone now found himself in a quandary. He would have been prepared to forfeit to Lypita in the hope that he would not find out, but Yokone's wife (Lypita's wife's sister's daughter) informed Lypita of the possibility of false dealing. Bokane was vulnerable to Ango, so he stole the pig from Yokone's house and gave it to Ango who was expecting it. Later Bokane and Yokone stole it back from Ango and gave it to Lypita. In the end, an informal court ordered that the pig be killed, and divided between Lypita and Ango, a settlement which satisfied neither.

Kokene was clearly at fault for asking *saandi* again for a pig already earmarked and "paid" for, and this incident was given by Yokone as the reason for his break with Kokene. Not only was this relationship affected, however, for the partnerships of Yokone/Lypita, Yokone/Bokane, and Bokane/Ango were also jeopardized. The relationship between Kokene and Yokone is not an important one, and the flow of pigs between them is small, so Kokene had felt that he could chance a default to him. The relationships of Yokone/Lypita and Bokane/Ango are more important ones, but Ango assured me that, if Bokane did not supply a pig in the future to replace his killed one, he would dissolve his partnership with him. Lypita was also vulnerable to the supplier of the pig to him, as was each partner in the sequence back to the original supplier. Ango had no further worry except for his own pig which he provided from his own herd.

While this may not seem to be a particularly subtle attempt to "break the end", it is more so than in other cases. A man will sometimes ask for and receive several initiatory payments, invest them, and when the return comes, give nothing back to the original donor, telling him bluntly that "these pigs did not come along your road, your investments will be reciprocated later". After asking the recipient several times to return the pigs, the donor eventually realizes that he has been deceived, and has little recourse other than to dissolve the partnership. I shall discuss later what other, few sanctions he has.

The great majority (see table 25) of dissolved partnerships result from this kind of default. But disputes may also arise from the simple failure of a partner to give a pig to another in the *tee*, whether or not an initiatory payment was made previously for it. If a request is made for a pig to invest as *saandi* and the request is refused, it is highly unlikely that this person would be given a pig later in the *tee*. However, when a *tee* is about to be made, persons who have not made initiatory payments ask to be given a gift anyway, and refusal may lead to dissolution. Failure to give means continuity in a relationship is broken, but this does not necessarily prevent its reinstatement in the next cycle of exchanges. Failure to make specific "non-*tee*" payments for death, child growth, or homicide compensation when they are due to *tee* partners may lead to dispute and eventual collapse of the partnership. This is especially so if the partners have been long-standing *tee* allies. Failure to reciprocate in equal, if not greater kind, to the initiatory payment may also lead to dissolution. The return of a smaller pig for a larger one given in *saandi* is a common complaint. This situation may lead to trouble even though the smaller pig was the actual return gained by the investment. A good exchange partner should make up the difference himself, even from his own herd, rather than simply pass on to valued partners inferior pigs he has received. Failure to add profit is sometimes cited as reason for a dissolved partnership though, as noted earlier, this in itself is not an essential aspect of *tee* giving. If this reason is cited, the partnership is probably declining for other reasons, and this becomes the ostensible cause rather than the actual one.

These obligations to give demonstrate the more general responsibility on the part of *kaita miningi* "to repay", or *ndenge nyingi*[9] as Tombema call it. Literally this phrase means "receiving or taking the corner". It applies typically to a situation when, after a person has been defaulted to, he accepts the loss himself and supplies a pig of his own so that he will not in turn default to his linked partner. Failure to repay in this way may lead a partner to break the relationship, saying that his partner obviously does not value his friendship enough to provide a substitute pig. An example will clarify the situation.

> Lakai (Mamagakini clan) and Tulyanga (Malipani) are *tee* partners of *imangi* status. Without any initiatory payment, Lakai sent a pig from his own herd as *mena yukupae* to Tulyanga. Later, when Lakai asked for *saandi* payments on two occasions, Tulyanga provided them: two sides of pork, and one live pig. Meanwhile, the pig that Lakai had sent was given by Tulyanga to his mother's brother and he sent it on to his mother's brother. A small *yae pingi* was held in 1976 (see previous chapter) and pigs killed by those men who had received them as *yukupae*. Lakai's pig was to be killed and since it was a pig originally from his own house, he expected to receive a side of pork to be returned by Tulyanga to him. He could then do with it as he chose. Tulyanga sent a message to Lakai's wife (his "daughter") to meet him and take the returned side of pork when he was given it. Lakai's wife waited at the designated spot, but the meeting never took place. Tulyanga's mother's brother's mother's brother defaulted to his own mother's brother and accordingly, Tulyanga defaulted to Lakai. Lakai was very upset and publicly announced that he would drop Tulyanga as an exchange partner.[10] He fully acknowledged that the fault was not Tulyanga's (a point I too made in discussing the case with him) but this did not in any way alter his view or intention. He also would not accept the argument that Tulyanga had given other pigs to him as *saandi*, and that perhaps he should think of these as partial repayment. Lakai countered with the point that each was a distinct transaction, and that each should be treated separately. His pig was lost and it mattered not at all what Tulyanga had given earlier. I doubt that Tulyanga heard any of Lakai's bitter words, but a day later, he called out for Lakai's wife to come. He had decided to kill a pig of his own and give the whole of it (that is, more than the one side required from Lakai's live pig payment)[11] to Lakai and his wife. He thereby demonstrated to Lakai the value he places on their partnership. His *ndenge nyingi* saved the partnership when it was clear that his failure to do so would mean collapse.

Men are not always in the financial position to do as Tulyanga did, and therefore lose relationships through no fault of their own. Tulyanga's statement to Lakai was that he valued highly the *tee* connection existing between them; he wanted it to continue and would kill a pig of his own to sustain it. *Ndenge nyingi* is thus a crucial aspect of the obligations of an exchange partner, especially an important one.

Finally, I consider certain non-*tee* obligations which *tee* partners should observe; ignoring them can lead to the collapse of a partnership.

It has been mentioned that public, personal defamation of a *tee* partner's performance is unbecoming conduct. When one hears such outbursts, one can be sure that a collapse is imminent. Tombema contrast two modes of conferring by saying that "*tee* partners talk easily and gently to each other", and do not speak insultingly or in a disparaging manner.

To bring charges against a partner into an informal court for any reason whatever, *tee* or not, are grounds enough for dissolution. If pigs of one partner damage the garden of another, the settlement should be informal and friendly rather than public and open for all to hear. One of several such cases I observed was an award of two pigs as damages by a court, from one *tee* partner to another. The defendant who gave the pigs warned his *tee* partner, "If you want to make *tee* with me again, reciprocate these pigs in the *tee*. If you eat them, we're finished". In the following *tee* they were not given, and the relationship dissolved.[12]

Another case which illustrates further the range of expected behaviour between partners concerns the fulfilment of domestic duties while a partner is away negotiating *tee* transactions with another partner. A man and his son left to visit a *tee* two days' walk away, in which they were to receive pigs directly. They asked the linked partner who was to receive the pigs subsequently, to look after their house and pigs and especially to care for the man's wife, who was pregnant and due to give birth soon. The *tee* was delayed and, in all, the man and his son spent a month away from home. This is not an unusual delay when *tees* are in progress. Rather than stay behind and patiently attend to the chores he was given, the waiting man decided to follow the two and visit the *tee*. When he arrived at the *tee* ground, his partner became annoyed and ridiculed him for being faithless and irresponsible. The three pigs he was to have received were given instead to another man. The man was asked to stay behind, for he had no direct connection at that *tee* and was due to receive no pigs. In addition to neglecting his duties at his partner's house, he had shown, or so it was thought, a lack of trust in the dealings of his linked partner, and was dropped as a *tee* partner then and there.[13]

Obviously, the above stated reasons for dissolution of *tee* partnerships are open to the criticism that rationalizations rather than root causes have been given. The strategies of default will be dealt with in the next section, but it is clear that "*tee* man" is not merely a strategist who defaults and breaks relationships only from a quest for maximized gains and minimized losses. He is also constrained and obliged by the morality of friendship in *tee*-making to give and behave properly to his partners in both *tee* and non-*tee* contexts.

Summarizing data on 42 adult men, table 25 classifies partnership dissolutions according to the three discussed cases, plus a fourth I mentioned earlier. The total number of collapsed partnerships for the sample of men is 312, an average of seven per man.

**Table 25**  Stated Causes of Dissolved *Tee* Partnerships

| Cause | Number | Percentage of Total |
|---|---|---|
| Simple default (*duna lakenge*) | 168 | 54% |
| Failure to repay (*ndenge nyingi*) reciprocate equally, give "profit" or make appropriate payments | 66 | 21% |
| Disputes over conduct | 19 | 6% |
| Death or divorce of linking woman | 59 | 19% |
| Total | 312 | 100% |

## Strategy and Timing in Defaults

Slightly more than half of all dissolved *tee* partnerships are caused by simple default. In any *tee*, it is unlikely that a person of whatever status has sufficient credits from finance and home production to meet all of his accrued debts. This may be so even if a person precisely figures his accounts, for his dependence on the dealings of linked partners will inevitably cause some shortages. If a man chooses to make further investments by giving profitable increases, the debt/credit discrepancy may be more severe. In short, a person is always faced with the decision of whom to give to (that is who to retain as a partner) and to whom default becomes necessary (that is, who to risk losing as a partner). A corollary to this situation is the possible use of delaying tactics: deferring to another time, another *tee*, with the promise that accounts will then be set right. Or, a man may simply try to avoid detection until the debt can be satisfied. As has been mentioned previously, each *tee* sequence is not a discrete series of transactions, but rather obligations and credits overlap between individual *tees*. Partners who have a history of strong, fruitful exchanges may not bother about a minor default, knowing that the debt will subsequently be paid. Partners who exchange few pigs, however, are more concerned should the return not be made. It has been shown that major partnerships are very stable.

There are several acknowledged strategies for attempting to avoid the appearance of default thereby averting potential disputes with partners. The most common is a procedure, or more precisely, it emerges from a situation known as the "bundling together of *tee* roads". Figure 6 illustrates the process:

**Figure 6** "Bundling together of *Tee* Roads"

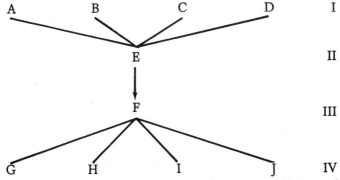

E has accepted initiatory gifts from, A, B, C, and D, and has given them to F, prior to a *tee*. F has in turn invested the four payments with G, H, I, and J. The donors of stage I do not usually know who the eventual recipients in stage IV are, nor do they know that they have all given pigs to E. Furthermore, they have little information of the volume or flow of pigs between E and F, or what other men in stage I have given pigs to E. When F makes the return *tee* to E, members of stage I who gave initiatory payments to E, will have competing claims over F's pigs through E. But many pigs from many different sources have previously gone to F from E, rather than to four different persons in stage III (where better accounting would be possible by A, B, C, and D). The recipient of stage I pigs is the same man (F), and so E can claim that F has not returned enough pigs to satisfy all men who have made initiatory payments to him. E can then, if he wishes, short-circuit ("shunt" in A.J. Strathern's [1971] terms) some of F's pigs to satisfy more pressing obligations, or give to persons who have promised greater return gains than A, B, C, or D. A man can also forestall criticism by declaring that these dealings were not of his own making.[14] The knowledge of "*tee* roads" is extremely limited and confusion can arise if each *tee* road is not separate and distinct. E may exploit this confusion by funnelling many pigs from different sources to the same man. In practice, most men have major partners and this strategy is often employed. E may well inform those to whom he has defaulted that their reciprocation did not come, but will do so later. He may offer a pearlshell or small pig from his own herd to appease them temporarily. The strategy is to delay if at all possible, and "float" one's debt until a later *tee*.

A man may also enter into a private agreement with an especially close exchange partner to withhold or substitute pigs before a *tee* is made, so that he can plead reciprocation did not come, or an inferior pig can be given instead of the better one which is held back. I witnessed instances when two partners agreed to substitute a boar for a sow and pass it down the line, with the idea that they would share the offspring and breeding potential of the sow instead of letting it pass out of their hands. Pigs withheld can be directed later to persons other than their rightful owners. But a partner who asks another partner to hold back a pig belonging to him and to give it privately later, carries an additional risk. In one incident, a bigman from Mamagakini well-known for his guile in *tee* dealings, asked his sister's husband to hold back five pigs and some pearlshells due to him, so that he could later, after the public *tee*, give them away to other than their rightful owners. The sister's husband dutifully did this, but when his brother-in-law went to collect them he found that he had sent them to his own friends. This partnership, between actual brothers-in-law in this case, immediately ended after the men nearly came to blows. With many pigs coming to a man from many sources, and with knowledge so restricted, he has considerable scope for manipulating his resources should he wish to do so. A person first makes sure his major partners are satisfied, perhaps by defaulting to a minor one. To this man he promises a bigger return later, or simply tells him that his pig is not lost and will be reciprocated shortly. The net outcome of a man's *tee* is likely to be a continuing, steady relationship with his major partners; and a few to whom he has blatantly defaulted and who will drop him as a partner.

Following a major *tee* and even during the proceedings of one, there may be a flurry of disputes between partners over alleged failures and infractions. It is not unusual for a wronged partner to try forcibly to pull pigs from the stakes of the giver, claiming the pigs really belong to him. Although the distribution is apparently well-sorted out in advance, partners who feel that they have been cheated may cause havoc and try to disrupt the proceedings. In a few cases I have recorded, disputed pigs were killed on the spot during a *tee* ceremony when the anger of an outraged partner became too great.[15] When a *yae pingi* follows a major *tee*, disputes between partners are more numerous and more dissolutions occur. A side of pork is expected for each live pig given in the *tee*. If they do not come, a man tries to discover where they have gone. An investigative search sometimes follows by informal means, as a man tries to find which step in the chain has diverted the pork from the proper return sequence. *Tee* disputes cluster around these two events; the live pig distributions and the return killed pig phase.

Tombema feel with justification that the number of disputes is greater than in times past, and ironically suggest that the ban on warfare and increased secure mobility may be the reason. Part of this explanation involves the increased ability of partners to move about and follow *tees* distant from their own clan areas. Men can now check on the destinations of their pigs and the performance of their partners. Infractions have no doubt always occurred, but are more easily detected now, and a person depends less on the word and goodwill of his linked partner than on his own inquiries and investigations.[16] Increased security in movement has also meant that the close interlocking network of individuals in contiguous clans has been somewhat upset. Some direct ties between partners now step over many intervening clans and long distances, and the once close intermeshing of near ties, and the dependability they offered has decreased. At one distribution I attended, a man from fifteen miles away, and at least ten individual steps distant in the chain of partners, was present to watch. He took many pork sides directly from a man who would normally have passed them to the first of the nine remaining links. This tenth man assured the giver that the sides of pork were intended for him and would eventually reach him anyway, so he would take them directly. The problems this kind of short-circuiting poses are obvious, for any one of the pigs may not rightfully have been his due. In the past, this man would not have been present, the pigs would have proceeded through each step, and possible infractions and confusions were less likely to occur. The pattern of warfare imposed a closer reliance on partners in nearby (enemy) clans, a pattern now undermined by increased mobility. More disputes today are also caused by the slowness in arrival of the major *tees*, due to the competing demands of time, production, and interest in other commercial and social pursuits. In some areas, though not in Kompiama, these are demoting the importance of the *tee*. As an end point in the major *tee* routes, Kompiama is in a precarious position, for other, more "developed" Enga areas send pigs to them. The causes of *tee* delays in Wapenamanda or Wabaga are not really understood by Kompiama people.

As I have mentioned, *tees* are becoming increasingly fragmented and more localized phenomena than perhaps was true in the past. The ban on interclan warfare has also taken some of the burden off the *tee* as a peace-keeping institution, and with it, some of its *raison d'etre*. Increasing *tee* disputes result from all of these circumstances.

During *tee lyunguna*, factions favouring one position or another cut right across every clan, and even former exchange allies were divided in their commitment to one side or the other. In this instance, withholding pigs and, more importantly, failure to reciprocate, were political statements of alliance or opposition. Some men, rather than passing pigs to those who had made initiatory gifts for them, "stepped over" these men and gave to others, for they were opposed to the smaller *tee*. They would not have passed pigs onward but instead would have held them, thus blocking the *tee's* progress. Men who decided to make this small *tee* gave pigs only to those partners who favoured it, disregarding other *tee* partners who had earlier invested with them. Obviously, disputes and dissolutions were more frequent than usual. In one example, a man gave not a single pig or pearlshell to partners in his mother's clan, for they were opposed to this smaller *tee*. They had in the recent past given many preliminary payments to their sister's son. He disregarded them entirely and sent the majority of his pigs to a sister's husband who later made this *tee* himself. During the *tee*, scuffles and fights developed over several pigs which were due to members of his mother's clan and, in the end, one was killed on the spot, and a disputed cassowary was stolen from him. In any *tee*, however, a person's performance has a partly political content, for gifts of pigs ally his interests with some and by withholding reciprocation, cancel his relations with others.

## Status of *Tee* Disputants

It was shown in chapter five that major *tee* partnerships are highly stable. This section presents additional information on the status and kinship relationships of individuals whose *tee* partnerships have dissolved. The same sample of 42 men, divided into four status categories is again used. Table 26 shows "major" versus "minor" dissolved partnerships. As mentioned earlier, the distinction between major and minor is not in all cases objectively agreed to, or absolute; a partnership might be characterized as major by one partner and minor by the other. The table is based on the value given the partnership by each person.

These data confirm the point that dissolutions involve mostly minor partners, while major ones in the *tee* remain steady and continuous. Bigmen and minor bigmen appear to drop major partners much less often than other men. A bigman's major partners are almost exclusively bigmen themselves. These dyads form relatively stable alliances in rivalry with similar networks of bigmen.

**Table 26**  Dissolution of Major Versus Minor *Tee* Partnerships

| Category of man | No. | Total dissolved Partnerships | Current Major Partners | Dissolved Major Partnerships | % | Current Minor Partners | Dissolved Minor Partnerships | % |
|---|---|---|---|---|---|---|---|---|
| Bigman | 16 | 152 | 104 | 5 | 5 | 1,015 | 147 | 14 |
| Minor bigman | 4 | 21 | 25 | 1 | 4 | 163 | 20 | 12 |
| Ordinary man | 19 | 122 | 83 | 9 | 11 | 559 | 113 | 20 |
| Rubbish man | 3 | 17 | 10 | 3 | 30 | 36 | 14 | 39 |
| Total | 42 | 312 | 222 | 18 | 8 | 1,773 | 294 | 17 |

To gain an idea of the percentage of total partnerships that do dissolve, current *tee* partnerships may be measured against remembered dissolutions. These figures can only be approximations. While current *tee* partnerships can be accurately enumerated, these are weighed against all remembered past dissolutions. Many *tee* partners of older men in the sample have died. All men in the sample have lost partners in good-standing through death. Their current *tee* networks represent, in some instances, only a fraction of the size they once were. Thus the percentages given in table 27 are high, I would estimate, by more than 5 per cent.[17]

**Table 27**  Dissolution of *Tee* Network by Status

| Category of man | Total Partnerships | Dissolved Partnerships | Average | Range | Percentage of remembered dissolutions to current partnerships |
|---|---|---|---|---|---|
| Bigman | 1,119 | 152 | 10 | 0 – 30 | 13% |
| Minor bigman | 188 | 21 | 5 | 0 – 10 | 11% |
| Ordinary man | 642 | 122 | 6 | 0 – 15 | 19% |
| Rubbish man | 46 | 17 | 5 | 3 – 10 | 37% |
| Total | 1,995 | 312 | 7 | 3 – 30 | 15% |

These figures demonstrate what I maintain is the general stability of *tee* relationships. Rubbish men have the highest turnover rate of partners, minor bigmen the lowest. Three of the four minor bigmen in the sample are young men whose networks have not yet fully proliferated and, it might be assumed, that their experience of dissolved partnerships is less than it will eventually be. Putting aside the figures on rubbish men, it is estimated that no more than 10 per cent of a person's total *tee* network, or, to state the figure positively, 90 per cent of all men with whom a man makes *tee* will remain partners until they die. In a system of exchange based essentially on the goodwill and integrity of individuals and lacking formal sanctions, this is quite remarkable.

It has been mentioned that it is often very difficult to distinguish in a dispute the defaulter from the person claiming default. When *tee* disputes were discussed with each man in the sample, in almost every case they considered themselves to be the wronged party. Without assessing blame, the following table sets out the frequencies of dispute between men of different statuses.

**Table 28** Disputes Leading to Dissolution Between *Tee* Partners of Relative Statuses

| Status of disputants | | Number of Disputes | Percentage of Total |
|---|---|---|---|
| Bigman | Bigman | 51 | 16% |
| Bigman | Minor bigman | 11 | 4% |
| Bigman | Ordinary man | 133 | 43% |
| Bigman | Rubbish man | 8 | 3% |
| Minor bigman | Minor bigman | 1 | < 1% |
| Minor bigman | Ordinary man | 18 | 6% |
| Minor bigman | Rubbish man | 1 | < 1% |
| Ordinary man | Ordinary man | 78 | 25% |
| Ordinary man | Rubbish man | 11 | 4% |
| Rubbish man | Rubbish man | 0 | 0 |
| Totals | | 312 | 100% |

Nearly half of the disputes are between ordinary men and bigmen. This appears to reflect the situation mentioned earlier in which bigmen frequently default to ordinary men who are their minor partners. Ordinary men are sometimes lured into a relationship with a bigman, in expectation of a good return from an initially small investment. Men acknowledged that this is a risk, for bigmen may use pigs from minor partners and channel these to other major, bigmen partners and fail to return the initial gift. A great majority of all disputes occur on the first transaction, when an initiatory payment is not returned.

Although no figures have been given, a large proportion of defaults amount to a discrepancy of only one pig. Ordinary men who are minor partners to bigmen are the most vulnerable to default.

Finally, table 29 shows the kinship categories of *tee* disputants.[18]

Partnerships between kinsmen in all categories are liable to dissolve. There is a slight trend however. In general, the percentages of partnerships and dissolved partnerships in each kinship category are similar (see chapter five). But dissolved partnerships in the *palingi, imangi,* and *apange* categories are less frequent than total partnerships between individuals in those kinship categories; dissolved partnerships in the *yangonge, takange,* and *kaingi* categories are more frequent. The data are limited, but partially support the point noted by Bulmer (1960b:10) that "if a man over-commits himself and is forced to let down some of his partners in order to satisfy others, he is most likely to abandon his cross-cousins and other cognates but honour his obligations to his brothers-in-law." I am also in agreement with the reasons he gives, namely, "to ensure the stability of his marriage, and the longterm benefits of the ties to his children." (Bulmer 1960b:10)

The most significant fact however, emerges when intraclan dissolutions and those between partners of different clans are compared. Of the 312 broken *tee* partnerships, 128 (or 41 per cent) of them are between partners of the same clan.[19] Yet intraclan *tee* partnerships account for just 24 per cent of the total. This figure might well be lower if information regarding all *tee* partners, past and present, was known.

This comparison does reveal, however, the relative instability of intraclan *tee* partnerships. Partners from the same clan account for under a quarter of the total current partnerships, yet account for over 40 per cent of all recorded dissolutions. This is further indication of a point made throughout: clansmen, especially subclansmen, are the major *tee* competitors. The competition which exists between clansmen leads to more disputes and these lead ultimately to the collapse of *tee* partnerships.

**Table 29** Kinship Categories of *Tee* Disputants

| Kinship Category | | Number of disputes leading to dissolution | | |
|---|---|---|---|---|
| palingi | ZH | 27 | | |
| | WB | 21 | | |
| | WMBS | 9 | | |
| | WFZS | 9 | | |
| | MZDH | 4 | | |
| | FZDH | 2 | | |
| | WMZS | 3 | | |
| | MBDH | 2 | | |
| | WFMSS | 1 | 78 | (25%) |
| apange | WB | 16 | | |
| | ZS | 12 | | |
| | MBDS | 2 | | |
| | MMZS | 2 | 32 | (10%) 110 |
| yangonge | MZS | 38 | | |
| | WZH | 22 | | |
| | WFZDH | 1 | | |
| | WMBDH | 3 | | |
| | WMZDH | 2 | | |
| | MHBS | 1 | | |
| | FFZSS | 1 | 68 | (22%) 178 |
| ikiningi | WZS | 9 | | |
| | WMZDS | 4 | | |
| | WBS | 8 | | |
| | MZSS | 2 | | |
| | MZDSS | 1 | | |
| | FFZSSS | 1 | 25 | (8%) 203 |
| imangi | DH | 11 | | |
| | WF | 5 | | |
| | WMZH | 4 | | |
| | WMB | 3 | | |
| | WZDH | 1 | | |
| | ZDH | 1 | 25 | (8%) 228 |
| takange | MZH | 10 | | |
| | FMZS | 10 | | |
| | FMBDH | 5 | | |
| | MMZDH | 1 | | |
| | FMS | 1 | | |
| | FZH* | 1 | 28 | (10%) 256 |
| kaingi | FZS | 29 | | |
| | MBS | 25 | | |
| | FMBDS | 1 | 55 | (18%) 311 |
| kauwange | FZH | 1 | 1 | (<1%) 312 |

\* see also *kauwange*

# Notes

1. *Tee* relations between partners are thought of as "straight" and never-ending. The metaphor of a "broken end" means that a pathway between men is no longer straight and that pigs cannot find their way along its crooked course.
2. *Tee* partners may also dissolve and then resume transacting later at a reduced level.
3. All things being equal, a mother's brother is usually a man's first exchange ally. His father has given a "child growth payment" to the mother's brother and *tee* relations between MB/ZS then begin.
4. The children of cross-cousins accounted for only nine partnerships in the sample, six interclan and three intraclan.
5. As a general trend, men who are just beginning to participate in the *tee* rely more heavily on maternal partners; gradually affinal partners assume ascendancy and when a man grows older, his partners through his daughters are most important to him, but not necessarily to them.
6. Often, younger mother's brothers, members or the subclan of the mother, become more important than actual, older ones. Some men actually seek near contemporaries as mother's brothers so that both may continue to transact together until old age.
7. By criticizing the performance of men in other groups, symmetrical schismogenesis (see chapter six) may be further checked, for men criticize each other's partners in neighbouring clans. But more often, a man makes accusations of another clan's performance only if his major partners are absent thus further reducing the likelihood that they might take offence for a remark meant for other men.
8. Yokone and Bokane are both members of the Kirapani clan but refer to each other as *palingi*, brother-in-law, Bokane married a "cross-cousin" of Yokone.
9. *Ndenge nyingi* "taking the corner" is the replacement pig from a "bend end" (*duna lakenge*).
10. I noted in a discussion with Lakai that he was at least two pigs ahead, that Tulyanga had given him three pigs, and Lakai had given him only one. However, Lakai steadfastly denied that it made any difference and while he was ahead in count, a pig of his had gone astray.
11. Tulyanga also gave the head, breast, backbone, and intestines of the pig, parts which are very rarely included in *tee* payments, or payments of any kind. These additions are a further indication from Tulyanga that he highly values the partnership, for he is willing to give much more than necessary to keep it alive.
12. However, *tee* partnerships sometimes begin through court cases. If two men, who are not *tee* partners, are involved in a dispute and the court directs one of the men to compensate with a pig, the recipient may suggest that the giver wait until a *tee* arrives to give the pig. In making this statement, he is offering to forego temporary payment for what he hopes will be a more longlasting *tee* partnership. This situation is also acceptable to the fine giver, for a pig he might have had to give at the more private court venue can instead be added to his row of pigs at his *tee*. He might then gain prestige from a fine he has to pay. This again reinforces the view that the *tee* is a general, debt-repaying institution which encompasses all other spheres of giving, even informal court compensation payments.
13. After the father's death, however, the son resumed *tee* dealing with the man, saying that the dispute was his father's not his. He and this man became *tee* partners again.

14. I have some examples of men whose wife and mother both came from clans to one side of them, that is, they do not stand between them in a *tee* sequence (see this strategy of marriage in chapter five). These men, like E and F, have not been able to find other partners who can operate at a high level of transactions, with many pigs passing between them. Thus, they take many pigs from one major partner and invest them with many different men. Men do not like to do this, it makes for difficult accounting, but in this example, its strategic value to E and F is noted.

15. The most unusual incident I recorded was that of a woman who took an axe and killed a pig at a *tee* ground when the giver tried to send it elsewhere. The woman is still alive and recounted the story to me while other men nodded in agreement.

16. The *tee* appears to work more smoothly when knowledge is restricted, but increased mobility and movement fosters a decline of trust, as partners may no longer be content to listen to explanations by linked partners. They may overstep that partner to investigate themselves.

17. The 5 per cent estimation is based on remembered partners who have died while in good standing. Some old men in the sample have lost more than two-thirds of all their partners through death. They have also probably failed to mention some of the long since dead.

18. Intraclan and intrasubclan *tee* disputants are again listed by emic kinship category.

19. These are from the following categories: *palingi* (26), *apange* (2), *yangonge* (61), *ikiningi* (15), *imangi* (2), and *takange* (22).

# EIGHT

# Conclusion: The Elaboration of Ceremonial Exchange

> Given any continuum, the chances are that the Enga will be found at one end rather than in the middle.
>
> (Barnes 1967:33)

I have remarked many times in this book that the Enga have elaborated ceremonial exchange to a degree not found elsewhere in the Papua New Guinea Highlands.[1] The systematic features of the *tee* institution are unmatched in other societies, and this fact leaves its impression on other Tombema–Enga institutions as well (Feil 1984). In this chapter, by way of conclusion, I examine some aspects of this elaboration and offer a quite speculative history of this process of Enga efflorescence of ceremonial exchange. I do this before summarizing the more general configuration and meaning of the *tee* for Tombema–Enga and their society.

## The Elaboration of Enga Exchange and Production

While the exchange of valuables, especially pigs, occurs everywhere in the Highlands, perhaps in all of Melanesia, and exchange relationships are crucial political and economic relationships as well, some societies clearly emphasize the importance of exchange more than others. Broadly speaking, Eastern Highlands societies do not possess or appear to place functional value on the kind of exchange arrangements which exist in certain Western Highlands societies. Pig exchange cycles of the scale of *tee* and *moka*, for example, which ramify and incorporate thousands of people and hundreds of distinct locales, are non-existent. Pigs are important in each area, but there is a differential balance on "finance" in the West versus "production" in the East to secure them (A.J. Strathern 1969a). Pigs must be produced before they can be financed of course, but Eastern Highlands societies do not stress extra-group sources for pigs, nor do they have elaborate credit, financial, and investment schemes to get them. Rather, pig festivals are the norm: a group raises as many pigs as it can at home, and then they are all killed (not given live) at one time. The use of killed pigs literally and symbolically stresses separateness and discontinuity in exchange relations between discrete groups. The reproduction of pigs is limited and severely curtailed in these systems, which conform more closely than in the Western Highlands to a domestic production focus. Relations outside the group are not utilized and the group sees itself as the unit which exchanges "its" pigs. The Siane (Salisbury 1962) and Maring (Rappaport 1967), though not of the Eastern Highlands, are good examples. Women do not provide the contacts which link production units through exchange in any systematic way as they do in Enga. The size of pig herds increases from east to west (for some details see Feachem 1973), and in general, excluding Chimbu, population densities also increase from east to west (Brown and Podolefsky 1976). As Sorenson as noted, there is a definite relationship between population density and the elaboration of pig exchanges in the Eastern Highlands itself, and more widely, from east to west (Sorenson 1972:361). Thus, the political significance and areal integration of pig exchange cycles are most pronounced in the Western Highlands. One might argue that the elaboration in the west of systems of economic exchange and underlying pig production is countered in some Eastern Highlands groups by the elaboration of a distinct ritual and initiation complex that has no Western Highlands parallel. This efflorescence of initiation practices also leaves its mark on a variety of other institutions as well (see again, Feil 1984).

Most Highlands societies exchange pigs. An important aspect of their production however, must be mentioned. Enga pigs forage, but the majority of their food is cultivated sweet potatoes. This, in varying degrees, is the pattern across the Highlands. While pigs have been in the Highlands for many thousands of years, sweet potatoes are, of course, much more recent. The impact of the introduction of the sweet potato (probably two to three hundred years ago in the Highlands) is much debated, but its consequences were not necessarily uniform across the Highlands. In the Western Highlands for example, where Tombema–Enga live, there is sound and increasing evidence that intensive cultivation, most likely of taro, is at least six thousand years old and, as S. Bulmer (1975:43) remarked, "modern Western Highlands cultivation patterns are over two thousand years old and are definitely not practices developed within the past few centuries in response to the introduction of the sweet potato". Populations in the Western Highlands may well have been substantial prior to sweet potatoes, but pigs no doubt were scarce. Pigs are not keen taro eaters and their production at that time must surely have been limited to little more than for domestic use and consumption.[2]

The introduction of sweet potatoes in the Western Highlands, on what appears to have been an increasingly intensive taro base, led to a great rise in food and especially pig production, probably to more dense populations, and migrations to other places of higher altitudes. Sweet potatoes withstand frosts better than other Highlands foods, and pigs thrive on them. The present size of Highlands pig populations can only be the result of increased food production of sweet potatoes, an "intensification" with wide ranging effects noted by Modjeska (1982). We can hypothesize then, in the Western Highlands, an expanding migrating population, human and porcine, and I would suggest, a crucial and momentous development from pig production for mere use to, gradually, the production of an expanded surplus for exchange. More pigs could be produced than ever before; sweet potatoes provided fodder, a sort of storage on the hoof (Vayda, Leeds and Smith 1971); pigs as a protein source became more frequent and secure, but beyond that, pigs became "more valuable" as objects of exchange. This is precisely how Tombema view them today: nice to eat, better to exchange. While caring for pigs thus became more onerous for both sexes, establishing social credit by sending them outwards along lengthy, expanding exchange networks, was a relieving solution. The Highlands, though some parts more obviously than others, were caught up as mentioned earlier, in the "Jones Effect" (Watson 1977): increasing production and pig exchanges in a widening social field. Competition increased, as Watson notes, for limited goods and benefits, "for every item or relationship for which pigs (are) essential coin. . . . Among them are brides and affines, partners and allies" (Watson 1977:64).[3] A system of exchange like the *tee* demands "investment" and financial opportunities abroad, and its complex chain-like arrangements involve more people and independent groups and locales than any other exchange system in Melanesia (see Rubel and Rosman 1978). Tombema are a people who originated in "core" population centres, who sent, propagated, or brought the *tee* themselves to their present location from more densely settled Southern Enga areas. They colonized an area that was previously only lightly and sparsely settled; proliferating exchange ties were the means. There are places north of Tombema where people today still recall that the complex of *tee*, pigs, and sweet potatoes all arrived together only a generation or two ago, as marriages with Tombema first took place and then expanded into fully fledged *tee* relations. The *tee* is a linear cycle of exchange (Feil 1980a), incremental expansion taking place at the ends as people in these areas seek partners further and further afield for the investment of pigs, the returns of which then become part of the wider, overall *tee* system. The *tee* continues to expand today, but only slightly, for in its present configuration as Tombema know, "it travels until there are no longer people, only uninhabited bush".

The expansion of pig production, after the arrival of sweet potatoes, to yield surpluses for exchange, meant that the autonomy of individual households, and in fact, the "underproductive" aspect of the domestic mode of production (or something like it, see Sahlins 1972) was breached for all time.[4] Exchange resolved the imminent "contradiction" between increasing production opportunities and potential, and the "need" to invest (or relieve oneself of) the products, that is, pigs. The *tee* system reached a level where no simple, locally oriented, subsistence economy could exist. All production decisions came to have the *tee* as backdrop. A circumscribed domain of domestic production or larger groups encompassing autonomous producing units, and the exclusiveness of these groups, could not be maintained. The political side of elaborated exchange in the Highlands adhered to these emerging, expanding economic processes. Exchange ties proliferated beyond the group when production opportunities increased. But, in Tombema at least, as mentioned earlier, the means necessary to produce pigs are everywhere locally available. They are not restricted nor controlled in any way. A basic equality among men stems from open access to the means of pig production. This equality however, engenders intragroup competition in exchange matters (Feil 1980, 1982); the only thing which separates men are their relationships, and the quality of them outside the group. Intragroup competition between "agnatic brothers" is the major political nexus in Tombema society. Ties of kinship and affinity, ties of women outside the group provide the means, in pigs, to gain superiority, if only temporarily, over "equal" clansmen.

The expansion of surplus production for widened exchange value, the elaboration of a strict, autonomous domestic economy has, I believe, given women a dominant role in Tombema exchange arrangements (Feil 1978b). While the very foundation of the *tee* system fundamentally rests on women's part in the production of pigs, the production of pigs for their own sake has no value at all in Tombema society. Only by exchanging them, by giving them away, does "social value" accrue to the producers of pigs. Thus, the production and ultimate exchange of pigs should be regarded as a single process (Frankenberg 1967:84). Relations of exchange are equally relations of production. Tombema women are essential for both aspects of this combined and inseparable process: the production of pigs for the exchange system, and *also* for the very partnerships which constitute the system. Pigs are the inalienable property of the women whose labour produced them;[5] relations of exchange are equally inalienable from them, for as has been shown throughout this book, men cannot form partnerships without women. The functional value of exchange must then be seen historically, and cannot be separated from that part of production and the ultimate exchange in which women are crucial participants.

## Historic Development of Economy and Exchange

It is widely held that the arrival of the sweet potato in New

Guinea, no more than three hundred years ago (Yen 1974, White and Allen 1980) entered the Highlands in the East, and spread westward through the Markham Valley (O'Brien 1972:360–61). Its rate of absorption and diffusion was however uneven. Particular areas appear to have adopted it more quickly than others, depending, it seems, on the level and intensity of existing agricultural regimes. In the Western Highlands as mentioned, the cultivation of taro was ancient and elaborate, with, for example, drainage works evident. Population densities were relatively high, and sweet potatoes may well have "served to release" societies "from the constraints imposed by the resources" of the existing taro dependent production system (Waddell 1972:219).[6] Sweet potatoes may have been adopted relatively early in the Western Highlands. At Kuk for example, there is evidence of sweet potatoes about two hundred and fifty years ago (Golson 1977). These societies, of which Tombema is likely an offshoot, represent an extreme end of a continuum: historical processes of economy and exchange are the most complex and elaborate of any in the Highlands.

Although sweet potatoes entered from the east, their impact there and rate of adoption seems in general, more gradual and significantly later than in the west.[7] While Watson reports an early arrival of sweet potato in Tairora (1965b), Sorenson (1972) believes its introduction among certain Fore groups was as late as about one hundred years ago; Wagner (cited in Watson 1965a) suggests sixty years ago for the Daribi; and in some Eastern Highlands societies, sweet potato arrived and was taken up "only within living memory" (Sorenson 1976:79). Sweet potato as a staple was the "economic foundation" of a "proto-agricultural" movement in parts of the Eastern Highlands (Sorenson and Kenmore 1974:71–72). These eastern areas clearly were, in general, less agriculturally intensive than the Western Highlands prior to the arrival of sweet potatoes. Watson (1965a) goes so far as to speculate that "the Central Highlands (*sic*) were occupied by a scattered band of hunters practising supplementary cultivation until the introduction of sweet potato cultivation" (1965a:301). While these "semi-nomads", possessing few if any pigs inhabited the east, the Western Highlands, as I have indicated, were experiencing expansionist pressures much earlier, resulting in widening exchange and colonization.

Watson (1965a) postulates an historical sequence, which seems generally applicable for the Eastern Highlands and, has recently, been supported with details by Sorenson (1972, 1976). He suggests that "patrilocal bands" (Steward 1955) existed prior to sedentism based on sweet potato cultivation. Low-density bands, dispersed to take advantage of hunting resources, later became localized, "identified", and separated by exogamy, and eventually, "patrilineal", Watson argues, from the prior condition of patrilocality. This sequence is highly speculative, and the evidence not overwhelming, but if, as seems the case, such a developmental process occurred relatively late in the Eastern Highlands, compared to the west, one can relate the manifest differences in exchange arrangements and other cultural detail which exist between the two regions, and were first noted by anthropologists many decades ago.[8]

The most important bases of these differences are that, prior to the arrival of the sweet potato, Eastern Highlands societies lacked a very long history (or none at all) of intensive cultivation. The population was small, scattered and not dense, and as the late adoption of sweet potato suggests, it was not seen as necessary to resolve any limitations of an earlier agricultural system. Intensive production of sweet potato did not immediately occur; its value as fodder was not acknowledged, and pig production did not therefore exceed, to any significant extent, production for use. The domestic mode of production, constraining, inward-looking, narrow, and with limited objectives, was not surpassed or expanded as it was so comprehensively in the Western Highlands. In the Western Highlands, adoption of sweet potatoes made expanded pig production possible, even necessary, and social units expanded there, and in turn, affected the intensification of pig production. In the Eastern Highlands, social units remained small, disconnected, more concerned with maintaining boundaries, and producing far less intensively (Brown and Podolefsky 1976). These societies are underproductive, not intensive pig producers, nor it appears, were they ever so in the past.

A strict dichotomy of Western versus Eastern Highlands cannot be maintained, for there are notable exceptions to the trends set out above. The argument here is for a broadly comparative proposition. Eastern Highlands societies are less involved in exchange cycles and are less intensive pig producers. Western Highlands societies, like the Enga, have heightened their commitment to exchange and concomitant production of pigs. Exchange dominates politics there, women have become more crucial to the exchange and production systems and have gained a respected social position as the result.[9] In the east, women remain peripheral to exchange arrangements and the means of production. In Tombema society, production and exchange have extra-domestic ramifications. As processes they cannot be separated, and as the economic unit widened, relations through women (the exchange relations of men) have become the fundamental economic relations of society. The contrasts between exchange systems in the Eastern and Western Highlands must be related to the historical developments of economic production. Highland New Guinea societies have been far from changeless and the rationale of contemporary economic configurations must be sought in historic processes.

## Enga Society and Exchange

The elaboration of ceremonial exchange in the Western Highlands, based on the intensification of pig production (see Modjeska 1982) has not been uniform in the societies most frequently compared in this book, the Melpa and the Enga. It was suggested in chapter three that the Melpa *moka* represents a profound transformation of a system of exchange like the Tombema *tee*. In it, pearlshells and nowadays money, built on the "indigenous" "principle of increment" (A.J. Strathern 1978) fostered the creation of rank (or sustained it), a pattern perhaps begun thousands of years earlier (Golson 1982). Writing more generally, A.J. Strathern recently made the point that there appears to be a "remarkable mapping of Highland systems of prestige gift-giving . . . on to an introduced capitalist system" (1982b:551). His implicit example is the *moka*. This remarkable fit must surely, however, undermine the status of *moka* as a system of gift exchange, as Mauss conceived the category. A.J. Strathern further notes (1982a:315) that "younger men frequently declare that they want to move out of *moka* altogether" and concentrate their efforts instead on making money in business, a further indication of their incresing cognitive equivalence.

Whatever the differences between the *tee* and *moka* in the pre-colonial period, the *moka* was shattered by the introduction of large quantities of imported valuables, and Mount Hagen society severely affected by the most pernicious colonial influences at an early date. I have perhaps downplayed the changes in Enga, especially Tombema, society and *tee* practice following European penetration of the Highlands, although much of Enga country was shielded until much later from colonial interference. Meggitt's work on the *tee* (1972, 1974) can provide a counterpoint. Putting aside theoretical differences (see chapters five and six), the elaboration of exchange in Mae society may have followed a different path. In Mae society, as described by Meggitt, competition for land and bloody continual warfare have overshadowed, it seems, aspects of the *tee* which my analysis of Tombema has put at the forefront. The *tee* for Meggitt, as mentioned earlier, is important essentially for communicating and receiving information to aid solidary clans in surviving a hostile, enemy environment. Individual ties apparently are minimized in a setting demanding necessary cohesion, where fighting forces are critical for clan survival. The Tombema area is not subject to such current pressures and it may be that individual ties of exchange have gained prominence, or have perhaps been bolstered by pacification which remains a reality in the Kompiama area today.

The essential nature of Enga society might be characterized by two diametrically opposed forces: a centripetal force and a centrifugal one.[10] Given a climate of warfare (as among the Mae) the centripetal forces prevail: corporateness in *tee*-making is linked to the collective strength of clans. The centrifugal pattern marks Tombema society and *tee* practice there. Individual ties of exchange weaken clan solidarity and lead to the patterns of exchange arrangements elaborated in this book. Exchange in the *tee* is given the highest cultural value and overrides the parochial wars of clans. Enga societies have, through history, been subject to these opposing forces.

While exchange throughout the Enga area is similarly practiced, and based on intensified pig production, its functional character alters in different settings, subject to local factors and differing historical influences.

## The Meaning of the *Tee*

"When we had no pigs and couldn't make *tee*, men slept in the bush like wild animals; we didn't gather to see other people" (Pimbiki, a Mamagakini bigman).

The *tee* has been shown to be a "total social fact" which simultaneously encapsulates and expresses many values and social practices of Tombema society and culture. In this book, only some have been examined: the political processes of prestige-seeking and competition, interpersonal friendship and morality, the role of women, and the economic features of production, credit, finance, and repayment. The *tee* is also a festive occasion, the focus and planning of which provide a diversion from the monotony and drudgery of work and mundane daily life. This aspect along with its religious and aesthetic components have been given little mention. The ways in which the *tee* contributes to the self-esteem and other psychological satisfactions of participants have also been omitted. These omissions from my analysis are inevitable, for the *tee* is the central institution of Tombema society and a comprehensive account of it would fall little short of a comprehensive account of the society itself.

The essence of the *tee* is that it provides the basis for unparalleled partnerships between men. *Tee* partnerships are relationships of choice. There are of course constraints, but men "freely" seek out other men as partners, and with the payment of a valuable, count them as friends. As in other societies where friendship is institutionalized (for example, "blood brotherhood" or "bond-friendship"), "ceremonial trappings" give it added meaning and significance. *Tee* partners observe codes of protocol, and they transact within a formal, orderly structure of giving and receiving. *Tee* partners must be linked by women and they must observe myriad social obligations only some of which are related to the *tee*. These ceremonial trappings do not signify the weakness of the bond, but demonstrate that partnerships are too valuable to be left to chance, they are a "dear thing to any man" (Van Baal 1975:53). To assume, as many government officials, missionaries, and some anthropologists have done, that *tee* transactions are avaricious and corrupt, is to fail to recognize that mutual exchange interests bind men into lasting alliances. There are heavy burdens on *tee* partners, but these give the relationship a high value, far removed from the connotation of a fragile contract. Other relationships in Tombema society are claustrophobic, ordinary, and predetermined; *tee* partnerships alone offer the possibility of choice.

In acknowledging choice as a critical element in the formation of *tee* relationships, Tombema appear to recognize and emphasize the "naturalness" of friendship in contrast to descent and kinship ties which are predominantly "cultural". This is a further elaboration. Although they are largely voluntary, *tee* partnerships are not impermanent: *tee* partnerships are enduring, and an individual's most important partners are his lifelong exchange allies. The substance of blood, transmitted by women, provides immutable connections between men who are *tee* partners. Women, by linking men, create inequality between them, and this inequality translates into safe, reliable partnerships, free from competitive tensions. There is a kinship basis for the *tee*, but the institution in turn adds an additional dimension to kinship and, it has been argued, without mutual *tee* interests, the social recognition of kinship is absent.

In praising the values of friendship rather than kinship, Montaigne in his essay "On Friendship" wrote that "between relatives, the expectation of the one depends on the ruin of the other". Montaigne was concerned with the covetousness and competition of brothers. In this revised formulation, the statement applies well to the competitive nexus of the *tee*. Fellow clansmen and subclansmen are the major competitors for prestige and renown in the Tombema *tee* arena. Clansmen are linked by other men, not women, and the substance they share is not of the same quality as that of *tee* partners. Their behaviour in the *tee* has been described as equality-maintaining: the *tee* is a challenge to other clansmen to prove they are equal. Clansmen are seldom partners, and when they are, their equal, agnatic relationship must be disguised (Feil 1978a). In Tombema society, the equality which derives from common clan membership leads to competition and the dissolution of relationships, while support in exchange is provided by partners who are outside the clan. Membership of clans appear to be highly fluid, clan histories show fissioning, and there is often instability in internal clan relations. It is significant that when clans break up, or members move away, it is *tee* relationships which provide the stability and refuge for those displaced.

Seeking exchange support from outside the clan extends the web of political alliances but simultaneously depreciates the value of intraclan relationships. In Tombema society and throughout the wider *tee* community, this fact has important implications for intergroup politics. *Tee* partners are members of enemy groups, but the hostility between groups is counter-balanced by the amity of individuals and thus *tee* partnerships reduce a group's war-making strength. *Tee* partners do not allow the competitions of intergroup relations to impinge on their personal exchange arrangements based on trust rather than expediency. Exchange, not warfare, is the ultimate value in Tombema society, and continuing *tee* transactions are a constant reaffirmation of that point. Groups make war, but individual exchange ties inhibit its escalation and ferocity.

My analysis of Tombema society counterposes two analytical principles: group/warfare and individual/exchange. When it is remembered that the *tee* links individuals and, through them, their communities over a wide area, and that hostilities between groups cease to allow an approaching *tee* to continue on its way, it is clear that parochial conflict between groups was often sub-ordinated to the universal interests of *tee*-making. Individual exchange partnerships take precedence and subdue the destruc-tive wars of clans. It is common to hear Enga speak of the *tee* as something universal, an institution which encompasses all com-munities. The Tombema economy is not inward-looking or narrow in design; the *tee* system is "global".

The analysis of the *tee* and relations based in it, have been set in the framework of the production of pigs and some historical developments of Highland New Guinea economy. The Enga *tee* rests at the complex end of any exchange continuum: production is geared to extra-domestic exchange, and women are crucial participants in both processes. In contrast to other Highlands societies, the efflorescence of Tombema exchange patterns is clearly marked.

It is difficult to demonstrate the central significance of the *tee* to the Tombema, but some indication can be gained from reaction to its temporary suspension.

During the late 1940s, many Kompiama clans participated in a cult which swept through the area from the west (Feil 1983). Four men visited each clan and told its members to kill all of their pigs and destroy their pearlshells, and to forego the evil ways of their ancestors. In return, when they died they would not be buried in the ground, but would ascend to a platform in the sky and continue life there. In exchange for killing their inferior pigs, new, bigger ones would arrive unnoticed and fill their pig houses overnight. The cult was successful and Mamagakini closely followed the instructions of the cult leaders. According to informants, they killed all of their pigs, not one was left alive.

Pimbiki of Mapete subclan recounted this story to me and spoke of life during that time. "There were no pigs, people became easily angered and didn't speak to other people. When people have pigs and can make *tee*, they gather together with their partners and see other people. But without the *tee* as we were then, men and women slept in the bush, didn't marry, and lived like wild pigs, fleeing from others. We were in a bad state." But Mamagakini men soon realized that they had been duped. They asked their partners in the Wapi to give them tree-oil (*topa*) which they sent to linked partners to the South where the cult had not spread, to secure new pigs in a *tee* (*topa tee*). With the return of the *tee*, Tombema lifted themselves out of a desperate situation. From the isolation of life like wild animals, men and women became a community again.

At other times, when the government or missions banned the *tee*, I suspect there was a similar void in the life of the Enga. Kleinig, a Lutheran missionary reports (1955:2) being questioned by a dissenting Enga man: "You have taken away our *Te*, now what are you going to give in return for what you have taken away?" The man was apparently seeking something in exchange for the institution whose central value was reciprocity.

In the accounts of Pimbiki and the disgruntled man is the core meaning of the *tee* for Tombema people and society: it is a model of and a model for their humanity. Without the *tee*, there is no community, no sociability, no reason for people to congregate. The mutual, reciprocal exchange interests of the *tee* bind men into secure, cooperative partnerships of trust. Without the *tee*, Tombema believe such relationships are impossible.

# Notes

1. This chapter is in part based on a paper read at the conference "Feminism and Kinship Theory" held in Bellagio, Italy, in August 1982. A.J. Strathern ed. (1982) appeared subsequently, and I have tried here and in earlier chapters to take those papers into account, especially as they extend or affect my arguments.

2. See again Golson (1982), for his arguments that wet-taro (swamp) agricultural areas in parts of the Waghi Valley provided favoured areas for raising pigs in the pre-Ipomoean period, giving rise to "inequality" at an early date (see chapter three).

3. Pig production and social organization affected each other; as forces and relations of production, defining the economic arrangement (see Modjeska 1982:56–57).

4. The focus of production shifted to the wider requirements of external exchange. Domestic production and exchange relations as productive relations, become exchange oriented and no longer typically "underproductive".

5. Although Modjeska (1982:96) has argued that "enchained" exchanges exemplified by the *tee* system separate a large percentage of pigs from women's control (see note nine).

6. Golson (1977:606–609) has noted the "limiting conditions" of Highlands agriculture prior to the introduction of the sweet potato. Not only taro, but other crops as well were limited by altitude, climate, fallow periods, soils, prolificity, and other factors. Sweet potatoes lift the "ceiling" imposed by previous agricultural systems. Advances in agricultural technology provided by the sweet potato were necessary to curb increasingly severe "ecological changes" brought on by, among other things, the shortening of fallow periods and intensifying use of land through increased population.

7. The east versus west distinction applied in the remainder of this chapter is not a strict one. I mean to imply trends, from east to west, not rigid geographical boundaries. Watson (1965a:301) suggests, for example, three frontiers, not strictly geographical, along which the sweet potato appeared and then advanced in the Highlands.

8. I am emphatically not arguing for a simple evolutionary sequence in the Highlands stemming from the differential rate of adoption of the sweet potato. Some societies took up sweet potato cultivation more quickly than others, and this had far-reaching implications on productive forces and for social relations which can be "seen" in the societal contrasts suggested here. Feil (1984) argues that increasing pig production for exchange based on sweet potatoes, led to elaborated exchange arrangements in the Western Highlands. This in turn fostered increasing emphasis on affinal and matrilateral relations of exchange, as emphasized in this book. Eastern Highlands societies, it is argued, stress the maintenance of group boundaries and give little value to affinal and matrilateral relations (see for example: Berndt 1962, Langness 1964, Mandeville 1979). Western Highlands societies utilize these relations much more fully (see for example: Ryan 1959, A.J. Strathern 1972, Feil 1978). Eastern Highlands groups, in their concern with boundaries (A.J. Strathern 1969b) appear to propound "patrilineal dogmas" more clearly than in the west. This includes stressing "male solidarity" and also "converting" outsiders more quickly to group status (see for example: Salisbury 1956, Langness 1964, Glasse 1969). Allen (1967) makes many of these same points. As well, concern with boundaries in the East, is reflected in the elaboration of cults and initiations which reflect male solidarity (see

for example: Read 1952, Berndt 1952, Salisbury 1962, Langness 1967, 1974; and Watson 1970). This emphasis on male solidarity and the isolation of females from their natal kin, creates greater "sexual antagonism" and, I would argue, that women in the Eastern Highlands are more severely treated, sexually segregated, and have a more devalued position than in the Western Highlands. Eastern Highlands males are more acutely aware of feminine danger and the maintenance of masculine purity than elsewhere. Sorcery seems more prevalent in the east (a further concern with boundaries, Lindenbaum 1971), warfare more intense, hunting more important, and villages not dispersed homesteads are the rule. These may all be related, in varying degrees of course, to the intensity of economic production, and the relations of production in the Western Highlands versus the Eastern Highlands. In the east as noted above, production is domestic-oriented; in the west, it is geared to the requirements of expanded exchange of surpluses in pigs.

9.  Modjeska (1982) has argued that with increased production (of pigs), for example in Enga and Melpa, and with the added features of "enchained exchanges", "principles of increment" and "pearlshell mystification", women in these intensified production systems are "more exploited" than in less intensified ones. Comparing Western Highlands societies with those in the Eastern Highlands, I have here argued the reverse, that where production for exchange has been elaborated as in Tombema, ties through and involving women have become the most valued and women's position enhanced, for they literally produce both pigs and relations of exchange. Affinal and matrilateral links are favoured in Western Highlands exchange systems, but severely curtailed in Eastern Highlands systems. Modjeska (1982:107–108) appears reluctantly to recognize if not fully accept this very point. One must clearly specify patterns and variations across the Highlands.

10.  I am indebted to Roger Keesing for suggesting this formulation to me.

# Appendix 1

## Mamagakini Pig Census — 1976
### Table 30

Pigs Per Subclan

| Subclan | Population | Total Pigs | Average per person | Range |
|---------|-----------|-----------|--------------------|-------|
| Mapete | 93 | 358 | 3.85 | 1 — 66 |
| Mupani | 50 | 226 | 4.52 | 0 — 41 |
| Munimi | 79 | 259 | 3.28 | 3 — 47 |
| Tareyane | 108 | 416 | 3.85 | 1 — 39 |
| Tayowe | 135 | 521 | 3.86 | 4 — 36 |
| Kopane | 9 | 31 | 3.44 | 2 — 19 |
| Yauwani | 38 | 144 | 3.79 | 2 — 27 |
| Angaleyani | 23 | 68 | 2.96 | 6 — 32 |
| Total | 535 | 2,023 | 3.78 | 0 — 66 |

Pigs Per Adult Man

| Subclan | Adult Male Population | Total Pigs | Average per man |
|---------|---------------------|-----------|-----------------|
| Mapete | 21 | 358 | 17 |
| Mupani | 17 | 226 | 13 |
| Munimi | 16 | 259 | 16 |
| Tareyane | 33 | 416 | 13 |
| Tayowe | 34 | 521 | 15 |
| Kopane | 3 | 31 | 10 |
| Yauwani | 13 | 144 | 11 |
| Angaleyani | 5 | 68 | 14 |
| Total | 142 | 2,023 | 14 |

| | | | | | |
|---|---|---|---|---|---|
| | Ango | 66 | Tuingi | 31 | |
| | Kama | 25 | Lyupa | 39 | *Total* |
| Pigs | Pimbiki | 36 | Nenakae | 14 | 545 |
| | Kepa | 35 | Pyawa | 16 | |
| Per | Opone | 41 | Kambi | 36 | *Average* |
| | Mumbi | 17 | Ngoo | 20 | 30 |
| Bigman | Kamambu | 47 | Leyambo | 26 | |
| | Suluwaya | 24 | Angale | 26 | *Range* |
| | Waipape | 14 | Laima | 32 | 14−6 |

Nonagnates had 1,040 pigs, an average of about 15 pigs per adult man. Nonagnatic bigmen had 248 pigs, an average of 31 per man. While bigmen had, on average, 30 pigs per person, the range of pigs for non-bigmen is 0−39.

Based on a smaller sample of men (the 44 men used in other samples), which has 16 bigmen, I estimate that approximately 185 pigs currently held (10 per cent of the total) are *mena yukupae* supplied by other men and these do not "belong" to Mamagakini men. They must be returned to their sources when the *tee* is made. However, approximately 315 pigs belonging to Mamagakini men have been given by them as *mena yukupae* and are currently outside Mamagakini territory. Subtracting 185 from 315 equals 130 and these can be added to the Mamagakini total making 2,153. Many more *mena yukupae* have been given by Mamagakini men, but these originated from other men in the direction the *tee* is coming and in advance of it.

Although it is not always possible to distinguish pigs that are "big enough" to be included in the *tee*, informants usually agreed that certain pigs were adequate for *tee* purposes, others not. Of the 2,023 pigs counted, roughly 75 per cent (1,535 of 2,023) were thought to be of adequate size for the *tee*. This equals about 2.9 *tee* pigs per head. There are potential errors, so this calculation is only an approximation.

# Appendix 2

## Major *Tees* Through Kompiama Area from 1925

The following diagram shows the major *tees* that have passed through the Kompiama area in the last fifty years or so. The dating is approximate only, but I believe the directions and names to be correct. There was little discrepancy among my informants' knowledge and recollections on this aspect. The dates are based on the estimated ages of informants and the knowledge of dates of some events in the past. The arrows indicate the direction in which the *tee* moved.

**Figure 7**   Major *Tees* through Kompiama area from 1925

| *Tee* coming from Wapenamanda (south to north) | | *Tee* coming from Wapi (north to south) |
|---|---|---|

"To sharpen with an axe" (*Tee waame tokapai*), also called "To fire or burn a garden" (*Tee kupi ee*), c.1925.

⟵ "**Small** *tee*" (*Koki tee*)

"*Wanepa* (light-wood) tree *tee*" (*Wanepa tee*), also called "Pearlshell *tee*" (*Tee mamaku*) c.1930 ⟶

⟵ "Pearlshell *tee*", also called "Red pandanus leaf *tee*" (red as in pearlshells) (*Tee kusai maina*), also called "*Tee* of pigs with short tails" (*Tee boro semai*) for men in the Wapi had cut their pigs' tails for this *tee*, c.1936

*Mena yae pingi* ⟶

"*Tee* of a pig's backbone" (*Mena alekiki tee*), c. 1940 ⟶

"Bird *tee*" or "*tee* enough" (*Yaka tee*), c.1942–43 ⟶

⟵ *Mena yae pingi*

"Dying pigs' *tee*, (*Mena tee kumingi*), also called *Tee kuma kuma*, early 1940s ⟶

**Figure 7** (cont'd)   Major *Tees* through Kompiama area from 1925

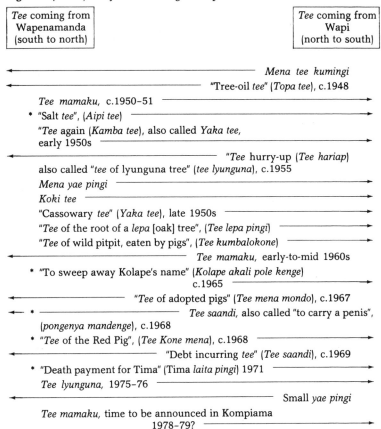

| *Tee* coming from Wapenamanda (south to north) | | *Tee* coming from Wapi (north to south) |
|---|---|---|

Mena tee kumingi

"Tree-oil *tee*" (*Topa tee*), c.1948

*Tee mamaku*, c.1950–51

* "Salt *tee*", (*Aipi tee*)

"*Tee* again (*Kamba tee*), also called *Yaka tee*, early 1950s

"*Tee* hurry-up (*Tee hariap*) also called "*tee* of lyunguna tree" (*tee lyunguna*), c.1955

*Mena yae pingi*

*Koki tee*

"Cassowary *tee*" (*Yaka tee*), late 1950s

"*Tee* of the root of a *lepa* [oak] tree", (*Tee lepa pingi*)

"*Tee* of wild pitpit, eaten by pigs", (*Tee kumbalokone*)

*Tee mamaku*, early-to-mid 1960s

* "To sweep away Kolape's name" (*Kolape akali pole kenge*) c.1965

"*Tee* of adopted pigs" (*Tee mena mondo*), c.1967

Tee saandi, also called "to carry a penis", (*pongenya mandenge*), c.1968

* "*Tee* of the Red Pig", (*Tee Kone mena*), c.1968

"Debt incurring *tee*" (*Tee saandi*), c.1969

* "Death payment for Tima" (Tima *laita pingi*) 1971

*Tee lyunguna*, 1975–76

Small *yae pingi*

*Tee mamaku*, time to be announced in Kompiama 1978–79?

*Tees* are frequently named after important events. The "dying pigs' *tee*" of the 1940s coincided with an epidemic which decimated Enga pig herds. Pigs were dying and some Enga wryly concede that this *tee* was made hastily to build up credits with other men before further pigs died at their houses. This was also a time of inflated bridewealth when more pigs were killed and invested in marriage payments. "Tree-oil *tee*" (c. 1948) followed a cult which had swept through the area. Tombema-Enga had killed most of their pigs in order to await superior beasts that never came. Soon realizing that they had been duped, they secured vast quantities of tree oil (*topa*) from the Wapi, and made a *tee* towards Wapenamanda that "brought" another *tee mamaku* downwards and replenished their pig herds. A couple of years later Europeans made their first appearance in the Kompiama area. "Hurry-up *tee*" (or *tee lyunguna*) was made after three *tees* from Wapenamanda failed to secure one *tee* from the Wapi. Police and luluais from Wapenamanda, dressed in trousers and sleeping in tents, invaded the Kompiama area and demanded that a *tee* be made quickly, "hurry-up" (*hariap*). Kompiama Enga had never seen such clothes and portable houses, and after some scuffles, Wapi and Tombema–Enga made a *tee* towards Wapenamanda.

A few *tee* names, like "pearlshell", "pig's backbone" and "*lyunguna* tree leaf" reappear and are conceived of as moving first in one direction and then the reverse, although other *tees* and many years may intervene. "*Tee* of Pearlshells" (*tee mamaku*) is currently moving towards Kompiama, and there is talk that "pig's backbone" will be the next *tee* from the Wapi, when that sequence is made. "Pig's backbone *tee*" came down earlier in the late 1930s or early 1940s. Some of the names are purely local ones, and the *tees* in the diagram marked with an asterisk are ones that began in the Kompiama area and apparently were not part of the wider *tee* community.

The diagram also shows that in the past, as well as more recently, double cycles that is, two successive *tees* in the same direction, were common. Informants say that such doubling usually occurs when *tees* are slow in coming, and those who are to start the *tee* feel that not enough initiatory payments have been made to warrant a return of pigs. Meggitt (1974:179) suggests that such double cycles were rare in the past but were necessitated in the 1940s by a great influx of valuables into the Wabaga area which allowed the Mae to send more initiatory payments eastward than Laiapo Enga could reciprocate in a single *tee*. The result was that two *tees* were sent back to satisfy accumulated debts.

*Topa tee* is a good example of the negotiable side of *tee*-making. Tombema quickly made this *tee* in the direction in which the cult had not spread, and where there were still pigs, duplicating the direction of the previous *tee*. This action prompted three downward *tees* before "hurry-up *tee*" was made in the 1950s.

These *tee* sequences also show that *yae pingi* phases, at least in the Kompiama area, are not frequent or inherent in *tee* cycles (compare Meggitt 1974). Informants could only remember three *yaes*; the last was made after "hurry-up *tee*" in about 1955.

"Salt *tee*" made in the mid-1950s, and the death payment for a Mamagakini man, Tima, in 1971, are examples of mini-cycles which are a local response to the fluctuation in the coming of big *tees*. Such small cycles seem to be common throughout the *tee* sphere. They help regulate the flow of pigs and the size of pig herds, as well as the build-up of credits and debts. There is a measure of unpredictability in the coming of a large *tee*, and the direction it takes. These mini-cycles are a check on the growth of Enga herds when a *yae pingi* is not forthcoming. A *tee*-type activity (see chapter two) circulates locally and eventually feeds back into the major *tee* when it arrives. However, pigs that would have been killed in a *yae pingi* are now variously disposed of in inflated bridewealth payments, in the practice of killing pigs to make "bisnis", and probably in eating them in greater numbers than before. Nevertheless, in the Kompiama area at least, there remains a surfeit of pigs which has lead to such increased investment that several *tees* from Wapenamanda will now be needed to reciprocate the accrued debts and those outstanding since the last *tee* came down. This situation has heightened fragmentation in *tee*-making and, as I have suggested, a more regional emphasis in the institution is predicted.

# Appendix 3

## Intraclan *Tee* Partnerships

Table 31 shows the *tee* partnerships involving fellow clansmen and sub-clansmen of a sample of men. The 539 partnerships listed involve men who are also genealogical agnates, yet each partnership hinges on a connecting female. All *tee* partners stress their kinship connections through women and downplay their agnatic status for exchange purposes. When fellow clansmen become *tee* partners, agnates become nonagnates, and they address each other by the appropriate term as shown in the table. Of the men in the sample, these 539 represent just over 24 per cent (539 of 2,176) of all recorded *tee* partnerships. Major partnerships, in terms of frequency and amount of wealth exchanged, are with men of other clans.

In this table, the connecting female link is further distinguished: one of different subclan, one of same subclan, or an actual (*angi*) relationship. For example, the relationship WFZS – different subclan intragenerational link – should be read: "own wife's father's different subclan sister's own son". The relationship MBDH – same subclan intragenerational link – should be read: "own mother's same subclan brother's own daughter's husband". The relationship WZH – actual link – should be read: "own wife's own sister's husband". The first intragenerational tie is denoted in the table. The "strength" of different subclan and same subclan connecting ties is assessed. Subclans are the units whose members make *tee* at the same time and at the same ceremonial ground.

**Table 31** Intraclan *Tee* Partnerships

Different Subclan Partnerships

| Category | Kinship Relationship | Different subclan intragenerational link | | Same subclan intragenerational link | | Actual link | | Total | |
|---|---|---|---|---|---|---|---|---|---|
| | WFZS | 23 | | 4 | | 0 | | 27 | |
| | MBDH | 15 | | 10 | | 2 | | 27 | |
| | WFZH* | 14 | | 2 | | 0 | | 16 | |
| | WMZS | 8 | | 3 | | 0 | | 11 | |
| *palingi* | WMBS | 4 | | 0 | | 0 | | 4 | |
| | MZDH | 2 | | 1 | | 0 | | 3 | |
| "WB-ZH" | FZDH | 2 | | 0 | | 0 | | 2 | |
| | MMBSDH | 1 | | 0 | | 0 | | 1 | |
| | WFMBSS | 0 | | 1 | | 0 | | 1 | |
| | WFMBDS | 0 | 69 | 1 | 22 | 0 | 2 | 1 | 93 |
| | MMZS | 4 | | 5 | | 0 | | 9 | |
| *apange* | FMBDS | 1 | | 0 | | 0 | | 1 | |
| | MZDS | 1 | | 0 | | 0 | | 1 | |
| "MB-Zch" | MMZDDS | 0 | 6 | 1 | 6 | 0 | 0 | 1 | 12 |
| | WZH | 56 | | 20 | | 3 | | 79 | |
| | MZS | 47 | | 22 | | 0 | | 69 | |
| | WFZDH | 9 | | 0 | | 0 | | 9 | |
| | MMZDS | 6 | | 1 | | 0 | | 7 | |
| | WMBDH | 6 | | 2 | | 0 | | 8 | |
| | WMZDH | 6 | | 1 | | 0 | | 7 | |
| *yangonge* | MMZSS | 2 | | 0 | | 0 | | 2 | |
| | FMBSS | 2 | | 0 | | 0 | | 2 | |
| "B" | MFZDS | 1 | | 0 | | 0 | | 1 | |
| | FMBDS | 1 | | 0 | | 0 | | 1 | |
| | MFZSS | 1 | | 0 | | 0 | | 1 | |
| | FMFZDSS | 1 | | 0 | | 0 | | 1 | |
| | FFZSS | 0 | | 1 | | 0 | | 1 | |
| | FBS | 2 | 140 | 0 | 47 | 0 | 3 | 2 | 190 |
| | WZS | 11 | | 8 | | 0 | | 19 | |
| | MZSS | 6 | | 5 | | 0 | | 11 | |
| | MBDS | 1 | | 0 | | 0 | | 1 | |
| *ikiningi* | WMZSS | 1 | | 0 | | 0 | | 1 | |
| | MZDSS | 2 | | 0 | | 0 | | 2 | |
| "S" | WFZSS | 1 | | 1 | | 0 | | 2 | |
| | MFZDSS | 1 | | 0 | | 0 | | 1 | |
| | WMMBSDS | 0 | 23 | 1 | 15 | 0 | 0 | 1 | 38 |
| | MZDDH | 2 | | 0 | | 0 | | 2 | |
| | WMZH | 1 | | 2 | | 0 | | 3 | |
| | MZSDH | 0 | | 1 | | 0 | | 1 | |
| *imangi* | WFMBS | 0 | | 1 | | 0 | | 1 | |
| | WBDH | 0 | | 0 | | 1 | | 1 | |
| "WF-DH" | WMH | 0 | | 0 | | 2 | | 2 | |
| | WMHB | 0 | | 0 | | 1 | | 1 | |
| | MBSWF | 1 | 4 | 0 | 4 | 1 | 5 | 2 | 13 |

\* WFZH may also be called *imangi*

**Table 31** (cont'd) Intraclan *Tee* Partnerships

Different Subclan Partnerships

| Category | Kinship Relationship | Different subclan intra-generational link | | Same subclan intra-generational link | | Actual link | | Total | |
|---|---|---|---|---|---|---|---|---|---|
| | MZH | 17 | | 10 | | 0 | | 27 | |
| | FMZS | 16 | | 6 | | 0 | | 22 | |
| *takange* | FMBDH | 2 | | 0 | | 0 | | 2 | |
| | MMZDH | 1 | | 0 | | 0 | | 1 | |
| "F" | FB | 4 | 40 | 0 | 16 | 0 | 0 | 4 | 56 |
| *kaingi* "CC" | FMZDS | 0 | 0 | 2 | 2 | 0 | 0 | 2 | 2 |

Same Subclan Partnerships

| Category | Kinship Relationship | Different subclan intra-generational link | | Same subclan intra-generational link | | Actual link | | Total | |
|---|---|---|---|---|---|---|---|---|---|
| | MBDH | 6 | | 4 | | 0 | | 10 | |
| | WFZS | 4 | | 1 | | 0 | | 5 | |
| | MZDH | 2 | | 0 | | 0 | | 2 | |
| *palingi* | MFZDH | 1 | | 0 | | 0 | | 1 | |
| | WMBDH | 1 | | 0 | | 0 | | 1 | |
| "WB-ZH" | WMZS | 0 | | 2 | | 0 | | 2 | |
| | WMBS | 0 | | 1 | | 0 | | 1 | |
| | FMBSDH | 0 | 14 | 1 | 9 | 0 | 0 | 1 | 23 |
| *apange* "MB-Zch" | MMZS | 1 | | 0 | | 0 | | 1 | |
| | MFZS | 0 | 1 | 1 | 1 | 0 | 0 | 1 | 2 |
| | WZH | 21 | | 6 | | 0 | | 27 | |
| | MZS | 17 | | 10 | | 0 | | 27 | |
| | MMZDS | 6 | | 0 | | 0 | | 6 | |
| *yangonge* | WMZDH | 2 | | 3 | | 0 | | 5 | |
| | MFZDS | 1 | | 0 | | 0 | | 1 | |
| "B" | WFZDH | 1 | | 0 | | 0 | | 1 | |
| | WMBDH | 0 | | 1 | | 0 | | 1 | |
| | FMZSS | 0 | 48 | 1 | 21 | 0 | 0 | 1 | 69 |
| | WZS | 8 | | 3 | | 0 | | 11 | |
| *ikiningi* | WFZSS | 2 | | 0 | | 0 | | 2 | |
| | MZSS | 1 | | 1 | | 0 | | 2 | |
| "S" | FMBSSS | 1 | 12 | 0 | 4 | 0 | 0 | 1 | 16 |
| *imangi* "WF-DH" | WFZH* | 3 | | 0 | | 0 | | 3 | |
| | WFFZS | 0 | 3 | 1 | 1 | 0 | 0 | 1 | 4 |
| | MZH | 15 | | 4 | | 0 | | 19 | |
| *takange* | FMZS | 3 | | 4 | | 0 | | 7 | |
| | MFZS | 1 | | 0 | | 0 | | 1 | |
| "F" | MFZDH | 1 | | 0 | | 0 | | 1 | |
| | FMBS | 0 | 20 | 1 | 9 | 0 | 0 | 1 | 29 |

\* WFZH may also be called *palingi*

## Summary of 2,176 partnerships

| | | |
|---|---:|---|
| Intraclan *Tee* Partnerships | 539 | (24% of total) |
| Different subclan partnerships | 396 | (18% of total) |
| Different subclan intragenerational link | 276 | (70%) |
| Same subclan intragenerational link | 110 | (28%) |
| Actual link | 10 | (2%) |
| Same subclan partnerships | 143 | (6% of total) |
| Different subclan intragenerational link | 98 | (69%) |
| Same subclan intragenerational link | 45 | (31%) |
| Actual link | 0 | (0%) |
| Different subclan partnerships, no known female link | 6 | (<1% ot total) |
| Interclan *Tee* Partnerships* | 1,631 | (76% of total) |
| Different subclan intragenerational link | 491 | (30%) |
| Same subclan intragenerational link | 962 | (59%) |
| Actual link | 178 | (11%) |

*   See chapter five

For intraclan partnerships, the set of relations through the mother (MZH/WZS-76; MZS-96; MZSS-11) account for one-third of the total intraclan partnerships. A complex of relationships through the wife (WFZS/MBDH-62; WZH-106; WMZS/MZDH-19; WFZH-19) account for nearly 40 per cent. It will also be noticed that clan and subclan *tee* partners use "different subclan" connecting links about 70 per cent of the time in reckoning relationships. Partners from different clans use different subclan intragenerational links much less often (30 per cent). Different subclan female links are sufficient to provide the basis for *tee* involvement with clansmen.

# Bibliography

Allen, M.R. 1967. *Male Cults and Secret Initiations in Melanesia.* Melbourne: Melbourne University Press.

Ambelaum, L. n.d. A History of Enga Housing. Unpublished Paper. 23pp.

Ardener, E. 1972. Belief and the Problem of Women. In *The Interpretation of Ritual,* ed. J. La Fontaine, 135–58. London: Tavistock.

Bailey, F. 1969. *Stratagems and Spoils.* Oxford: Blackwell's.

Barnes, J.A. 1962. African Models in The New Guinea Highlands. *Man* 62:5–9.

———. 1967. Agnation Among The Enga: a Review Article. *Oceania* 38:33–43.

Barth, F. 1966. *Models of Social Organization.* Royal Anthropological Society Occasional Paper no. 23. London.

Bateson, G. 1936 (1958). *Naven.* Stanford: Stanford University Press.

Berndt, R.M. 1954. Kamano, Jate, Usurufa and Fore Kinship of the Eastern Highlands of New Guinea: A Preliminary Account. *Oceania* 25:23–53, 146–87.

———. 1962. *Excess and Restraint: Social Control among a New Guinea Mountain People.* Chicago: University of Chicago Press.

Bloch, M. 1971. The Moral and Tactical Meaning of Kinship Terms. *Man* (n.s.) 6:79–87.

Boissevain, J. 1968. The Place of Non-Groups in the Social Sciences. *Man* (n.s.) 3:542–56.

———. 1974. *Friends of Friends.* Oxford: Blackwell's.

Bowers, N. 1968. The Ascending Grasslands. Unpublished Ph.D. dissertation. Columbia University.

Brain, R. 1977. *Friends and Lovers.* St Albans: Paladin.

Brennan, P. 1977. Let Sleeping Snakes Lie: Central Enga Traditional Religious Belief and Ritual. Unpublished manuscript. 51pp.

Brookfield, H.C., and Brown, P. 1963. *Struggle for Land.* Melbourne: Oxford University Press.

Brown, P. 1964. Enemies and Affines. *Ethnology* 3:335–56.

Brown, P., and Buchbiner, G., eds. 1976. *Man and Woman in The New*

*Guinea Highlands.* Special Publication of the American Anthropological Association.

Brown, P., and Podolefsky, A. 1976. Population Density, Agricultural Intensity, Land Tenure, and Group Size in the New Guinea Highlands. *Ethnology* 15:211-38.

Brunton, R. 1975. Why Do The Trobriands Have Chiefs? *Man* (n.s.) 10:544-58.

Bulmer, R.N.H. 1960a. Leadership and Social Structure Among the Kyaka People of the Western Highlands District of New Guinea. Unpublished Ph.D. dissertation. Australian National University.

————. 1960b. Political Aspects of the Moka Ceremonial Exchange System Among the Kyaka. *Oceania* 31:1-13.

————. 1962. Chimbu Plume Traders. *Australian Natural History* 14: 15-19.

————. 1965. The Kyaka of the Western Highlands. In *Gods, Ghosts and Men in Melanesia,* eds. P. Lawrence and M.J. Meggitt, 132-61. London: Oxford University Press.

————. n.d.a. Ethnographic Notes on the Sau Valley Region. Unpublished manuscript. 13pp.

————. n.d.b. A Pinaye Word-List. Unpublished manuscript. 4pp.

Bulmer, S. 1975. Settlement and Economy in Prehistoric Papua New Guinea: A Review of the Archaeological Evidence. *Journal de la Societe des Oceanistes* 31:7-75.

Burridge, K. 1957. Friendship in Tangu. *Oceania* 27:177-89.

Bus, G.A.M. 1951. The *Te* Festival or Gift Exchange in Enga (Central Highlands of New Guinea). *Anthropos* 46:813-24.

Carlson, R. 1977. Sex Differences in Ego Functioning: Exploratory Studies of Agency and Communion. *Journal of Consulting and Clinical Psychology* 37:267-77.

Chodorow, N. 1974. Family Structure and Feminine Personality. In *Woman, Culture, and Society,* eds. M. Rosaldo and L. Lamphere, pp. 43-66. Stanford: Stanford University Press.

Chowning, A. 1966. The Choice of Kin Roles in Lakalai. Unpublished manuscript. 19pp.

Clammer, J., ed. 1978. *The New Economic Anthropology.* London: Macmillan.

Cohen, A.P., and Comaroff, J.L. 1976. The Management of Meaning: On the Phenomenology of Political Transactions. In *Transaction and Meaning, Directions in the Anthropology of Exchange and Symbolic Behaviour,* ed. B. Kapferer, 87-108. Philadelphia: Ishi Press.

Cohen, Y. 1961. Patterns of Friendship. In *Social Structure and Personality,* ed. Y. Cohen, 351-86. New York: Holt, Rinehart and Winston.

Cook, E.A. 1970. On the Conversion of Non-Agnates into Agnates Among the Manga, Jimi River, Western Highlands District, New Guinea. *Southwestern Journal of Anthropology* 26:190-96.

Criper, C. 1967. The Politics of Exchange. Unpublished Ph.D. dissertation. Australian National University.

Crotty, J. 1951. First Dictionary of Tchaga Language, Central Highlands, New Guinea. *Anthropos* 46:933–63.

Dornstreich, M. 1973. An Ecological Study of Gadio Enga Subsistence. Unpublished Ph.D. dissertation. Columbia University.

Eisenstadt, S.N. 1956. Ritualized Personal Relations. *Man* 96:90–95.

Elkin, A.P. 1953. Delayed Exchange in Wabag, Sub-district Central Highlands of New Guinea. *Oceania* 23:161–201.

Ernst, T. 1978. Aspects of Meaning of Exchanges and Exchange Items among the Onabasulu of the Great Papuan Plateau. *Mankind* 11(3):187–97.

Evans-Pritchard, E.E. 1933. Zande Blood Brotherhood. *Africa* 6:369–401.

Faithorn, E. 1975. The Concept of Pollution Among the Kafe of the Papua New Guinea Highlands. In *Toward an Anthropology of Women*, ed. R. Reiter, 127–40. New York: Monthly Review Press.

———. 1976. Women as Persons: Aspects of Female Life and Male-Female Relations Among the Kafe. In *Man and Woman in the New Guinea Highlands*, eds. P. Brown and G. Buchbinder, 86–95. Special publication of the American Anthropological Association.

Feachem, R. 1973a. The Religious Belief and Ritual of the Raiapu Enga. *Oceania* 43:259–85.

———. 1973b. The Raiapu Enga Pig Herd. *Mankind* 9:25–31.

Feil, D.K. 1976. Pigs, People and Punishment. *Australian Natural History* 18:444–47.

———. 1978a. Straightening the Way: An Enga Kinship Conundrum. *Man* (n.s.) 13:380–401.

———. 1978b. Women and Men in the Enga *Tee*. *American Ethnologist* 5: 263–79.

———. 1978c. Enga Women in the *Tee* Exchange. *Mankind* 11:220–30.

———. 1979. From Negotiability to Responsibility: A Change in Tombema-Enga Homicide Compensation. *Human Organization* 38: 356–66.

———. 1980a. Symmetry and Complementarity: Patterns of Competition and Exchange in the Enga *Tee*. *Oceania* 51:20–39.

———. 1980b. When a Group of Women Take a Wife: Generalized Exchange and Restricted Marriage in the New Guinea Highlands. *Mankind* 12:286–99.

———. 1981. The Bride in Bridewealth: A Case from the New Guinea Highlands. *Ethnology* 20:63–75.

———. 1982. From Pigs to Pearlshells: The Transformation of a New Guinea Highlands Exchange Economy. *American Ethnologist* 9:291–306.

———. 1983. A World Without Exchange: Millenia and the *Tee* Exchange System in Tombema Enga. *Anthropos* 78:89–106.

———. 1984. Beyond Patriliny in the New Guinea Highlands. Paper presented at the conference "Feminism and Kinship Theory", Bellagio, Italy, 1982. To be published in *Man* 19(1).

Firth, R. 1936. Bond Friendship in Tikopia. In *Custom is King*, ed. L.H.D. Burton. London: Hutchinson.

Forge, J.A.W. 1972. The Golden Fleece. *Man* (n.s.) 7:527–40.

Fortes, M. 1969. *Kinship and the Social Order.* Chicago: Aldine.

Fortune, R. 1947. The Rules of Relationship Behaviour in One Variety of Primitive Warfare. *Man* 47:108–110.

Frankenberg, R. 1967. Economic Anthropology: One Anthropologist's View. In *Themes in Economic Anthropology,* ed. R. Firth, 47–90. London: Tavistock.

Gitlow, R. 1947. *Economics of the Mount Hagen Tribes, New Guinea.* Seattle: University of Washington Press.

Glasse, R.M. 1969. Marriage in South Fore. In *Pigs, Pearlshells, and Women,* eds. R.M. Glasse and M.J. Meggitt, 16–37. Englewood Cliffs: Prentice-Hall.

Glasse, R.M., and Meggitt, M.J., eds. 1969. *Pigs, Pearlshells, and Women.* Englewood Cliffs: Prentice-Hall.

Glick, L.B. 1967. The Role of Choice in Gimi Kinship. *Southwestern Journal of Anthropology* 23:371–82.

Gluckman, M. 1965. The Peace in the Feud. In *Custom and Conflict in Africa,* 1–26. Oxford: Blackwell's.

Golson, J. 1977. No Room at the Top: Agricultural Intensification in the New Guinea Highlands. In *Sunda and Sahul, Prehistoric Studies in Southeast Asia, Melanesia and Australia,* eds. J. Allen, J. Golson, and R. Jones, 601–638. New York: Academic Press.

_____. 1982. The Ipomoean Revolution Revisited: Society and the Sweet Potato in the Upper Waghi Valley. In *Inequality in New Guinea Highlands Societies,* ed. A. Strathern, 109–136. Cambridge: Cambridge University Press.

Goodenough, W. 1965. Rethinking "Status" and "Role": Toward a General Model of the Cultural Organization of Social Relationships. In *The Relevance of Models in Social Anthropology,* ed. M. Banton, 1–24. London: Tavistock.

Hallpike, C.R. 1977. *Bloodshed and Vengeance in the Papuan Mountains.* Oxford: Oxford University Press.

Hogbin, H.I. 1963. *Kinship and Marriage in a New Guinea Village.* London: Athlone Press.

Holzberg, C.S. 1973. Friendship: The Affective Manipulation. In *Learning and Culture.* Proceedings of the 1972 Annual Spring Meeting of the American Ethnological Society, eds. S. Kimball and J. Burnett, 245–64. Seattle: University of Washington Press.

Hughes, I. 1977. New Guinea Stone Age Trade. *Terra Australis* 3.

_____. 1978. Good Money and Bad: Inflation and Devaluation in the Colonial Process. *Mankind* 11:308–18.

Jackson, G. 1971. Review Article of The Huli. *Journal of Polynesian Society* 80:119–32.

Kapferer, B. 1976. Introduction: Transactional Models Reconsidered. In *Transaction and Meaning,* ed. B. Kapferer, 1–22. Philadelphia: Ishi Press.

Keesing, R.M. 1976. *Cultural Anthropology: A Contemporary Perspective.* New York: Holt, Rinehart and Winston.

Kleinig, I.E. 1955. The Significance of the *Te* in Enga Culture. Unpublished paper 21pp.

Kompiama Patrol Report. 1948. Held at the Kompiama Patrol Post no. 1.

_____. 1950. Held at the Kompiama Patrol Post no. 3.

Lacey, R. 1975. Oral Traditions as History: An Exploration of Oral Sources Among the Enga of the New Guinea Highlands. Unpublished Ph.D. dissertation. University of Wisconsin.

Lang, A. 1973. *Enga Dictionary*. Pacific Linguistics Series C, no. 20. Canberra: Research School of Pacific Studies, Australian National University.

Langness, L. 1964. Some Problems in the Conceptualisation of Highlands Social Structure. *American Anthropologist* 66:162–82.

_____. 1967. Sexual Antagonism in the New Guinea Highlands; A Bena Bena Example. *Oceania* 37:161–77.

_____. 1974. Ritual Power and Male Dominance in the New Guinea Highlands. *Ethos* 2:189–212.

Leahy, M., and Crain, M., 1937. *The Land That Time Forgot*. London: Hurst and Blackett.

Lepervanche, M. de. 1967–68. Descent, Residence, and Leadership in the New Guinea Highlands. *Oceania* 38:134–58; 163–89.

Lewis, I. 1965. Problems in the Comparative Study of Unilineal Descent. In *The Relevance of Models for Social Anthropology*, ed. M. Banton, 87–112. London: Tavistock.

Leyton, E. ed. 1974. *The Compact: Selected Dimensions of Friendship*. St John's Newfoundland: Memorial University of Newfoundland.

Lindenbaum, S. 1971. Sorcery and Structure in Fore Society. *Oceania* 41: 277–87.

Luzbetak, L.J. 1954. The Socio-Religious Significance of a New Guinea Pig Festival. *Anthropological Quarterly* 2:59–80; 102–128.

Mandeville, E. 1979. Agnation, Affinity and Migration among the Kamano of the New Guinea Highlands. *Man* (n.s.) 14:105–123.

Marshall, M. 1977. The Nature of Nurture. *American Ethnologist* 4: 643–62.

Mauss, M. 1954. *The Gift*. Translated by I. Cunnison. London: Routledge and Kegan Paul.

Mayer, A. 1966. The Significance of Quasi-Groups in the Study of Complex Societies. In *The Social Anthropology of Complex Societies*, ed. M. Banton, 97–120. London: Tavistock.

McArthur, M. 1967. Analysis of the Genealogy of a Mae–Enga Clan. *Oceania* 37:281–85.

Meggitt, M.J. 1957. House Building Among the Mae Enga, Western Highlands Territory of New Guinea. *Oceania* 28:161–76.

_____. 1958a. The Enga of the New Guinea Highlands: Some Preliminary Observations. *Oceania* 28:253–330.

_____. 1958b. Salt Manufacture and Trading in the Western Highlands of New Guinea. *Australian Museum Magazine* 12:309–13.

_____. 1964a. The Kinship Terminology of the Mae Enga of New Guinea. *Oceania* 34:191–200.

_____. 1964b. Male–Female Relations in the Highlands of Australian

New Guinea. *American Anthropological Association Special Publication on New Guinea* 66:204–24.

_____. 1965a. *The Lineage System of the Mae-*Enga of New Guinea. New York: Barnes and Noble.

_____. 1965b. The Mae Enga of the Western Highlands. In *Gods, Ghosts and Men in Melanesia,* eds. P. Lawrence and M.J. Meggitt, 105–31. London: Oxford University Press.

_____. 1967. The Pattern of Leadership Among the Mae Enga. *Anthropological Forum* 2:20–35.

_____. 1971. The Pattern of Leadership Among the Mae-Enga of New Guinea. In *Politics in New Guinea,* eds. R.M. Berndt and P. Lawrence, 191–203. Perth: University of Western Australia Press.

_____. 1972. System and Subsystem: The *Te* Exchange Cycle Among the Mae-Enga. *Human Ecology* 1:111–23.

_____. 1974. Pigs are Our Hearts. *Oceania* 44:165–203.

_____. 1976. A Duplicity of Demons: Sexual and Familial Roles Expressed in Western Enga Stories. In *Man and Woman in the New Guinea Highlands,* eds. P. Brown and G. Buchbinder, 63–85. Special Publication of the American Anthropological Association.

_____. 1977. *Blood is Their Argument.* Palo Alto: Mayfield.

Meillassoux, C. 1972. From Reproduction to Production. *Economy and Society* 1:93–105.

_____. 1978. The Economy in Agricultural Self-sustaining Societies: A Preliminary Analysis. In *Relations of Production,* ed. D. Seddon, 127–58. London: Cass and Co.

Modjeska, C.N. n.d. Duna Kinship Terminology: An Atrophied Iroquois System. Unpublished manuscript. 24pp.

_____. 1982. Production and Inequality: Perspectives from Central New Guinea. In *Inequality in New Guinea Highlands Societies,* ed. A. Strathern, 50–108. Cambridge: Cambridge University Press.

New Guinea Lutheran Mission. 1968. *Anthropological Study Conference* (Amapyaka). Mimeo.

_____. 1970. *Exploring Enga Culture.* ed. P. Brennan. Mimeo.

New Guinea Reports to the League of Nations. 1935–1940. Hagen–Sepik Patrol 1938–1939. 139–49.

O'Brien, P. 1972. The Sweet Potato: Its Origin and Dispersal. *American Anthropologist* 74:342–65.

Ortner, S. 1974. Is Female to Male as Nature is to Culture. In *Woman, Culture and Society,* eds. M. Rosaldo and L. Lamphere, 67–88. Stanford: Stanford University Press.

Paine, R. 1974. Anthropological Approaches to Friendship. In *The Compact: Selected Dimensions of Friendship,* ed. E. Leyton, 1–14. St John's Newfoundland: Memorial University of Newfoundland.

Panoff, M. 1970. Marcel Mauss's The Gift Revisited. *Man* (n.s.) 5:60–70.

Parsons, T., and Shils, E.A. 1951. *Towards a General Theory of Action.* Cambridge, Mass.: Harvard University Press.

Radcliffe-Brown, A.R. 1950. Introduction. In *African Political Systems,* eds. A.R. Radcliffe-Brown and D. Forde, 1–85. Oxford: Oxford University Press.

Rappaport, R.A. 1967. *Pigs for the Ancestors*. New Haven: Yale University Press.

Read, K.E. 1952. The Nama Cult of the Central Highlands, New Guinea. *Oceania* 23:1–25.

Reay, M.D. 1959. *The Kuma*. Melbourne: Melbourne University Press.

Rosaldo, M. 1974. Women, Culture and Society: A Theoretical Overview. In *Woman, Culture and Society*, eds. M. Rosaldo and L. Lamphere, 17–42. Stanford: Stanford University Press.

Rosaldo, M., and Lamphere, L., eds. 1974. *Woman, Culture, and Society*. Stanford: Stanford University Press.

Ross, W. 1936. Ethnological Notes on Mt. Hagen Tribes (Mandated Territory of New Guinea). *Anthropos* 31:341–63.

Rubel, P., and Rosman, A. 1978. *Your Own Pigs You May Not Eat*. Chicago: University of Chicago Press.

Ryan, D. 1959. Clan Formation in the Mendi Valley. *Oceania* 29:257–89.

_____. 1961. Gift Exchange in the Mendi Valley. Unpublished Ph.D. dissertation. University of Sydney.

_____. 1969. Marriage in Mendi. In *Pigs, Pearlshells, and Women*, eds. R.M. Glasse and M.J. Meggitt, 159–75. Englewood Cliffs: Prentice-Hall.

Sahlins, M. 1963. Poor Man, Rich Man, Big-Man, Chief: Political Types in Melanesia and Polynesia. *Comparative Studies in Society and History* 5:285–300.

_____. 1965. On the Sociology of Primitive Exchange. In *The Relevance of Models for Social Anthropology*, ed. M. Banton, 139–236. A.S.A. Monograph 1. London: Tavistock.

_____. 1972. *Stone Age Economics*. Chicago: Aldine.

Salisbury, R.F. 1956. Unilineal Descent Groups in the New Guinea Highlands. *Man* 56:2–7.

_____. 1962. *From Stone to Steel*. Melbourne: Melbourne University Press.

Schieffelin, E.L. 1980. Reciprocity and the Construction of Reality. *Man* (n.s.) 15:502–517.

Schwimmer, E. 1974. Friendship and Kinship: an Attempt to Relate Two Anthropological Concepts. In *The Compact: Selected Dimensions of Friendship*, ed. E. Leyton, 49–70. St John's Newfoundland: Memorial University of Newfoundland.

Sillitoe, P. 1978. *Give and Take: Exchange in Wola Society*. Canberra: A.N.U. Press.

Sorenson, E.R. 1972. Socio-Ecological Change among the Fore of New Guinea. *Current Anthropology* 13:349–83.

_____. 1976. *The Edge of the Forest. Land, Childhood and Change in a New Guinea Protoagricultural Society*. Washington D.C.: Smithsonian.

Sorenson, E.R., and Kenmore, P. 1974. Proto-Agricultural Movement in the Eastern Highlands of New Guinea. *Current Anthropology* 15:67–73.

Steward, J.H. 1955. *Theory of Culture Change: The Methodology of Multilinear Evolution.* Urbana: University of Illinois Press.

Standish, W. 1978. The "Big Man" Model Reconsidered: Power and Stratification in Simbu, The Papua New Guinea Highlands. Unpublished manuscript.

Strathern, A.J. 1966. Despots and Directors in the New Guinea Highlands. *Man* (n.s.) 1:356–67.

———. 1969a. Finance and Production: Two Strategies in New Guinea Highlands Exchange Systems. *Oceania* 40:42–67.

———. 1969b. Descent and Alliance in the New Guinea Highlands: Some Problems of Comparison. *Proceedings of the Royal Anthropological Institute* 1968: 37–52.

———. 1971. *The Rope of Moka.* Cambridge: Cambridge University Press.

———. 1972. *One Father, One Blood.* London: Tavistock.

———. 1978. Finance and Production Revisited: in Pursuit of a Comparison. *Research in Economic Anthropology* 1:73–104.

———. 1979. Gender, Ideology and Money in Mount Hagen. *Man* (n.s.) 14:530–48.

———. 1982a. The Division of Labour and Processes of Social Change in Mount Hagen. *American Ethnologist* 9:307–319.

———. 1982b. Alienating the Inalienable (correspondence) *Man* (n.s.) 17:548–51.

———. ed. 1982. *Inequality in New Guinea Highlands Societies.* Cambridge: Cambridge University Press.

Strathern, A.J., and Strathern, A.M. 1969. Marriage in Melpa. In *Pigs, Pearlshells and Women,* eds. R.M. Glasse and M.J. Meggitt, 138–58. Englewood Cliffs: Prentice-Hall.

Strathern, A.M. 1972. *Women In Between.* New York: Seminar Press.

Swartz, M.J. 1960. Situational Determinants of Kinship Terminology. *Southwestern Journal of Anthropology* 16:393–97.

Uberoi, J.S. 1962. *Politics of the Kula Ring.* Manchester: Manchester University Press.

Van Baal, J. 1975. *Reciprocity and the Position of Women.* Amsterdam: Van Gorcum.

Vayda, S., Leeds, A., and Smith, D. 1961. The Place of Pigs in Melanesian Subsistence. *Proceedings of the American Ethnological Society* 69–77.

Vicedom, G., and Tischner, H. 1943–48. *Die Mbowamb.* 3 vols. Hamburg: Cram, de Gruyter.

Village Directory. 1973. Prepared and published by the Department of the Chief Minister and Development Administration, Konedobu.

Waddell, E. 1972. *The Mound Builders.* Seattle: University of Washington Press.

———. 1973. Raiapu Enga Adaptive Strategies: Structure and General Implications. In *The Pacific in Transition,* ed. H.C. Brookfield, 25–54. London: Edward Arnold.

Wagner, R. 1967. *The Curse of Souw.* Chicago: University of Chicago Press.

Watson, J.B. 1965a. From Hunting to Horticulture in the New Guinea Highlands. *Ethnology* 4:294-309.

———. 1965b. The Significance of Recent Ecological Change in the Central Highlands of New Guinea. *Journal of the Polynesian Society* 74:438-50.

———. 1970. Society as Organized Flow: The Tairora Case. *Southwestern Journal of Anthropology* 26:107-123.

———. 1977. Pigs, Fodder and the Jones' Effect in Postipomoean New Guinea. *Ethnology* 16:57-69.

Weiner, A. 1976. *Women of Value, Men of Renown.* Austin: University of Texas Press.

———. 1978. The Reproductive Model in Trobriand Society. *Mankind* 11:175-86.

Westermann, T. 1968. *The Mountain People.* New Guinea Lutheran Mission. Mimeo.

White, J.P., and Allen, J. 1980. Melanesian Prehistory: Some Recent Advances. *Science* 207:728-34.

Williams, F.E. 1937. The Natives of Mount Hagen, Papua: Further Notes. *Man* 37:90-96.

Wirz, P. 1952a. Die En-ga. Ein Beitrag Zur Ethnographie eines Stammes im Nordöstlichen Zentralen Neuguinea. *Zeitschrift für Ethnologie* 77:7-56.

———. 1952b. Quelques notes sur la cérémonie du Moka chez les tribus du Mount Hagen et du Wabaga Sub-district, Nouvelle-Guinée du nord-est. *Bulletin de la Société Royale Belge d'Anthropologie et de Préhistoire* 63:65-71.

Wolf, E.R. 1966. Kinship, Friendship, and Patron-Client Relations in Complex Societies. In *The Social Anthropology of Complex Societies,* ed. M. Banton, 1-22. London: Tavistock.

Yen, D. 1974. The Sweet Potato and Oceania. *Bernice P. Bishop Museum Bulletin* 236.

Young, M.W. 1971. *Fighting with Food.* Cambridge: Cambridge University Press.

# Index